COLONIAL TO POSTCOLONIAL STUDIES

A LITERARY INSIGHT

COLONIAL TO POSTCOLONIAL STUDIES

A LITERARY INSIGHT

S. Sujaritha

AUTHORSPRESS

Worldwide Circulation through Authorspress Global Network
First Published in 2022
by
Authorspress
Q-2A Hauz Khas Enclave, New Delhi-110 016 (India)
Phone: (0) 9818049852
E-mail: authorspressgroup@gmail.com
Website: www.authorspressbooks.com

Colonial to Postcolonial Studies: A Literary Insight
ISBN 978-93-5529-197-4

Printed in India at Thomson Press (India) Limited

Dedicated to my beloved Madam Prof. H. Kalpana
Head, Department of English, Pondicherry University

Preface

Prof. H. Kalpana, my mentor, shared an article around three to four years ago. The article titled "The Case for Colonialism" by Prof. Bruce Gilley, Associate Professor of Political Science at Portland State University shook me. It led to many questions within me regarding the standpoint of the writer. When the postcolonial scholars/critics (from Fanon to Ngugi) speak about the colonisation of the mind and loss of culture and language, how could one support colonisation? Is Gilley trying to romanticise colonisation? As he happened to be a white from the present-day so-called imperial country, can he take everything for granted? Has he not gone through the information regarding the mayhems that happened during the process of colonisation? How could he accept erasing one's culture, language or religion as civilisation or enlightenment? From the ideological framework of the first world nations, many from all around the world may share the views of Gilley, which is considered as 'public discourse' by Martin A. Klein.

Gilley begins the article with a question why Western colonialism has had a bad name for the past century. He is of the view that colonialism could not be seen always in a negative way. According to him, "The case for Western colonialism is about rethinking the past as well as improving the future" (1). He wants to look at colonialism as a positive thing to the third world countries and moreover he believes that the third world countries' living conditions improved during the period of Western colonisation. The highlight of the essay is his suggestion to 'reclaim the colonial toolkit' and he states that this could be done in three ways to reclaim colonialism as it may enable the colonies to enjoy the benefits again. They are 1. Poor countries self-governing should be changed with 'colonial governance agenda', 2. Recolonising the areas, 3. 'To build new Western colonies' from scratch. His suggestion that this new colonisation can happen with the consent of the decolonised countries, indicates his firm belief on the positivity of colonisation. Contradictorily Western colonialism is seen in three perspectives by the anti-colonialists. They are 1. Harmful 2. Illegitimate 3. Offends the sensibilities of the colonial society.

Gilley trusts that colonialism is usually seen as something negative by the neo-colonists which destroyed the good done by the colonisers. Some research found that some of the episodes of Western colonialism were beneficial to the colonies like,

> "social, economic and political gains under colonialism: expanded education, improved public health, the abolition of slavery, widened employment opportunities, improved administration, the creation of basic infrastructure, female rights, enfranchisement of untouchable or historically excluded communities, fair taxation, access to capital, the generation of historical and cultural knowledge, and national identity formation, to mention just a few dimensions" (4).

He believes that the above mentioned factors fail the anti-colonial criticism. It is an established fact that mostly colonialism happened mentally under the disguise of civilisation and enlightenment. Illogically he argues that actually colonisation was accepted by the colonised as less number of people could colonise more populated countries. He claims, "... the most serious threat to human rights world peace was not colonialism – as the United Nations declared in 1960 – but anti-colonialism". Finally, he suggests recolonisation of places to the policy makers by following one of the three given separate methods: 1. 'To make colonialism acceptable to the colonised;' 2. 'To motivate Western countries to become colonial again;'3. 'To make colonialism achieve lasting results'.

Gilley believes that colonialism has improved the condition of the colonised countries. By forgetting about the injustice done to human kind during colonisation, he supports it by stating that it has given justice for women in the colonised countries. He further supports colonisation by stating that researches prove that even before colonisation, a country like Nairobi had comparatively weak institutions and divided societies. Here he was ignorant /imperialistic about the rewriting of histories (his-stories) of such countries. Another absurd factor is Gilley's projection of colonisation as a saviour of human rights which abolished slavery. Everyone knows that colonialism paved the way for slavery. The European colonisers in order to expand their plantations in the settled lands were in need of manpower. Around the 16th century, the colonisers transported the slaves to the colonies and they preferred physically strong Africans to do more work with less food and rest. In the 18th century, slavery and slave trade became a well organised business. Actually, it bloomed when colonisation flourished. Hence his opinion about the abolition of slavery as a benefit of colonisation is a fabricated one.

In reality colonialism improved the economy of the colonisers by exploiting the economy of the colonies. The colonisers used the natural resources, manpower and wealth of the colonies to develop themselves. In a way they pillaged the wealth of the colonies under the disguise of development. When he mentions 'historical and cultural knowledge, and national identity formation' as a benefit of colonisation, it is understandable that his views are subjective. He completely conceals or manipulates the fact about the education policy of Europe in the colonies. Macaulay's education system in India aimed to produce only clerical servants for the British. In Australia the children of Aboriginal and Torres Strait Islanders were forcibly removed from the parents by the Australian government from 1910 to 1970, who are still known as the stolen generation. The same kind of attempt was made in all the colonies by the colonisers that actually aimed to make the colonised to forget their cultural and historical information. In the case of national identity, the natives of many colonies especially in the settled colonies, lost their national identity and lived as a marginalised community in their own nation.

This article was published as viewpoints in the *Third World Quarterly* journal in 2017, which was soon removed from the journal due to protests from academicians. But still some supported Gilley's imperialistic views. As they belong to the imperial countries, their views are also imperialistic. It seems that they have forgotten easily and quickly about the pain colonialism has created. Reading this article, rekindled my interest in postcolonial criticism. It gave me an interest to write this book. Though many books are available on postcolonial criticism, this work attempts to give information from the period of colonisation to decolonisation and the relevance of postcolonial studies.

The book attempts to provide information about the background of colonisation, focusing on the colonisation of Britain, its political condition and most importantly the crucial role of English literature in constructing the binary division of the colonisers and the colonised. The first section of the book gives a detailed study of colonisation and the major role of literature in it. The second section presents the transformation of Commonwealth Literature to

Postcolonial Studies. The third section elaborates different meanings and forms associated with the term postcolonialism with and without a hyphen. Under Postcolonial Studies, the book focuses more on the concept of 'colonial discourse analyses' and its transformation under the thinking of the key intellectuals of postcolonial studies. Important terms and concepts of postcolonial studies are discussed in section four. Section five lists the key thinkers of postcolonial studies and outlines the important works of seven key thinkers. The book aims to give a summary of the key books in postcolonial studies than analysing it in order to present the ideas of the great thinkers. Section six provides the interdisciplinary nature of postcolonial studies and its scope for the future research.

The objective of this book is to enable the readers especially the student community to understand the impact of colonisation and the influence of mental colonisation. This book attempts to give a detailed historical and literary image of colonisation, specially focusing on the British imperialism on its colonies, its impact, decolonisation, postcolonial experiences, important concepts, theories, thinkers, and future scope of postcolonialism.

As history can be changed/re-written by powerful nations or people as done by Gilley, I hope that this work will enable the readers to know/realise the reality and the pain of the past situation.

Dr. S. Sujaritha

Acknowledgment

My first and foremost thanks to the Almighty, for Her constant blessings.

Mere thanks is not sufficient to express by indebtedness to the two important persons. Both of them played an enormous role in my transformation. My deep sense of gratitude to my mentor Prof. H. Kalpana and my husband P. Saravanan. Without my madam's encouragement and concern, I am nothing in the academics. My sincere thanks to my madam Prof. H. Kalpana for her never- ending care, moral support and inspiration.

Better-half is not a mere word as its role is huge in my life. Without my husband P. Saravanan's endless support and understanding, balancing both personal and professional life is impossible. My sincere thanks to him for his suggestions with regard to this book and for typing the entire text for me.

I acknowledge my heartfelt thanks to Prof. Sujatha Vijayaraghavan, Dean, Pondicherry University, who introduced Colonial and Postcolonial studies during my P.G. and M. Phil. days. Her lectures created a great impact on me which resulted in my research on Postcolonialism. Her knowledge and expertise in Literature is always a wonder. Thanks Mam for being such a great inspiration.

My sincere thanks to Prof. N. Natarajan (Former Head, Pondicherry University), who stimulated different ways of thinking in class. It is his class that inspired and motivated me towards teaching profession. I thank Prof. Clement S. Lourdes for his blessings.

My sincere gratitude to my teachers Dr. Kalaiselvi (late), Dr. Suguna Manikam, Dr. Susheela Jayanthi, Dr. Jyothi Laila, Dr. Sreelatha, Dr. Shanthi, Dr. Kalpalatha and Dr. Fathima from C. Kandaswamy Naidu College for Women, Cuddalore for finding my potential and guiding me to reach it.

Two dominant spaces, Pondicherry University campus and Pondicherry University Community College campus crafted my life positively. I thank these two campuses for providing positivity around me. I thank my friends from PUCC for their support and academic discussions. I owe a debt of gratitude to Ananda Rangapillai Library for its support in providing knowledge since 2001.

I thank Authorspress, New Delhi for their immediate responses and co-operation.

S. Sujaritha

Contents

CHAPTER 1

History of British Colonisation

"His Majesty's dominations, on which the sun never sets"

John Wilson

Human interest towards expanding their power and territories is a never-ending avaricious act. The greed towards expanding landscape and gaining power can be witnessed in the history of any century or even in the contemporary time. As the concept "the survival of the fittest" has become the motto of humans, the interest to expand the power and territory is haunting them. As power has been the driving force, the world has witnessed several conquests. In such wars an empire that lost the battle might have faced transformation under the new empire. As it did not/does not create much impact upon the rest of the world, war and its impact upon others was not mostly read in great detail and neglected by the rest of the world. The Expansion of the British Empire which was proudly called as the Empire where 'the sun has never set' was different from the earlier imperial reigns. Furthermore this expansion of landscape by a single country, almost throughout the world in different manners with a single purpose, created an immense physical and psychological impact for at least three to four centuries.

The word colonialism is from the Latin word 'colonus' means farmer. Till the 19th century, the word was used with a positive meaning by projecting the images of the Roman colonisation but later the pain undergone by the colonised changed its meaning as negative. Collins English Dictionary defines colonialism as, "the policy and practice of a power in extending control over weaker peoples and areas". The etymology of the term imperialism is from the Latin word, 'imperium' means supreme power/to command. It is defined as "… the formation of an empire and as such has been an aspect of all periods of history in which one nation has extended its domination over one or several neighbouring nations" (Ashcraft and eds., 2013: 122). According to Edward Said imperialism is, the practice, the theory and the attitude of a dominating metropolitan centre ruling a distant territory (1993: 8). The earlier conquerors and conquering had been attributed with the term imperialism. The expansion of the British Empire was/is also addressed by many as imperialism. But some scholars consider British expansion as colonisation rather than imperialism. Peter Childs and Patrick Williams state that there is considerable difference between imperialism and colonialism. McLeod cites their opinion and states,

> imperialism is an ideological concept which upholds the legitimacy of the economic and military control of one nation by another. Colonialism, however, is only 'one form of practice' which results from the ideology of imperialism, and specifically concerns the 'settlement' of one group of people in a new location. Imperialism is not strictly concerned with the issue of settlement: it does not demand the settlement of different places in order to work (7&8).

Since the 15th century, the European countries had been obsessed with the urge to discover lands apart from their homelands. The rivalry among Portugal, Spain, France and Britain resulted in the colonisation of many countries and continents. Colonisation occurred due to various reasons and the primary one was to increase their power. The British kingdom wanted to show its superiority over its rival countries, especially upon France. The expansion of its colonies made it as a powerful empire all around the world. Moreover, the Black Death of the 14th century and the agricultural depression of the 15th century left the British economy in a poor condition. Furthermore the growing population, land shortage and low wages were the additional problems faced by the government. This was the time when the industrial revolution happened and Britain's desire to conquer colonies began. The colonies were considered as a source of raw materials and also as markets to sell its products. It persuaded colonies to supply raw materials for the industries and food products. At the same time, it had used the natural resources from the colonies. Thus, Britain became the richest empire in the world. Though Britain wanted to have colonies for its own economic and space requirements, it had manipulated the reasons by stating that it had its duty as a civilised society to enlighten the barbarians about civilisation.

The Age of Discovery paved the way for agents to travel across the globe to fetch wealth (also information about trade or natural resources of other countries) for their home country. Though Columbus landed in America in the 15th century, the British arrived there approximately three decades later. One of the main reasons for the mass migration from Britain to North America was religious freedom. Puritans chose to migrate to America with the hope of establishing their own communities and to breathe freedom in worshipping God in their own way. Britain, by initiating its colonisation in America turned out to be a great empire in the world. It had colonised almost the whole world by creating some differences among the colonies. The colonies can be broadly divided into two types 1) the settler's colonies – (North America, Australia, New Zealand and South Africa) enjoyed the special attention as they were colonies of settlements for the colonisers, and 2) colonies to enrich the economy of Britain – Africa, some parts of Asia and the Caribbean Islands.

1. America

The Native Americans (indigenous people) had been living in their home country for thousands of years. But history books taught the world that Columbus discovered America in 1492. (Which gives an impression that it was a bare land without people and with the discovery of Columbus the land was brought to the knowledge of the world.) After this Spain and Portugal established their colonies in North America, whereas Britain did not show much interest in it. Later, around 1600 with the advance of travel and discoveries, Britain showed interest to expand the territory. King James I, in 1606, supported the travellers to explore new lands for settlements. As naming is one of the strategies followed by the colonisers to acquire a land to be theirs (by naming, they try to have ownership over something mostly places), the British when they tried to explore America, named a river as 'James River' and a place where they stayed as 'James Town' in honour of their king and the entire territory was named Virginia after their late virgin queen. Virginia was the first established colony of Britain. Initially, they had survival problems like hunger, diseases and attacks by the natives. During this time, in England there was unrest between the Roman Catholics and the Puritans. As the King was a follower of Roman Catholicism, the Puritans did not have religious freedom in their country. In order to escape from religious persecution, they decided to move to the new world in 1620. Though they worried about leaving their home country by knowing that they would never come back, the freedom for religious practices motivated them to take that strong decision of leaving. They departed in a ship named 'Mayflower' from Plymouth, England. In memory of their home country, they named the place where they settled as Plymouth, Massachusetts. Their success story attracted many Puritans from England to leave for the new land. The natives in Plymouth were less in number and they helped the white settlers with plantation.

Interest in cultivation motivated the settlers to cultivate crops, tobacco and cotton which minted huge wealth. Initially, unlike the other Europeans, the British were friendly with the Native Americans. They worked together on the fields. Slowly, the British exploited the natives by acquiring more land from them. Thus, Britain expanded its colonial territory by colonising thirteen colonies in America. The list of those thirteen colonies is: Virginia, New York, Massachusetts, Maryland, Rhode Island, Connecticut, New Hampshire, Delaware, North Carolina, New Jersey, South Carolina, Pennsylvania and Georgia. In around 170 years, the white population in North America was approximately 2.5 million which paved the way for the marginalisation of the Native American population. Later the Americans revolted for freedom from Britain and the wars related to it made Britain to declare freedom in 1783. It was a great loss for Britain to lose thirteen colonies in North America. In order to compensate the loss, Britain had decided to establish a colony in Australia.

2. Australia

The natives of Australia are called as Aboriginals, who have lived in Australia for around 70,000 years. More than 500 indigenous groups (the most ancient group in the world) lived in Australia. In 1770, Lord James Cook explored Australia and recommended Britain to colonise it. Though Lord James Cook recommended colonising, he knew that those people were happier than the British (which proves William Wordsworth's saying 'Ignorance is Bliss'). James Cook in his logbook commented on the aborigines and Australia thus,

> From what I have said of the natives of New Holland they may appear to be the most wretched people on earth, but in reality they are far happier than we Europeans, being wholly unacquainted not only with the superfluous, but with the necessary conveniences so much sought after in Europe; they are happy in not knowing the use of them. They live in tranquillity. The Earth and the Sea of their own accord furnish them with all things necessary in life... (Quoted in https://www.britishempire.co.uk/maproom/pacific.htm)

In 1788, the British decided to establish a colony in Australia with dual purposes: to alleviate the overcrowded prisoners and to expand the empire. The first fleet of British with around 730 convicts reached Australia. The Aboriginals were fighting to send the British out but they failed in their attempt. Christopher Warren states that the outbreak of small pox in 1789 was a deliberate act by the British marines, due to the lack of ammunition and to extend their settlement. They treated the Aborigines with cruelty. In three decades 40-60 percentage of the Aboriginals died due to the spread of disease and killing by the British. Later when the British reported that the Aborigines were less in numbers in Australia, the world knew how their population had reduced. William Westgarth in his work *The Colony of Victoria* (1864) stated, "The case of the Aborigines of Victoria confers… it would seem almost an immutable law of nature that such inferior dark races should disappear" which proves the evil nature of the settlers. Moreover from 1788-1868 approximately 1, 61, 700 convicts were transported to Australia and they were used to do agricultural works and as labours. Slowly Australia emerged as the biggest business spot for Britian and so many business companies showed interest to start their business there.

3. New Zealand

The native people of the South Pacific Island group, which was later named as New Zealand after the Dutch king, were Maori people. Though it was found by a Dutch navigator in 1642, till the late 18th century, New Zealand did not attract the attention of the Europeans. The English explorer, Lord James Cook travelled to New Zealand and wrote in detail about the land especially about the chance to import timber from the new land to Britain. By the 1840s, based on a treaty between the British and the Maori people, 2000 white people settled in the island. Later, the British settlers occupied the main land and marginalised the natives by following the strategy they exercised in North America and Australia. Initially New Zealand was not a profitable colony like Australia as it provided only frozen meat, dairy and agricultural goods. Later, gold mines and agricultural growth transformed New Zealand also as a wealthy settlers' colony.

4. South Africa

South Africa was colonised in 1652 by the Dutch East India Company. In 1806, the British acquired the colony in order to prevent the French colonising it and also to maintain its trade with Asia. Initially, they showed interest to protect this and by 1820, the British started to migrate in more numbers to South Africa. However, in the later period South Africa too turned as a market and also as a source of raw materials for Britain. Wine from the Cape was shifted to Britain, Merino sheep growing was introduced in South Africa in order to supply wool to British textile mills.

5. Africa

Colonisation in Africa began as a need for humans due to the development of the industrial revolution and the findings of new colonies in North America. Due to the rapid production of goods with the help of industries, Britain needed more production of agricultural products. It led them to use the colonies for cultivation and native population and the white criminals as labours. Additionally, Britain traded Africans as slaves for plantation work in its colonies. Later when slavery was abolished, and the American colonies got independence from Britain, it made Africa its colony. Chinweizu states

> When Europe pioneered industrial capitalism, her demands upon the resources of the world increased tremendously. In addition to obtaining spices for her tables and manpower for her mines and plantations in the Americas, Europe set out to seize for her factories the mineral and agricultural resources of all the world. Her need to take African manpower to the Americas declined. She needed instead to put African labour to work in Africa, digging up for her the riches of African mines; the trading companies that had for centuries bought and sold on Africa's coast were found inadequate for seizing and carting off the raw materials of the African hinterland. Europe now felt a need to export her power into Africa's interior to reorganise the farms, mines and markets for Europe's greater profit. Her adventures banded together, obtained charters from their national governments, and came to seize the African markets, from the African middlemen with whom for centuries Europe had been content to trade. Africa's coastal rulers naturally resisted all encroachments and battled to maintain the status quo. They strove to retain their position as middlemen, importing and distributing European wares to the hinterland, and collecting produce from the hinterland markets and selling it to European merchants who came to the coast. The new breed of European merchants, however, wanted direct access to the hinterland markets so that, by eliminating the profits of the African middlemen, they could enlarge European profits and directly supervise African production. The situation was ripe for conflict.

Slowly Africa was under the control of the British Empire. As done in the settler colonies, in Africa too lands were confiscated from the Africans and moreover heavy taxation was implemented which left the Africans to work as labourers in their own land.

6. India

The British entered India with a trading disguise and slowly showed their true colours by conquering some places especially the provinces of Bengal. In 1858, the rule of India was transferred from the East India Company to the Crown (Queen Victoria). Since then the British started to conquer all the states of the nation. Like the Africans, the Indians were taxed heavily by the British and the British Indian army with Indian sepoys who were controlled by the British officials were used to control the revolters against the British rule.

7. The Pacific Island

The countries in the Pacific islands attracted the attention of the Europeans and the U.S.A. France had a dominant position in the Pacific Islands. Slowly Britain showed its concern towards those countries but was successful only to get Fiji in 1874 as the native authority had broken down. As usual the British set aside the vast majority of land for Fijians initially but later imported thousands of Indian indentured labourers for plantation. Slowly it extended its rule over the Crown Colony of the Gilbert and Ellice Islands, the Protectorate of the British Solomon Islands, the Protectorate of Tonga or the Friendly Islands.

8. South East Asia

The Europeans were interested to trade in the Asian countries. The wealthy trading of the Portuguese with China and South East Asia, increased Britain's desire to trade with South East Asians. The British conquered Burma by fighting three wars (from 1824-1886), Penang in 1786, Singapore in 1890 and Malacca in 1824, as British strait settlements.

Along with the above-mentioned important colonies of Britain, in all the colonies the empire collected huge taxes for the benefit of its mother country apart from the extraction of natural resources and the human resources. It collected various forms of taxes like personal tax, income tax, 'hut' tax and import tax. Though the prime motive of colonisation was its economic growth, the British justified it by giving various reasons. They killed many native people and confiscated their land and natural resources. Regarding such kind of mass killing of the natives in Australia, what Edward Wilson said could be applied to all the colonies.

> In less than twenty years we have nearly swept them off the face of the earth. We have shot them down like dogs. In the guise of friendship we have issued corrosive sublimate in their damper and consigned whole tribes to the agonies of an excruciating death. We have made them drunkards, and infected them with diseases which have rotted the bones of their adults, and made such few children as are born amongst them a sorrow and a torture from the very instant of their birth. We have made them outcasts on their own land, and are rapidly consigning them to entire annihilation (quoted in Harris: 209).

Yet they called it as their responsibility to colonise those nations. Their superiority complex led them to think it as the 'white man's burden' to civilise barbaric or uncivilised natives of the colonies (colonisers' constructed ideas about the native). Thus, they morally justified their brutal expansion of colonies. The British came in the disguise of giving civilisation to the colonies, nevertheless it had created negative impacts such as environmental degradation, spread of disease to the natives, economic instability, and moreover human rights violations. Added to that, the method of forced labour and slavery crippled the colonies further.

According to the British, civilisation was, "the triumph and development of reason, not only in the constitutional, political and administrative domains, but in the moral, religious and intellectual spheres" (Conklin: 14). The British in order to maintain their superiority projected the natives of various colonies with the same name. By doing so they indirectly wanted to create a truth that all the colonised people were the same level in their barbaric nature. This homogenisation of the natives across the globe in spite of the cultural and geographical differences indicates the ultimatum of the colonial power.

> Since Columbus's time, it had been a European practice to use the term 'Indian' to name all the native peoples of the Americas and the Pacific… So, too, the term 'nigger' used by the Europeans in India was exported to Africa. The device of travelling name again underlines that prevailing quality in colonial interpretation of sameness bridging difference (Boehmer: 50).

Even though the British considered all the colonised as the same, still they followed a hierarchy among the colonised. They considered the Africans as culturally and racially inferior. Dr. Nott in his lecture in the U.S.A. before colonisation stated that the races based on colour have a different level of intellect. "…deep-rooted intellectual and physical differences seen around us, in the White, Red, and Black Races, are too obvious and too important in their bearings, to be longer overlooked" (3). He further states that though they lived for several centuries, still the Africans could not be civilised. He believed that the Africans are incapable of civilising themselves.

> There Africa stands with her fifty millions of blacks, and there she has stood for the last five thousand years, with this people occupying the same countries, without one step towards civilisation; and all the experiments in the United States, the West Indies, and elsewhere have failed (19-20).

Such kind of ideas led the British to take responsibility of civilising the uncivilised.

The British wanted not only to colonise the land or the people physically but they intended to colonise the people mentally. To do so it was necessary for them to make the natives believe they were inferior and they should be ruled by the superiors, i.e. the British. Hence it became the duty of the whites to mentally colonise the natives. It was done in two ways. First, they made the natives accept that they were uncivilised. Ashis Nandhi's *The Intimate Enemy* (1983), talks about two types/levels of colonisation. He makes a distinction between the two as, "the first, …was relatively simple-minded in its focus on the physical conquest of territories, whereas the second was more insidious in its commitment to the conquest and the occupation of minds, selves, culture" (15). Second, the British made the natives to think that English language and Christianity could civilise them. Along with missionaries and English education, Colonial Narrations too played an ugly role in colonising the psyche of the colonised as well as to give a superiority complex to the British.

Bill Ashcroft in *The Empire Writes Back* observes that the growth of the empire and study of English are correlated. The colonisers showed their imperial power by controlling the language of the colonised countries. Through their power they enslaved the minds of the colonised to accept the colonisers' language and education as the standard one and the other languages as "impure" (7). They created an ideology that their language was the only language, which worked as a vehicle to convey 'truth', 'order' and 'reality'. For the imperialists, other cultures and languages were non-existent and believed theirs as real. McLeod in *Beginning Postcolonialism*, elaborates this idea that the British Empire did not rule by military and physical force alone, but it made the colonised to see their world in a particular way, that is to look negatively upon their people, their culture and themselves. It is considered as an effective way of disempowering people which became possible through English education and English language.

Imperialism through language paved the way for death of many native languages and oral literatures of the colonies. The colonised people's perception on the superior position of the whites developed interest towards English language. In the settler colonies new varieties of English languages were developed by the native speakers. The total number of English speakers before 1800 was less. As the colonies grew in size, the English speakers also rose in number. In the 21st century, English is the third most spoken language in the world.

> Language is the primary mode of comprehending, contextualising and communicating reality: without it one can neither name nor distinguish what one perceives. ...thoughts are as much shaped and expressed by language as that language is shaped by its specific context. The lives of the people who speak it, the terrain which they inhabit, their cultural, social and religious practices, their economic activities – all contribute to the development of a language (Sarbani Chowdhury: XV)

The British decided to teach English and educate the colonised countries through the English language. Thus, English language was systematically imposed on the colonise as they know very well that language is not a simple tool used merely for communication, added to that it plays a vital role in creating and maintaining culture. Language carries cultural, geographical, traditional and historical elements. For example, the countries, where the cold season prevails most of the time, cherish warmth and heat. As opposite to that, countries with hot climate celebrate chillness. Thus, climatic condition of the places change people's attitude towards chillness and heat. It is reflected in their language and thinking. As heat is favoured by the cold country people, they associated positive feelings and things with warmth and negative feelings and things with chillness. Hence, we have sayings like 'warm welcome', 'gives warmth', 'cold-blooded murder'. Contrarily, countries like India use heat related words for negative things or feelings and chillness for positive feelings or things. Sayings like 'good news brings chillness to my heart', 'bad news burns my heart/stomach' proves it. Hence imposing a language from a foreign country upon the native people of the colonised was not only for trading but to cripple the cultural practices of those colonies as well as to colonise those natives eternally though not physically but at least mentally. Consequently, the colonisers in some places forbid the natives to talk in their mother tongue that resulted in many getting educated in English.

The reasons stated by the British government for the formation of English education were different from reality. They stated that only through English language scientific developments could be achieved and thus the colonised would get civilised. However the reasons behind implementing English education were 1) it was difficult for the British to rule the colonies without the knowledge of the local languages. 2). to break the cultural and traditional practices of the nation. Thus by hiding the fact with false justification the British implemented English education in the colonies. Judith Brown in the Epilogue to Volume IV of *The Oxford History of the British Empire* states that, "the most significant of all is the legacy of the school and the University" (706). Though the British wanted to impose the English language on the colonisers, they were unaware about the method to do so: they were bothered about investing in colonial education and uprising of the colonised in knowledge. Thus, they decided not to give scientific education to them but educate them only to do clerical jobs.

In the settler colonies, as the British occupied a superior position, implementing English language and education went hand in hand with their settlement. In the colonies the British created a need for English language and education. In India Macaulay's "Minute upon Indian Education" (1835) played a major role in implementing English education. It shows how language is conjoined with imperial power to leave colonialism in a stable position. Moreover it is considered as a subtext of strong political agenda. Macaulay's Minute which is in 32 paragraphs changed the educational history of India. He suggested that as the natives are inferior, it is unnecessary to get the opinion of the natives regarding education and the ruler has to make a decision. English is the only language which promotes science and the oriental language will fail in it. Thus, teaching oriental languages like Sanskrit or Arabic is similar to cheating the Indians. He states,

> ...we ought to employ them in teaching what is best worth knowing; that English is better worth knowing than Sanskrit or Arabic; that the natives are desirous to be taught English, and are not desirous to be taught Sanskrit or Arabic; that neither as the languages of law, nor as the languages of religion, have the Sanskrit and Arabic any peculiar claim to our engagement.

Moreover, he says that publishing oriental literary works are waste of money and they are not worth the effort.

> I have conversed both here and at home with men distinguished by their proficiency in the Eastern tongues..... I have never found one among them who could deny that a single shelf of a good European library was worth the whole native literature of India and Arabia. Thus, English education was imposed upon the Indians. In Africa and Pacific Islands, missionaries were instrumental in starting English education for the native people. Christian missionaries had opened many elementary and secondary schools in Africa between 1820-1881. Fifty years after Macaulay's Minute, Sir Richard Temple, the former Governor of Bombay stated regarding the importance of English education to the natives as, "English or Western education has greatly elevated the character of natives who have come within its influence" (quoted in Boehmer: 49).

This ideology again intensified the interest of the colonised towards English education.

The other justification which the British gave to colonise, especially, Africa was Christianity. The British treated unfamiliar native religious practices as savage. To the British, Christianity is not only the religious practice but basis for morality and this led them to believe that they were superior to the rest of the world. "Mid and late nineteenth century Europeans were generally convinced that their Christian, scientific and industrial society was intrinsically far superior to anything that Africa had produced" (Fage: 322). The missionaries play a pivotal role in the expansion of colonies. They established churches in the colonies with a vision to convert many people. Even before legally colonising Africa and colonies in the Pacific Islands, the British established missionaries to break the native culture by imposing Western culture, ideas and education. By the end of the 19th century around 10,000 missionaries were established in the colonies of Britain. Edward Andrews states the role of Christian missionaries in the expansion of colonies as, "Visible saints, exemplars of ideal piety in a sea of persistent savagery. Many historians accuse Christian leaders and Christian doctrines for justifying violence against the native people in the colonies" (14). In India, the missionaries had moderate success, whereas in America they played a key role in converting most of the African slaves. Later those converted Africans were utilised/assigned to convert the people in Africa. In Africa, the missionaries found that they could provide medical and educational services to the Africans as they were not very strict with theological appeals. The British missionaries achieved success through its agreeable means and persuaded the Africans to accept Christianity.

> The Christian missionaries were much part of the colonising forces as woe the explorers, traders and soldiers. There may be room for arguing whether in a given country the missionaries brought other colonialist forces or vice versa, but there is no doubting the fact that missionaries were agents of colonialism in the practical sense whether or not they saw themselves in that light (35).

As mentioned earlier, British education and colonisation go hand in hand to colonise the natives mentally. In many places colonisation happened without much violence due to the constructed knowledge about the British. The colonial education by teaching English slowly deviated the mind of the colonised from their culture. They were unknowingly mimicking their masters. The colonial education and colonial narratives simultaneously achieved the task of the coloniser: creating the differences between the coloniser and the colonised.

Similar to the enforcement of English language and the spread of missionary, colonial writing too played a seminal role in expanding territories. The colonial writing can be in any form of writing as mentioned by Elleke Boehmer, "political treaties, diaries, acts and edicts, administrative records and gazetteers, missionary reports, notebooks, memoirs, popular verse, government beliefs, letters 'home' and letters back to settlers" (14). Colonial narratives can be considered as a discursive text, where a belief is constructed and later which is produced as truth by power. These writings try to convey "the myths of power, the race of classifications, the imagery of subordination" (Ibid: 3). Later those constructed truths were circulated in the society. Thus, colonial narratives produced knowledge about East and West by the West.

The colonial narratives helped in developing power to control the colonies and also gave justification for colonisation. As these works were produced during the colonial period, they are imperial narratives which always hide the real motive and reality. Through these narratives the British wanted to create the binary: white and non-white. They did not bother about the differences that existed among various communities in a country. Nevertheless, they homogenised the entire colonised countries as one. Tamara explains this thus, "This range of competing labels reflects increasing taxonomic differentiation within the overarching constructs of non-white

Others as the British Empire attempted to subsume and incorporate multiple cultures in Africa and Asia" (3).

Colonial narratives initially started in the form of travelogue. To the already existing world, the Europeans developed maps claiming that many countries and continents were discovered by them. Map making and naming are very crucial in exhibiting their power and establishing themselves as the master of the world. Naming is an act of possessing and self-perpetuation. The British named their colonies after their Kings, Queens, Lords, and places from home. It is in a way of acquiring the land as theirs. Travel writing is a dense one, which is not only about visiting places and travel experiences but it talks more about cultural practices, products, important trades and political information. Thus, it supplies information about a country's wealth to the colonisers. Ironically most of the travellers were functionaries of the empire. Henry Lord, a traveller makes his appeal to the Archbishop of Canterbury and to the Governor of the East India Company to colonise India. He urges the Archbishop of Canterbury to redeem the Indians as they were,

> violating the divine law of the dread Majesty of Heaven, and with notable forgery Coyning Religion according to the Mint of their own Tradition, abusing that Stamp which God would have to pass current in the true Church (A2-A3) and to the Governor he states "this sect of Banians suggested unto me something novel and strange, and gave me hopes it would be a present worthy and welcome to your" [Governor's] hands (IV).

Another feature of travelogue is that it constitutes a system of cultural behaviour of the West as a standard one and by interpreting and representing the 'other' culture (it tries to claim its domination over the 'other'). Moreover, the native people would be homogenised and projected as barbaric in nature.

Literature is perceived as a mirror of the society. Some go to the extent of considering literature as a piece of history. However when the truthfulness of history itself is doubted in new historicism, the same can be applied to literature. Literature especially the Western literature which was produced during colonisation was with a purpose. Here literature did not mirror the society but it was constructed with a purpose. The superiority complex and the dominant nature enabled the British to look down on the 'others'. It used its literary works to stereotype the colonised as 'barbaric', 'stupid', 'ugly', and 'uncivilised'. Many literary works of the British directly or indirectly showed their discursive writings. English literature of the 18th and the 19th century played a pivotal role in constructing ideologies about the natives. Most of the literary works though appeared very naive; they constructed the stereotypes about the colonies.

Teaching of English slowly led to the teaching of English literature, which is considered as a strong source to convey the English ideologies. Gouri Viswanathan has noted that the goal of imperialism in constructing 'knowledge' was adored with teaching English literature for the civil service and other administrative positions: English literature was seen as a representation of the ideas and qualities that should be replicated by the colonies. Consciously or unconsciously the writers produced the societal changes in Britain and their so-called responsibility to civilise the colonised. Colonial writings were produced with two purposes. One is to enable the British to believe that they are superior to rule over the world and the second is to make the colonised accept their need for civilisation with the help of the British. Lord Meath is of the opinion that the superiority feel of the British has to be sustained,

> . .. the continuance of the British race as one of the dominant peoples in the world is dependent on the sustained possession of a virile spirit which makes light of pain and physical discomfort, and rejoices in the consciousness of victory over adverse circumstances, in which regard the performance of duty, however difficult and distasteful, as one of the supreme virtues… (20).

Among the British writers some were for imperialism/colonisation and some were against it. They believed that Christ was against dominating fellow human beings. "For Christ, imperialism is a moral evil incompatible with the flourishing of true civilisation, and empire is the opposite of peace, liberty, piety and culture" (O' Brien: 270). Milton expresses the above said view in his *Paradise Regained III.* Though Milton was against colonisation, he could not come away from the superiority complex. His work *Paradise Lost* is filled with imperialistic views where he perceives the new colonies as a place of Satan, which attracts the merchants of Britain with its spices, pearls and gold. He indirectly projects Vasco da Gama as Satan as he explores places (ibid: 276).

Charles Cameron suggested to introduce John Milton to colonial education to project English literature as superior to Sanskrit literature. Milton's works were taught with another purpose that is,

> ...government institutions officially committed to secularism realised they were in effect teaching Christianity through Milton, a 'standard' in the literary curriculum whose scriptural allusions regularly sent students scurrying to the Bible for elucidation. (*The Bible* was in every library and was easily accessible to any student who cared to read it) (Viswanathan: 85).

John Milton's *Paradise Lost* is considered as a Eurocentric poem. He presented India as exotic. In Book I, he describes Arabian countries and India as the pandemonium. In Book II, India is projected as Satan's private hall. "High on a throne of royal state, which far/ Outshone the wealth or Ormus and of Ind, /or where the gorgeous east with richest hand/ showers on her kings barbaric pearl and gold, / Satan exalted sat..." (Milton: 1-5). Again, in Book II from line 630 to 643 Milton describes the voyage towards the colonies especially to 'Bengala' from where the merchants bring spices, he describes Satan's exploration to those places. In Book IX, from line 1099 to 1118, the Banyan tree is referred. In India the Banyan tree is associated with eternity and moreover considered as a place of angels. In *Paradise Lost* Milton made it as a sight of shame, a thick tree with endless branches is presented as a hiding place for Adam and Eve after committing the sin. The fallen leaves of the Banyan tree are compared to the fallen angels.

> ... there soon they chose
> The fig-tree, not that kind for fruit renowned,
> But such as at this day to Indians known
> In Malabar or Deccan spreads her arms...
> There oft the Indian herdsman shunning heat
> Shelters in cool, and tends his pasturing herds
> At loopholes cut through thickest shade: those leaves
> They gathered, broad as Amazonian target (Milton.9. 1100-11)

In Book XII Milton for the first time introduces the concept 'the white man's burden' (that is to civilise the world) in literature. Though Adam says that man should not rule over men (69-70) but in 95-96 he states, "Tyranny must be; through to the tyrant thereby no excuse". This approves Milton's approval of the Western domination over the East. Moreover in *Areopagitica*, Milton's statement that god speaks with the English and He does not have anything to discuss with the others, projects his superiority feeling over the other races.

Following Milton, many writers of English literature, have started to project the colonies as evil and also waiting for colonisation/enlightenment. Consciously or unconsciously the writers produced the societal changes in Britain and their so-called responsibility to civilise the colonised. James Thomson's *The Seasons* (1726-30 revised 1746) presents England as Eden and the recently discovered nations are ready for colonisation. "With superior Boor may your rich soil, /Exuberant, Nature's better Blessings pour/ O'er every Land, the Naked Nation's Cloth, /And be the exhaustless Granary of a world" (18)

John Dryden's influential work *Annus Mirabilis* (1667) projected the wealth, capturing of places and free trade with the Eastern countries.

> Thus to the eastern wealth through storms we go;
> But now, the cape once doubled, fear no more:
> A constant trade-wind will securely blow,
> And gently lay us on the spicy shore (11)

Dryden's works attempted more to defame India by projecting it as uncivilised. His play *Aureng-zebe* (1675) was claimed to be based on the life of the Mughal King Aurangzeb. Contrarily many historians claim this work has many historical anachronisms. Instead of projecting the true picture of the Mughal Empire, Dryden presented the kings as very weak personalities who always fall for women. Without even visiting India, writing a historical play can be considered as a good example to show how a literary text can be used as a source to imply colonial knowledge. The purpose of writing this play was to impress Charles II as well as to show Charles II as an ideal king and Aurangzeb as a fiend. The play projects illicit relationships which was Dryden's imagination: father Shahjahan and his son's (Aurangzeb) love for the same girl Indamora, Empress Noor Mahal's (Aurangzeb's step grandmother), love for Aurangzeb. Among the Mughal empresses Noor Mahal was the only empress with absolute power in the court. However in the play Dryden makes her fall in love with her grandson. Noor Mahal states that she and Aurangzeb are like Adam and Eve created from the same source and at the end, rejection of her love by her step grandson results in her suicide. This kind of fictional element makes the play a farce. Balachandra Rajan in his book *Under Western Eyes*, says that "Mughal history is treated by Dryden with a disrespect that no writer would have thought of bringing to bear on the Greek and Roman past. Such a disrespect points to a stubbornly resident devaluation of the Orient" (76). Dryden wrote this play with a purpose to use it as a colonial text to construct India to the British.

British literature of the 19th century presents the Empire and colony related political / economic / societal information at least as a backdrop. Jane Austen's *Mansfield Park* (1814), presents sugar plantations in the West Indies, from where Sir Thomas Bertram derives his wealth. His visit to West Indies is mentioned in the course of the novel. In W. M. Thackeray's *Vanity Fair* (1847), Jos Sedley, who is a coward and stupid returns from India with enormous amount of money. In Dickens' *Great Expectations* (1860-1), (will be discussed in detail in another chapter) the criminal Magwitch is transported to Australia, where he makes a fortune. Though he is rich and leads a decent life in Australia, he is seen as an inferior in Britain as he is from Australia. In *David Copperfield* (1849-50), too Dickens presents the hopeless Mr. Wilkins Micawber immigrating to Australia, where he becomes successful. In Elizabeth Gaskell's novel *Mary Barton* (1848), towards the end of the novel some of the characters move to a new life in Canada.

Charlotte Brontë's *Jane Eyre* (1847) projects the British society and its connections with its colonies. The novel is named after the protagonist who in the later part of the novel falls in love with her master Edward Rochester. Rochester is already married to Bertha Mason from West Indies. Rochester was sent to the West Indies where he marries a rich girl named Bertha but very soon finds that she is insane and their marriage was a failure which indicates the ideology that natives of the colonies are inferior. Bertha's insanity is associated with her place which is barbaric and wild. Later Jane is presented as a perfect match for Rochester. Another character St. John Rivers' visit to India for spreading Christianity projected the way of life led by the British during colonisation. Moreover the novel depicted India as a dangerous place for the British and subsequently St. John Rivers dies in India.

During this time many adventurous stories for children were produced. Almost in all these novels a British man or a group of British men explore the colonised places and civilise the native people. These colonial writers produced adventurous stories to justify colonisation and mainly to perpetuate it among the children especially to the boys as they are seen as the future potential imperialists. The adventure stories follow a similar pattern that the heroes were safe in the homeland at the beginning of the novel and they were made to undergo a journey always in an 'exotic' setting which is filled with mystery.

> In addition to the stereotypical setting, the British characters and the indigenous people are a stereotypical construction of colonial discourse because the former represent the "idealised" Western values, whereas the latter represent their negations. Throughout the novels, the natives are othered and the civilising impact of conversion to Christianity is emphasised... The narrators justify British violence upon the natives which at the same time signifying the colonised as "savage", set off with a domestic issue on the surface, material reasons in reality, the British heroes end their journey by achieving their imperialist ends; they benefit from the lands and "civilise" the indigenous people. (Ayyildiz: IX-X).

Daniel Defoe's *Robinson Crusoe*, a popular adventure story was published in 1719. Superficially this novel is characterised as adventure literature and even as children's literature. When the texts are seen at a deeper level, one finds the imperialistic ideologies: which represent a prototype of a culture, religion and ideology. The story not only tells the protagonist's adventure but also it focuses on the issue of race, power, and identity formation. This story could be seen parallel with the British colonialism, where like the British Robinson Crusoe too extended his control over the island and resembling the British, Crusoe too wanted to expand his belt. Like the British who mentioned America, Australia and even New Zealand as deserted places, Crusoe too leaves for Africa in order to acquire a deserted Isand. He built his hut symbolically which means his possession of the island. He saved a man whom he always described as 'negroes', named him Friday (through naming Crusoe tries to possess the ownership of the person), taught him Christianity, English language and tried to civilise him. Throughout the text Defoe describes the island people as barbaric and savages. The incident of saving Friday and his reaction is described by Crusoe thus, "laid his head upon the ground, and taking me by the foot, step my foot upon his head" (147) and immediately without even asking his name, Crusoe named him Friday; which is not even a human name that indicate Crusoe's mindset that the boy is less than human. Through this work Defoe has created some colonial discourse about the Caribbean island. He describes those people as cannibals,

> ...for I heard that people of the Caribbean coast were cannibals or man eaters, and I know by the latitude that I could not be far from that shore. Then supposing they were not cannibals, yet they might kill me, as many Europeans who had fallen into their hands had been served, even when they had been ten or twenty together – much more I, that was but one, and could make little or no defence; ... (160).

Ballantine's *The Coral Island* is another adventurous novel for children. The three British boys land on a remote island after a shipwreck. They settle on the island and their peaceful settlement is interrupted by the two groups of indigenous people. The British boys help one of the groups by fighting with the other group. This projects the talent of the boys in solving the problems of the indigenous people. Later, there is a comparison between people converted to Christianity and the rest. They teach the British cultural values to them before leaving for Britain.

King Solomon's Mines (1885) is a famous novel written by an English adventurer Sir H. Rider Haggard. The plot of the novel is a search by a group of white adventurers for a missing brother in Africa as well as to find a hidden mine. It is considered as the first English adventurous novel set in Africa. Though it is an adventurous story, it projects colonial narratives. The writer presents some of the African characters as barbarians and as usual the whites solve the problems of Africans. When compared with other colonial texts this novel carries less of a colonial attitude as it projects some blacks as heroes.

Three Sailor Boys: or Adrift in the Pacific was written by the British Victorian explorer Verney Lovett Cameron. He served the British Empire as an explorer to Africa. Based on his travel experiences he has written this novel focusing on children's adventurous journey to Africa. It is an imperial text which projects the Africans in negative stereotypes especially as 'cannibals'.

Kingston's *In the Wilds of Africa* is an adventurous novel set in Africa. Even in this novel a crew travels to Africa for their domestic needs. Their adventures in Africa present Africa as an uncivilised and dangerous world filled with wild animals and indigenous people. It also projects some of the Africans who try to behave like the white yet they fail to reach their level. In the novel Portuguese colonisers are also presented and they are also othered like the Africans. While justifying the British colonisation, the novel criticises the Portuguese slave trade. Throughout the text Christianity is also preached by stating that the crew members (including a native named Timboo) were keeping the Bible close to themselves.

Sanders of the River (1911) was written by Edgar Wallace. This work is actually a collection of short stories which is loosely tied together through the projection of experiences of the protagonist Commissioner Sanders in Africa. The protagonist is in charge of the

British administration in West Africa and spent most of his time in Africa which results in taking the Africans seriously. He tells them, "I am as your father and mother" and tries to perform a strict paternal role. This novel too portrays the Africans as barbaric and gives justification for the British rule. "In the good old times before the English came there were many wars, tribe against tribe, people against people. There were battles, murders, raiding and wholesale crucifixions, but the British changed all that. There was peace in the land."

Along with the above mentioned adventurous stories one could also join the life and mission of David Livingstone, a famous 19th century pre-colonial missionary-cum-explorer, who wanted to find the source of the river Nile. His aim during his first journey was to spread Christianity and to convert the Africans. Later along with that he was interested in exploring places. Mr. Jeal in his work *Livingstone* (1973) projected Livingstone as a 'complicated man' who wanted the empire to trade in Africa. Commerce, Christianity and Civilisation are the three C's which motivated Livingstone. His work *Missionary Travels and Researches in South Africa* and his speech at Cambridge University calling for "Opening Africa for Commerce and the Gospel" reveals him as an imperialist.

> I beg to direct your attention to Africa. – I know that in a few years I shall be cut off in that country, which is now open; do not let it be shut again! I go back to Africa to make an open path for commerce and Christianity; do you carry out the work which I have begun. I leave it with you (Monk: 24).

By stating this he believed that this might benefit the Africans. He assumed that educating Africans would improve their lives. Moreover, such thinking projected him as a beneficiary of Africans. However he was attacked by the critics for his imperialistic ideology of helping humans. Cecil Northcott states, "Livingstone was the colonialist and was not ashamed of it. He was in Africa to offer the benefits of the white man's civilisation, and no latter day beliefs in black man's freedom liberation and independence may be read into his action" (74).

From 1865-1869 no one knew about the whereabouts of Livingstone. At that time Henry Morton Stanley took a mission to find Livingstone in Africa. For his exploration to search Livingstone, Stanley travelled around 750 miles in the Dark Continent. His successful journey took around 1000 days to complete this mission.

Stanley published his adventure as *How I Found Livingstone* which again gives an imperialistic view of the Africans.

The British were very particular about maintaining the difference between the natives and themselves. In colonial literature the natives were presented as inhuman, uncivilised, wild, beastly and stupid. In most of the colonial literature colonial people are presented as a group with no individuality and mostly when it deals with the British characters the natives are absent in their own land. Similarly the British were afraid of the mixed race. Thus they made the native women die or cause problems in the mixed race marriages. Often they present white women as the nobler ones who redeem the troubled soul of the white male as in *Jane Eyre.*

A sensational work of this category which was successful in creating a negative image of the natives back home is *Confession of a Thug* (1839) by Philip Meadows Taylor. This novel was the most sensational ethnographic fiction as well as the most influential novel about India. This novel was an assumed confession of an Indian thug to a British narrator. The thug, Amir Ali, is projected as a devotee of Goddess Kali, has killed more than 700 people covertly for money. The novel was written with an intention to project India as a dangerous place where innocent travellers were murdered by thugs and their religious practices as barbaric. Mary Poovey observes that *Confession of a Thug* was written

> ...as an unequivocal justification for British rule in India – but as an oblique critique of the East India Company and everything it represented: assumptions about the racial superiority of the English, the conviction that Christianity is morally superior to various Indian religions, and the belief that Western bureaucracy is more efficient and rational than its Eastern counterpart (4).

Rudyard Kipling another important imperial writer spent most of his time in India. Thus his stories centre on the Indian and Anglo-Indian characters. Kipling's protagonists are generally Indian Civil Service officers or army soldiers who worked for the native people as a representation of the empire. The important characters of Kipling are British, Indian and Anglo-Indian. Throughout his work Kipling consciously maintains the hierarchy of characters. He does not allow the British to mingle closely with the Indians. In some of his stories he gave voice for the better treatment of Indian women by Indian men and also other problems faced by Indians. However he maintained the prejudices in his novels which left him as a political writer.

Kipling's famous poem 'The White Man's Burden' projects the imperialist notion vividly. He is of the view that to civilise the non-white is a moral burden of the white. He states, "Take up the white man's burden-/ Send forth the best ye breed-/ Go bind your sons to exile-/ To serve your captives' need;/ To wait in heavy harness/On fluttered folk and wild-/ Your new-caught, sullen peoples,-/ Half devil and half child." Through this poem Kipling presents the common thought of the British as the white are sent with a purpose to civilise the non-white. Kipling's view is criticised by many critics stating his appreciation of the empire indicates the exploitation of the poor nations by the empire.

Most of Kipling's stories are set in rural India which is mixed with fantasy and myth. Though Kipling lived in India for several years he failed to project India in its true colours. Nevertheless he intended to present India with negativity so that Britain is seen in a positive light. David Cody says that Kipling's writings imply,

> ...that the Empire existed not for the benefit – economic or strategic or otherwise – of Britain itself, but in order that primitive peoples, incapable of self-government, could, with British guidance, eventually become civilised (and Christianised). The truth of this doctrine was accepted naively by some, and hypocritically by others, but it served in any case to legitimise Britain's acquisition...

His novel *Kim* (1901) is a story of the titled character. Kim, an orphaned son of Irish parents, lives in the streets of Lahore. Kim is accustomed to the native culture and only a few could realise him as a white child. The novel is about young Kim's development from a cheap native-like boy to a serious, dedicated and intelligent member of the British Indian secret service. Kim joins Lama who is in search of a river, for a spiritual journey. Though the journey is undertaken by Lama, accompanied by Kim a fourteen-year-old boy, kim is projected as more intelligent than Lama, an old native man. While travelling by allowing Kim to take all the major decisions, Kipling presents a white child as superior than an elderly native man. Kipling was criticised severely by many for his imperialistic attitude. One such comment is from George Orwell, who called Kipling "a jingo imperialist," who was "morally insensitive and aesthetically disgusting."

George Orwell's comment projects him as anti-imperialist yet one of his novels shows that he too has grown the seed imperialism in his work. George Orwell's *Burmese Days* (1934) is set in British Burma which was ruled from Delhi and considered as a part of British India. Orwell served as a police officer in Burma from 1922 to 1927. Based on his experience in Burma, Orwell wrote this novel. It was written with the purpose to project the helpless condition of the natives under the control of the imperialists. Contradictorily the novel presents imperialistic ideas through the native characters. Flory, a British timber merchant is in support of the Burmese. Flory describes imperialism as, "the lie that we're here to uplift our poor black brothers rather than to rob them" (39). But an Indian character Dr. Veraswamy contradicts this view that British rule enlightened them. Dr. Veraswamy, "would maintain with positive eagerness that he, as an Indian, belonged to an inferior degraded race" (40). Other White characters too approve imperialism. Ellis, a white character, says,

> ...good God what are we supposed to be doing in this country? If we are not going to rule, why the devil don't we clear out? Here we are, supposed to be governing a set of damn black swine who've been slaves since the beginning of history, and instead of ruling them in the only way they understand, we go and treat them as equals (25).

By projecting contradictory characters, Orwell struggles with the complexity of emotion. Racist ideas are sprinkled through almost all the characters except Flory and Mr. MacGregor. However though Flory mingles with the Burmese and has a Burmese lady as his mistress, his willingness to marry an English woman indicates the hierarchy of race. Regarding Orwell's oscillation, Trilling states,

> ...he has spoken with singular honesty of the ambiguousness of his attitude in the imperialist situation. He disliked authority and the manner of its use, and he sympathised with the natives; yet at the same time he saw the need for authority and he used it, and he was often exasperated by the natives (61).

The most important work of the 20th century, still much celebrated work in academic circles is Joseph Conrad's *The Heart of Darkness*. Earlier the work was read in a different perspective and later from the Nigerian author Chinua Achebe's rereading of the text from the postcolonial view showed its potential as a colonial text. It is a novella which is based on Conrad's personal experience in Congo. The title of the text *The Heart of Darkness* represents the protagonist's journey to Central Africa, which strengthens the ideology that Africa is dark with regard to civilisation and development. The protagonist Marlow's character is based on Conrad's experience of voyage and the story is presented as Marlow talking about his experience in

Congo and how he became the captain of a boat to his friends in England. Mr. Kurtz, a dealer of trade is seen as the representative of European interest in the exploitation of natives in trade. Mr. Kurtz travels to Africa with the intention of enlightening the Africans but in reality to trade ivory. This work enables the readers to understand that colonisation did not help the natives in getting enlightened, whereas it benefited the whites in trade.

Most of the British colonial writers through their works tried to justify colonisation as primarily for the goodness of the colonised. The white man's duty is carried over by the British to compel their normal duty that is to civilise the natives. In Kipling's work one finds the dedicated service of the British officers for the good management of the empire in India.

Like the British men, the British women too wrote about the colonies. Many of them who stayed with their families in the colonies created their perception/understanding of the colony as real to others through their writings. Most of such British women wrote informal writings such as sociological studies, memoirs, diaries, letters, and they are called as Memsahib Writings. They preferred informal writings because it is not bound to any structure and it is based on the power of desire and knowledge. In order to overcome their loneliness, boredom and homesickness they started to write. They were not publishing their works but wrote it to their friends who stayed in England. Through their writings they constructed the native men and women as dangerous, ignorant, stereotypes, etc. These works created an interest in Britain to know their superiority over the colonies which resulted in them worshipping the colonial heroes. The interest to know their powerful position in the colonies, the public developed curiosity to know about the missionaries, explorers and adventurers. Thus works dealing with these themes became bestsellers. Moreover these works created a vision of their home countries as well as the colonies. It highlights that the British writing in any form explicitly projected the natives in negative form.

Not only literature even history is written with the subjective views of the British. History is mocked now as His+Stories by many. *The History of British India* (3 volumes) gave the stories of an imperialist James Mill. He took the task of writing India's history in 1803 but took 12 years to finish the three volumes with his imagination. The purpose of writing this history was to defend Britain for colonising India. He believes that India was the backward nation and the Indians as uncivilised. In the Preface of this work he claims proudly that without visiting India he could write three volumes of Indian history.

> "A duly qualified man can obtain more knowledge of India in one year in his closet in England than he could obtain during the course of the longest life, by the use of his eyes and ears in India" He used this book to register his attack on the culture, tradition, language, art, people and laws of India. He projected Hindus as, "under the glossing exterior of the Hindu, lies a general disposition to deceit and perfidy... in truth, the Hindu like the eunuch, excels in the qualities of a slave" (150).

This book became a famous reference work to know about India. No one dared to question the authenticity of the text but praised it as a genuine history.

Similar to Mill, Hegel a much acclaimed philosopher wrote *Philosophy of History* and in the work he was trying to look at the history of Philosophy. His intention in writing this work is to construct the colonised and their philosophy as inferior and consequently by doing so to promote the Western philosophy. He views the violent colonisation and slaughter of the natives in America as justified. He is of the opinion that the reason for such violence was to teach culture to the colonised. He states that till the Europeans arrived, America did not have history. Only through European rule the Americans and the Africans were educated. To teach the meaning of freedom, Africans were enslaved by the British.

> Another characteristic fact in reference to the Negroes is slavery. Negroes are taken into slavery by Europeans and sold to America. Despite this, their lot is even worse in their own country, where an equally absolute slavery is present; for the overall foundation of slavery is that man has no consciousness of his freedom yet, and so sinks down to a mere thing, a worthless object. .... Slavery is in and for itself wrong [Unrecht], for the essence of humanity is freedom; but for this man must first become mature [reif]. This is why the gradual abolition of slavery is therefore more appropriate and more right [Richtigeres] than its sudden removal (96-97).

Moreover Hegel mentions the reason for colonisation as "The English, or rather the East India Company, are the lords [Herren] of the land; for it is the necessary fate of Asiatic empires to be subjected [unterworfen] to Europeans; and China will also, some day, have to submit to this fate" (142-143). He wrote a volume on India and Indian philosophy without visiting India and understanding Indian philosophy. He describes India as a corrupt nation and Indians as corrupt and deceitful. Further he states that like other colonised countries, India too does not have a proper history. According to him the Africans are better than the Indians as the Africans were educated about freedom and other moral values through slavery.

The above mentioned literary and non-literary works projected its implicit role in the construction of 'the white man's burden' in the mind of the colonised. Moreover as a part of missionary zeal, English medicine played a crucial role by getting colonised people as lab rats for testing the English medicines and to develop their research. Slowly the native medicine practices in the colonised nations were forgotten and the English medicine started to rule the colonies. It is clear from the statement of the Nobel Laureate Sir Ronald Ross, "in the coming century, the success of imperialism will depend largely upon success with the microscope". (Rohan Deb Roy).

CHAPTER 2

Commonwealth Literature to Postcolonial Studies

> "Let us therefore brace ourselves to our duties, and so bear ourselves that if the British Empire and its Commonwealth last for a thousand years, men will still say, this was their finest hour."
>
> Winston Churchill

Since colonisation the thinking process of almost the entire world has changed to a greater level. Most of the decolonised countries, though become independent before seven to eight decades, still find difficulty in decolonising themselves mentally. The inferiority complex or the position of subordination altered their thinking process, lifestyle and culture. It is visible through their fascination for English language and Western culture. As Sujata Bhatt states in her poem "A Different History", the present generation of the decolonised nations are showing an interest towards the language which killed their grandparents.

> Which language,
> has not been the oppressor's tongue?
> Which language
> Truly meant to murder someone?
> And how does it happen
> that after the torture,
> after the soul has been cropped
> with a long scythe swooping out
> of the conqueror's face-
> the unborn grandchildren
> grow to love that strange language.

As stated above, the citizens of decolonised nations, instead of retrieving one's culture and language after colonisation, are willingly choosing their former master's culture and language over their own. Slowly the decolonised nations started to believe that everything from the West is superior and theirs as inferior which results in people mimicking the West. Already with the help of the colonial rule and education, English has become the official language or one of the official languages of the former colonies of the British Empire. Now with the term of globalisation and language of technology, English has started to dominate the world. As rightly warned by the cultural thinkers, distancing from one's mother tongue also results in the isolation from one's own and specific cultural practices. Arjun Appadurai projects this by warning the world's change towards 'monoculture'. It is interesting to note that all these mass changes are the aftermath of colonisation.

Thinkers and critics are taking tremendous measures to stop the damage of monoculture. One such measure taken by the theorists and critics is to project the importance of cultural history to the people. Here the role of postcolonial critics and theorists is essential as their part in retrieving one's own cultural history is tremendous. Partly they initiated to present the culture of a nation before colonisation and juxtaposed it with the present. Thus postcolonialism has become one of the buzz words in the 20th century. When postcolonialism as a new branch in academics was started in the Western universities, many universities opposed to having a separate department. They were worried that studying colonial and postcolonial literature or theories may create enmity towards the American whites or the British. Hence primarily there was opposition on this initiation. Postcolonialism was not the first type to start with, actually it was initiated and developed from the Commonwealth Literature. Literature produced from the once colonised countries have different names like Commonwealth Literature, New English Literature, Third World Literature and Postcolonial Literature.

Commonwealth Literature was a very popular literature in the middle of the 20th century. It refers to the literary works produced from the former colonies of Britain. The Commonwealth Nations, also known as Commonwealth is a political association of 54 former colonies of the British Empire. Salman Rushdie defines it as, "...that body of writing created...in the English Language, by persons who are not themselves white Britons, or Irish, or citizens of the United States of America" (63). The term British Commonwealth of Nations was given by Jan Smuts in 1917 with a vision of the "future constitutional relations and readjustments in essence" (Crafford: 142). The term Commonwealth was officially used to denote the community which was explicit from the 1926 Imperial Conference where the declaration of Britain and its dominations as "equal in status, in no way subordinate one to another in any aspect of their domestic or external affairs, though united by common allegiance to the crown, and freely associated as members of the British Commonwealth of Nations" (Olson: 297-298). The British Commonwealth of Nations, comprised of Australia, Canada and New Zealand started in 1931. These countries agreed to be self-governing as well as to allegiances to the British Crown. Later in 1949 it faced some transformation by leaving 'Britain' from the title and adding some more former British colonies, that is around 53 countries to be 'free and equal'.

Literary works produced from the former colonies of Britain that is the Commonwealth countries are termed as Commonwealth Literature. "Commonwealth Literature was a term literary critics began to use from the 1950s to describe Literatures in English emerging from a selection of countries with a history of colonialism" (McLeod: 10).The specific feature of Commonwealth Literature is the literary works produced from the postcolonial countries of Britain were written in English. According to Rushdie, "What seems… to be happening is that those people who were once colonised by the language are now rapidly remaking it, domesticating it, becoming more and more relaxed about the way they use it – assisted by the English language's enormous flexibility and size, they are carving out large territories for themselves within its frontiers" (64). This literature serves with the purpose of spreading a country's unique cultural and cross-cultural practices of the world. Rushdie comments regarding this as,

> What commonwealth literature finds interesting in Patrick White is his Australianness; in Doris Lessing, her Africanness; in V.S._ Naipaul, his West Indianness.... Books are almost always praised for using motifs and symbols out of the author's own national tradition or when their form echoes some traditional influences at work upon the writer can be seen to be wholly internal to the "culture" from which he "springs" (66).

In spite of being very popular, Commonwealth Literature had its own limitations. The biggest limitation is despite it being written from the different corners of the world with distinct cultural practices, it was generalised as Commonwealth Literature. Another major problem with commonwealth literature is that it was seen separately as a new type of writing but not combined with the mainstream British Literature. Henry Louis Gates cites this as,

> ...sometimes vulgar nationalism implicit in would-be literary categories such as 'American Literature' or the not so latent imperialism implied by the vulgar phrase 'Commonwealth Literature' are extra-literary designations of control symbolic of material and concomitant political relations rather than literary ones (quoted in Bryden: 7).

Many writers do not feel comfortable to be fixed under some terms or theories. They fear that those terms may limit their themes in order to produce a uniform kind of literature which also lead to categorise it as a sub-kind of literature away from the mainstream. Rushdie in *Imaginary Homelands* criticises it stating, "Isn't this the very oddest of beasts... a school of literature whose supposed members deny vehemently that they belong to it? Worse these denials are simply disregarded! It seems the creature has taken on a life of its own". He further states that it means 'master-slave relationship' and he titles this essay as "Commonwealth Literature Does Not Exist". Rushdie disapproves of Commonwealth Literature as it is just an attempt to create an exclusive literary ghetto. He further adds that the "effect of creating such a ghetto was, is, to change the meaning of the far broader term 'English literature' which I'd always taken to mean simply the literature of the English language – into something far narrower, something topographical, nationalistic, possibly even racially segregationist" (63). Meenakshi Mukherjee in her essay titled "Interrogating Postcolonialism" offers the difference between Commonwealth Literature and Post-colonial Literature. She states that commonwealth literature is named for the "comprehensive label for all English writing that came out of the various British colonies, but during and after the era of imperial control" (5) and moreover it has British literature as its centre. On the other hand post-colonial literature is free from the "centralist undertones" (6). In *The Empire Writes Back: Theory and Practice in Post-Colonial Literatures*, Ashcroft, Griffiths, and Tiffin reject the term Commonwealth as it rests "purely on the fact of a shared history and the resulting political grouping" (23). Consequently, due to its limitations, scholars prefer the term Postcolonial Literature rather than Commonwealth literature.

Postcolonial literature is the non-Western literature with a common historical experience. Under this title literature written in other languages and the former colonies of other European empires are included.

CHAPTER 3

Postcolonial Studies

"Until the lion learns how to write, every story will glorify the hunter."

— J. Nozipo Maraire

The term 'Postcolonial' is still under a discussion with regard to its meaning. Some scholars prefer to use the hyphenated term post-colonial. In *The Empire Write's Back,* Bill Ashcroft, Gareth Griffiths and Helen Tiffin prefer to use the term post-colonial to denote the period after colonisation. Here 'post' is about after, the temporal period. They state,

> We use the term 'post-colonial', however, to cover all the culture affected by the imperial process from the moment of colonisation to the present day. This is because there is a continuity of preoccupations throughout the historical process initiated by European imperial aggression. We also suggest that it is most appropriate as the term for the new cross-cultural criticism which has emerged in recent years and for the discourse through which this is constituted. In this sense this book is concerned with the world as it exists during and after the period of European imperial domination and the effects of this on contemporary literatures (2).

Hamza Alavi (1972) and John S. Saul too preferred to use the hyphenated term. But since the publication of Edward Said's *Orientalism*, many prefer to see postcolonialism as a single term to denote ideological response to Euro-centricism.

Homi Bhabha rejects the idea that postcolonial is historical. According to Bhabha,

> Postcolonial criticism bears witness to the unequal and uneven forces of cultural representation involved in the context for political and social authority within the modern world order. Postcolonial perspectives emerge from the colonial testimony of Third World countries and the discourses of "minorities" within the geopolitical divisions of East and West, North and South. They intervene in those ideological discourses of modernity that attempt to give a hegemonic "normality" to the uneven development and the differential, often disadvantaged, histories of nations, races and communities peoples. They formulate their critical revisions around issues of cultural differences, social authority, and

political discrimination in order to reveal the antagonistic and ambivalent moments within the "rationalisations" of modernity (171).

Also Helen Gilbert and Joanne Tompkins in *Post-Colonial Drama: Theory, Practice, Politics* (1996), reject the usage of it with a hyphen. They state that,

> The term post-colonialism – according to a too-rigid etymology – is frequently misunderstood as a temporal concept, meaning the time after colonialism has ceased, or the time following the politically determined Independence Day on which a country breaks away from its governance by another state. Not a naïve teleological sequence, which supersedes colonialism, post-colonialism is, rather, an engagement with, and contestation of, colonialism's discourses, power structures, and social hierarchies... A theory of post-colonialism must, then, respond to more than the merely chronological construction of post-independence, and to more than just the discursive experience of imperialism.

According to Robert J.C. Young postcolonialism is,

> … simply the product of human experience, but human experience of the kind that has not typically been registered or represented at any institutional level. More particularly, it is the result of different cultural and national origins, the ways in which the colour of your skin or your place and circumstance of birth define the kind of life, privileged and pleasurable, or oppressed and exploited, that you will have in this world. Postcolonialism's concerns are centred on geographic zones of intensity that have remained largely invisible, but which prompt or involve questions of history, ethnicity, complex cultural identities and questions of representation, of refugees, emigration and immigration, of poverty and wealth – but also, importantly, the energy, vibrancy and creative cultural dynamics that emerge in very positive ways from such demanding circumstances. Postcolonialism offers a language of and for those who have no place, who seem not to belong, of those whose knowledges and histories are not allowed to count. It is above all this preoccupation with the oppressed, with the subaltern classes, with minorities in any society, with the concerns of those who live or come from elsewhere, that constitutes the basis of postcolonial politics and remains the core that generates its continuing power (13-14).

Leela Gandhi defines postcolonialism as "a theoretical resistance to the mystifying amnesia of the colonial aftermath. It is a disciplinary project devoted to the academic task of revisiting, remembering and, crucially, interrogating the colonial past". Thus many scholars preferred the term postcolonialism without a hyphen as it is sensible to denote a long period of consequences of colonialism. Moreover the decolonisation period of the formerly colonised countries varies. Some scholars rejected –ism as it may attach the academic dogma (just like other –isms) and preferred 'postcolonial'.

Postcolonial Studies includes literatures from the formerly colonised nations such as African countries, Australia, Bangladesh, Canada, Caribbean Islands, India, Malaysia, New Zealand, Singapore and Sri Lanka. It also uses concepts from other critical practices like Post Structuralism, Feminism, Marxism, Psychoanalysis, Deconstruction and Linguistics. The situation of all the colonised countries are not the same. Some of the countries got independence very early and other countries got independence very late. The case of America, Australia, New Zealand, South Africa, and Canada is different from the African countries. The literature of America is not included in the postcolonial literature due to its powerful position and its condition of colonisation was different from the other colonies. In the decolonised countries, the class or caste hierarchy exist which further lead to different hierarchies. Terry Eagleton states, "Postcolonial thought is allowed to talk about cultural differences but not – or not much about economic exploitation". Ania Loomba in her third edition of her work *Colonialism/Postcolonialism* states that many conservatives in the higher position of academics are not happy with the field of Postcolonialism. They even go to the extreme to blame Postcolonialism as a reason for people turning anti-American.

> Till the 1970s the term Postcolonial Studies was not available in academics but instead its content was read as historical, political, economic and social studies. Later after the emergence of the term Postcolonial Studies, it occupied an important position in the universities of Europe, America and many of the formerly colonised countries. With so many scholarships, journals and conferences, Postcolonial Studies has become a buzz word. Though it was mostly linked with the English department, it was actually an interdisciplinary studies with cultural studies, history, anthropology, arts and other disciplines. The major characteristic of Postcolonial Studies is that it depends upon other disciplines as it is an interdisciplinary study. It has borrowed various important concepts and ideas from other disciplines like cultural studies, history, anthropology, geography, sociology, feminism, political studies, postmodernism, post structuralism, psychoanalysis, Marxism and environmental studies. Thus postcolonial studies is 'highly interdisciplinary in the synoptic sense, borrowing freely from a wide range of fields in a desire both to challenge received assumptions as well as to shed light on the configurations of the present and the future' (Quayson: 25).

Some scholars divide postcolonialism in two waves. Julian Go locates the period from anti-colonialism to postcolonialism as first wave postcolonialism. He includes W.E.B. Du Bois, Aimé Césaire, Frantz Fanon, Amilcar Cabral, C.L.R. James, Léopold Sédar Senghor, Benoy Kumar Sarkar, Albert Memmi and Anouar Abdel-Malek as thinkers of the first wave. They moved history from the Euro-centric perspective by providing history of the colonies.

> "First-wave thinkers extended the idea of a mutually constituting relationship between coloniser and colonised, or metropole and colony, to global history in its entirety. They thereby subverted dominant stories about the exceptionality and agency of Western development. "Europe," the first-wave showed, is not an isolated agent. It is constituted by its imperial peripheries. History is not the history of single nations but of metropoles and colonies, empires and peripheries, interlocked and enchained in international and transnational relations" (Go: 26).

Along with protesting against the empire they also gave insight into the standpoint of the colonised and their culture. They provided the subjective view of colonialism by transforming from the position of object to subject. Mukherjee claims that "[F]irst-wave postcolonial theorists stressed [...] the importance of the historical specificity of literature and culture. Yet, frequently, their very notion of "history" and "culture" remained textualist/linguistic in conception and their own institutional location [was] under theorised".

The second wave has started to emerge in the 1980s. It is actually an extension of the first wave with respect to the analysis of culture but it focused more on colonial discourse. The key thinkers of the wave are Said, Bhabha, Spivak and Dipesh Chakrabarty.

> The very critique of the imperial episteme that the second-wave offered was itself a move in the right direction towards postcolonial knowledge... There is no consensus here; no singular approach. Instead, there are a variety of tactics and methods. Not all of them are consistent with each other. But they all endeavour to cultivate knowledge that challenges the imperial episteme rather than reproduces it (Go: 59).

Now, some critics state that the postcolonial studies are exhausted/ dead or the next stage of the theory, Post-postcolonial Studies has emerged. The third wave or the future of postcolonial studies is given in detail in the last section of the text.

Till the emergence of postcolonial studies, the imperialists presented their point of stories where they projected the colonised as primitive, who needed to be civilised. The postcolonial writers changed this and they have started to present their point of view/ counterviews which decentred the position of logo-centralism under Western knowledge. Postcolonial studies aims to dismantle the

Euro-centric discourse by placing the societies from the periphery to the centre that is in subjective position. Reconstruction of national culture and reclaiming tradition paved the way for the social articulations. It resulted in the variety of works related to the histories of minorities which is addressed as 'intellectual evolution' by U.Y. Mudimbe.

The emergence of postcolonial studies changed the way of reading metropolitan writing. The primary methodology to deconstruct the colonial constructed images of the colonised is through colonial discourse analysis. This important way of reading played an influential role in the development of postcolonial studies. Colonial discourse analysis presents "how colonialism suggests certain ways of seeing, specific modes of understanding the world and one's place in it that assist in justifying the subservience of colonised peoples to the (oft-assumed) 'superior', civilised order of the British colonisers. These ways of seeing are at the root of the study of colonial discourses" (McLeod: 18). Through colonial discourse, the colonisers justified their act of colonisation and made the colonised to accept it as proper to be under control. Sam Selvon, in one of his lectures in 1979, recollects that in his youth he considered white people as superior and the non-white as inferior.

> When one talks of colonial indoctrination, it is usually about oppression or subjugation, or waving little Union Jacks on Empire Day and singing 'God Save the King'. But this gut feeling I had as a child, that the Indian was just a piece of cane trash while the white mam was to be honoured and respected – where had it come from? I don't consciously remember being brainwashed to hold this view either at home or at school (211).

The main intentions of colonial discourses are to show how colonialism made certain ways of seeing and understanding.

The term 'discourse' has been used since the 16th century to describe any sort of speech, conversation or talk on any subject. Foucault believes that the term discourse is not simply a speech but it means more. He states that, "a discourse is a strongly bounded area of social knowledge, a system of statements within which the world can be known. The key feature of this is that the world is not simply 'there' to be talked about, rather, it is through discourse itself that the world is brought into being" (62). He used this concept in his work on madness, where he intends to recover the voices of the insane people than to believe others' opinion about them. He analysed how madness as an identity produced and reproduced by rules and procedures which became institutionalised. He called such systems as 'the order of discourse'. He believed that humans produce certain ideas as normal and some as deviant. According to him power exists everywhere in a society. "Power is everywhere; not because it embraces everything, but because it comes from nowhere' (93). Such power produces knowledge as per its desire. Here language is used in a particular way that is rooted in practices and actions.

Reading colonial literature by applying colonial discourse is colonial discourse analysis.

> Colonial discourse theory is that theory which analyses the discourse of colonialism and colonisation; which demonstrates the way in which such discourse obscures the underlying political and material aims of colonisation; and which points out the deep ambivalences of that discourse as well as the way in which it constructs both colonising and the colonised subject (Bill Ashcroft and Pal Ahluwalia: 15).

It projects how the stereotypes, images and knowledge about the colonised and their culture is connected with the desire and power of the imperials. Their desire leads to the construction of binary division among humans. Europeans presented the non-Europeans as negative in order to get positive image of themselves. Young defines it as, "colonial discourse analysis ... forms the point of questioning of Western knowledge's categories and assumptions" (11). Edward Said used Foucault's concept of 'discourse' to understand the production of discourses about the orient. According to Said, the study of the Orient "was ultimately a political vision of reality whose structure promoted a binary opposition between the familiar (Europe, the West, "us") and the strange (the Orient, the East, "them")" (43). Said denied the innocence of Oriental studies and Western scholarship. He believed that each field (now celebrated as interdisciplinary courses with postcolonialism) has its own objective to project the non-West as primitive.

Colonial discourse analysis tends to project the presence of oriental discourse. Since the publication of *Orientalism* in 1978, many works have started to project the orientalist (Eurocentric) discourse. Said was a pioneer in the colonial discourse analysis especially in using literary work to discuss history. Homi Bhabha considers Said as an important figure in colonial discourse analysis as his work, "focused on the need to quicken the half-light of Western history with the disturbing memory of its colonial texts that bear witness to the trauma that accompanies the triumphal art of Empire". Ania Loomba comments regarding it thus,

> ... it was new in its wide sweeping range and focus, in its invocation of Foucault's work to make connections between the production of knowledge and the exercise of power, and innovative also in its use of literary materials to discuss historical and epistemological processes. In many ways Said's use of culture and knowledge to interrogate colonial power inaugurated colonial discourse studies (63).

Said defines Orientalism as "the corporate institution for dealing with the Orient – dealing with it by making statements about it, settling it, ruling over it: in short, Orientalism as a Western style for dominating, restructuring, and having authority over the Orient" (3). The work presents the Western representation of the non-Western cultures in the constructed discipline named Orientalism which is supported by other disciplines like philosophy, history, anthropology and literature. It examines literature and cultural texts to present how the certain way of seeing and thinking helped the colonial power. Moreover these discourses are central in the creation of the 'orient'. Said states,

> Most important, such texts can create not only knowledge but also the very reality they appear to describe. In time such knowledge and reality produce a tradition, or what Michel Foucault calls a discourse, whose material presence or weight, not the originality of a given author, is really responsible for the texts produced out it (94).

Said believes that the power of colonisation led to the construction of information about the orient: how the orient has to be viewed and controlled.

The book *Orientalism* is considered as a political work by many critics as it wanted to reverse the 'gaze' by the orients. The book consists of three parts: 1. 'The Scope of Orientalism' presents the establishment of characters and qualities of orients through the similarities in the representation of 'Oriental despotism, Oriental sensuality, Oriental modes of production, and Oriental splendour' (47). 2. 'Orientalist Structures and Restructures' analyses how historical and creative texts of the 19th century constructed the Orient textually which resulted in the colonial administration. 3. 'Modern Orientalism' presents America as a new imperialist country that followed the imperialist principles of the then Britain and France.

Said elaborates the construction of the 'Orient' by projecting the connectivity between the expansion of the empire and the study of Orients. For example colonisation of Egypt was justified thus,

> England knows Egypt; Egypt is what England knows; England knows that Egypt cannot have self-government; England confirms that by occupying Egypt; for the Egyptians, Egypt is what England has occupied and now governs; foreign occupation therefore becomes 'the very basis' of contemporary Egyptian civilisation. (34)

Construction of the Orient was important to define themselves (Occident). Whatever is the nature of the orient, its opposite is the Occident. Europeans homogenised the behavioural nature, geography and culture of the orients and their landscape across the globe.

> 'the Orient' is itself a constituted entity, and the notion that there are geographical spaces with indigenous, radically 'different' inhabitants who can be defined on the basis of some religion, culture or racial essence proper to that geographical space is equally a highly debatable idea (322).

Said expects the intellectuals of the postcolonial nations to be active to erase the misrepresentation of themselves by the colonisers.

Later day critics found some limitations in the work *Orientalism.* Dennis Porter is of the view that by using Foucault's concept of discourse, Said has created some methodological problems. Said actually homogenised the Orient and could not elaborate the process how counter discourse could emerge. He states that

> … in the end to suggest alternatives to the discourse of Orientalism is not difficult to explain. First, because he overlooks the potential contradiction between discourse theory and Gramscian hegemony, he fails to historicise adequately the texts he cites and summarises … Second, because he does not distinguish the literary instance from more transparently ideological textual forms he does not acknowledge the semi-autonomous and over determined character of aesthetic artefacts. Finally, he fails to show how literary texts may in their play establish distance from the ideologies they seem to be reproducing (160).

Aijaz Ahamed in his work *In Theory: Classes, Nations, Literature* explains that Said was inconsistent about Orientalism as representation or as misrepresentation by the Europeans. 'The line between representation and misrepresentation is always very thin' (164). Robert Young in his work *White Mythologies* comments that *Orientalism* fails to give any alternative to the phenomenon it finds and it falls prey to what it finds.

Though some critics presented the limitations of the work *Orientalism*, Said's colonial discourse analysis was celebrated widely by the scholars and translated in many languages. Homi Bhabha and Gayatri Chakravorty Spivak used this approach with some diversions and contributed their knowledge to enrich this field.

Homi Bhabha accepts Said as a pioneer in colonial discourse analysis but feels that he has focused too much on the concept 'binary'. According to Said, the binary division between the coloniser and the colonised is definite and fixed one. Said could not consider that there could be any intermediary space between these two. For Said colonial discourse represents colonial subjects and helped to study the 'other'. The colonial discourse space was created for the colonised. Bhabha disagrees with Said's arguments here. He extended his research from Said to present the manner how Orientalism became a tool of colonial power and administration. "My reading of colonial discourse suggests that the point of intervention should shift from the ready recognition of images as positive or negative, to an understanding of the processes of subjectification made possible (and plausible) through stereo-typical discourse" (67).

Bhabha is of the view that colonial discourse is not masterful as it fails to produce the inferior 'other' and nevertheless it contains the seeds of rebellion. For Bhabha colonial discourse is created by the coloniser due to their fear. The colonisers depended upon the colonised to show their superiority. Bhabha uses the terms 'ambivalence' and 'mimicry' to define colonial discourse. He believes that in colonial discourse, ambivalent space exists that consequently produces counter-discourse. He believes that lack and desire of the colonised resulted in the construction of the 'other'. The colonial subject is a strange creature, a curious object, who is always positioned outside the Western knowledge but observed under the Western knowledge.

> The objective of colonial discourse is to construe the colonised as a population of degenerate types on the basis of racial origin, in order to justify conquest and to establish systems of administration and instruction. Despite the play of power within colonial discourse and the shifting positionalities of its subjects (for example, effects of class, gender, ideology, different social formations, varied systems of colonisation and so on), I am referring to a form of governmentality that in marking out a 'subject nation', appropriates, directs and dominates its various spheres of activity. Therefore, despite the 'play' in the colonial system which is crucial to its exercise of power, colonial discourse produces the colonised as a social reality which is at once an 'other' and

> yet entirely knowable and visible. It resembles a form of narrative whereby the productivity and circulation of subjects and signs are bound in a reformed and recognisable totality. It employs a system of representation, a regime of truth, that is structurally similar to realism (70-71).

Bhabha wanted colonial power relation to be understood from the semiotic and psychoanalytic level.

The next important key thinker in colonial discourse analysis is Spivak, who fought for the space for the subalterns by questing 'Can the Subaltern Speak?' The notion of subaltern in postcolonial studies created a great impact. According to Ranjith Guha, the founder of the idea 'subaltern', denoted the colonised who were marginalised by the coloniser. He is of the view that the colonised subjects especially the peasants were made absent in the works of the colonisers and the elite colonised; but they continuously resisted the imperial power which purposely darkened their protests. Guha in *Elementary Aspects of Peasant Insurgency* (1983) claims that, "parallel to the domain of elite politics, there existed... another domain...in which the principal actors were not the dominant groups of the indigenous society or the colonial authorities, but the subaltern classes and groups constituting the mass of the labouring population... – that is, the people". Spivak used Deconstruction, Marxism and Psychoanalysis to present the colonial discourse analysis. She projected the postcolonial literary works from the decolonised countries to question the colonial representations of the colonised and specifically to present the exploited condition of the subalterns in the era of globalisation. Her colonial discourse analysis aims to question the totalising presentation of the colonisers about the colonised and to present the resistance movements of the colonised especially about the subalterns. Spivak writes in *A Critique of Postcolonial Reason*, "Colonial Discourse studies, when they concentrate only on the representation of the colonised or the matter of the colonies, can sometimes serve the production of current neo-colonial knowledge by placing colonialism/imperialism securely in the past" (1). Along with producing colonial discourses, she offered "various manifestations of counter-discourse' (Moore-Gilbert: 75) by rereading the British classical literatures from the 18th and the 19th century.

Re-reading the classic works written during colonisation by applying colonial theories is a part of colonial discourse analysis. Under this, several classics were re-read by the postcolonial scholars to project the transformation of innocent writing into a construction of discourses. Spivak in her famous essay "Three Women's Texts and a Critique of Imperialism" warned that, "The role of literature in the production of cultural representation should not be ignored". Edward Said re-read many of the British classics in his works. In *Orientalism,* he re-read Aeschylus's *The Persians* and Euripides's *The Bacchae* to project how these works constructed Asia as a hostile 'other' world across the sea. In *Culture and Imperialism* he reread important classics like Kipling's *Kim,* Austen's *Mansfield Park,* Conrad's *Heart of Darkness,* Forster's *A Passage to India* and Verdi's *Aida* (detailed study of it is given in chapter 5). Elleke Boehmer in *Colonial and Postcolonial Literature* analyses Conrad's *Lord Jim* to project, in spite of Jim being a flawed character, he was given another chance to prove his ability as he happened to be a white. According to Boehmer, both Conrad and Kipling "subscribed to theories of racial difference and supremacy, manifested in the main as the hierarchies of command which dominate their narratives. Despite his failings, Marlow sees Lord Jim as possessing an internal nobility and quality of leadership that distinguishes him from the people of Patusan" (86). Spivak in "Three Women's Texts and a Critique of Imperialism" re reads Bronte's *Jane Eyre* and Mary Shelley's *Frankenstein.*

Similar to re-reading, re-writing of classics by postcolonial writers gave voice to the marginalised. Voiceless communities/characters from the colonies in the European novels gained their voices through such re-writing and also questioned what they have constructed as 'truth'. The classic work of Shakespeare, *The Tempest* was rewritten by Aime Cesaire titled *A Tempest* (discussed in detail in Chapter 5). George Lamming's *Water with Berries* (1971), a rewriting of Shakespeare's *The Tempest,* is a political resistance. Lamming used this work to rewrite a canonical work to register the revolt of the colonised. Dereck Walcott rewrote Defoe's *Crusoe,* especially the ship wreck in his drama *Pantomime* (1978). This drama is written with an anti-colonial theme which has resistance seed. He is of the view that after getting freedom the best of both cultures (natives' and colonisers') has to be mixed to get a new culture. His view is very clear from his statement, "If we continue to sulk and say, look at what the slave-owner did, and so forth, we will never mature. While we sit moping or writing morose poems and novels that glorify a non-existent past, then time passes us by". Peter Carry's *Jack Maggs* (1997) is a rewriting of Charles Dickens' *Great Expectations.* He rewrote the novel by changing the name of the main character from Magwitch to Jack Maggs and narrated it from the third person point of view than from Pip's point of view. Being an Australian, through this rewriting, he represents the proliferation of Australia as an antipodean penal colony. Such rewritings of the canonical texts are actually a challenge to the imperial texts and through that imperial ideology itself is challenged. These re-readings and re-writings could be seen as counter-discourse.

CHAPTER 4

Key Concepts

> "... the language of the criminal can contain only the goodness of the criminal's deed. The language of the criminal can explain and express the deed only from the criminal's point of view. It cannot contain the horror of the deed, the injustice of the deed, the agony, the humiliation inflicted on me."
>
> — Jamaica Kincaid

Postcolonial studies could be well understood with the knowledge of the terms/concepts associated with it. These terms are used specially to denote the condition of colonialism or postcolonialism. Most of the postcolonial terms are borrowed from other fields or disciplines which are used with specific usage to describe or to denote the conditions associated with colonisation. Some of the significant terms/concepts are elaborated here (Terms such as Imperialism, Colonialism, Postcolonialism, Post-colonialism, Discourse, Orientalism, Subaltern are omitted here as those terms are discussed in detail in the chapters).

1. Aboriginal/ Indigenous People

The term aboriginal means 'inhabitant of a place' (noun) and 'inhabiting or existing in a land from the earliest times or from before the arrival of colonists; indigenous' (adjective) in the Dictionary of Oxford Languages (DOL). "The term 'indigenous' derives from the late Latin 'indigenus' and 'indigena' (native) and from the Old Latin 'indu' that is derived from the archaic 'endo' (a cognate of the Greek 'endo'), meaning 'in, within' and the Latin 'gignere' meaning 'to beget', from the root 'gene' meaning 'to produce, give birth, beget.' 'Indigena' in Latin means 'native' used to denote plants, animals and people who come from a particular region. Its first known use was in the 1640s when it was applied to plants and cultures in the New World. The general sense of the term applied to that produced, growing, living, or occurring naturally in a particular region or environment; also sometimes used as a synonym for 'native,' 'innate,' 'aborigine,' 'endemic,' and 'inborn."' (Peters, A. Michael: 1229). The term Aboriginal is Euro-centric as it was used to produce a binary to the Europeans. This term has been used approximately since the 17th century from the time of exploration of the British. Being dense with colonial connotations, this term was used to include all the natives of the British colonies. The British intentionally used the term aboriginal in a homogeneous way to group all the natives of their colonies to omit/hide their heterogeneity. The thousands of different ethnic communities irrespective of their differences were seen as the same by the British and the latter considered the aboriginals as inferior.

> It is estimated that there are more than 370 million indigenous people spread across 70 countries worldwide. Practising unique traditions, they retain social, cultural, economic and political characteristics that are distinct from those of the dominant societies in which they live. Spread across the world from the Arctic to the South Pacific, they are the descendants – according to a common definition – of those who inhabited a country or a geographical region at the time when people of different cultures or ethnic origins arrived. The new arrivals later became dominant through conquest, occupation, settlement or other means (Quoted in Peters, A. Michael: 1232).

The British visited and conquered those lands since the 17th century and projected the people as half human/uncivilised as the latter did not have any written history or record. In North America, the first settler colony of Britain, the natives were addressed as Red Indians by the British. In Australia, the natives were called aboriginals. It was stated by the British that initially the British explorers considered the Australian natives as animals and in order to safeguard themselves they killed many of them. The people of New Zealand were addressed as Maori. Later all these terms were united and all the natives of the colonised nations were addressed as aboriginal/indigenous people. Presently as the term aboriginal is considered derogatory, the native people wish to restore their uniqueness and identity.

2. Abrogation and Appropriation

The above mentioned two terms are used as conjunction which aims to discard the idea of standard language. Firstly, rejection of the concept of 'standard' and 'correct' English by the postcolonial writers is called an abrogation. The postcolonial writers preferred to deviate from the standard English and introduced a variety of 'Englishes' in their works (works of Chinua Achebe, Salman Rushdie and in particular *The Colour Purple* by Alice Walker). This act could be considered as one of the important political stances taken by the postcolonial writers which results in the formation and usages of many 'Englishes' such as Indian English, African English, American English, etc. Thus, with the concept of abrogation, the postcolonial writers dismantled the concept of 'centre' and 'periphery' which means the removal of 'the English' and the emergence of 'many Englishess'. As the English language played a major role in dominating/controlling the colonies, the postcolonial writers with a view to dismantle its power, used the concept abrogation to state that all English languages and its dialects are correct.

Secondly the term 'appropriation' denotes the ways of postcolonial societies' use of the coloniser's culture, language and even their thoughts in their own way. During colonisation the coloniser's language, education and cultural practices were projected as superior and as a result there was a desire among the colonised to follow those. Moreover, the cultural and language invasion upon the colonised were also severe. In particular, the imposition of the English language and English education upon the natives was the main ambition of the British. Through this most of the colonised were made to accept the English language and the coloniser's culture over theirs. However, in the postcolonial era two sets of ideas were/are shared by most of the postcolonial writers. Some reject the former-colonial language and culture to go back to their native language (for example, Ngugi wa Thiong'o who rejected the English language to write in his native language Gikuyu). Some others appropriated the English language to spread their cultural diversity to the world. They were particular about using the foreign language in their own style as a popular tool to represent their realities to a wider audience across the globe.

Through the first concept 'Abrogation' the Postcolonial critics erased the division between correct and incorrect language, which is actually the centre and the periphery distinction. Subsequently they appropriated/used the coloniser's tool (which they used for colonisation) in their own way to undo the dominance of the past.

3. Ambivalence

The term ambivalence is adapted in postcolonial studies by Homi K. Bhabah in his seminal work *The Location of Culture*. The term ambivalence is used in psychology to present the oscillation between choosing two opposite things. Bhabha while talking about the term ambivalence in colonial discourse perspective, he projects the complexity of attraction and repulsion experienced by the colonised towards the coloniser. The relationship between the coloniser and the colonised is always ambivalent because they always have the fluctuation reaction. The colonised sometimes mimic the coloniser and at times mock them. Thus, resistance against the coloniser did not occur in a full hearted way. The emotion of hate and envy towards the coloniser oscillated in the mind of the colonised.

Similarly, the colonisers too oscillated between the mindset of civilising and not-exactly civilising the colonised. Initially the colonisers quoted civilisation as the main motif of colonisation. Hence the colonised were provided English education, medicine and Christianity through missionaries. Nevertheless, the colonisers did not want the colonised to be the 'same' as themselves as they felt it would be a threat. Thus, the coloniser wanted to civilise as well as not to civilise the colonised. This fluctuation of thoughts and desire is explained as ambivalence by Homi K. Bhabha. (Refer: *Of Mimicry and Man: The Ambivalence of Colonial Discourse*).

4. Binarism

The word binary means "relating to, composed of, or involving two things." (D.O. L) which is a common word used in several fields with different meanings. In postcolonial studies it is used with distinct meaning. The concept 'Binarism' was first introduced by a French structural linguist Ferdinand de Saussure, who explained that a sign has its meaning not by a simple explanation/reference to it. But it could be well understood when it is explained/compared with the other from which it differs. That is a word could be well understood by stating its opposite, which leads to the construction of Binarism. The problem with the Binarism system is instead of explaining a sign clearly, its opposite is projected as the negative of it. Thus, it leads to the construction of hierarchy such as white/black, man/woman, day/night, where the first words of the binary sets are perceived as superior over the other.

The concept 'binarism' is used in a successful way by the imperialists to construct the binary ideology between the coloniser and the colonised like coloniser/colonised, civilised/uncivilised, beautiful/ugly, gentle/brutal, knowledgeable/stupid, active/lazy, saviours/demon, which results in colonising the people easily. From the above-mentioned set of binary words, the first words were used to denote the coloniser and the latter words were used to denote the colonised. Thus, Binarism was used successfully by the colonisers to construct ideologies about their superiority and their moral obligation to save the colonised.

5. Cartography

In postcolonial studies, the act of map making is presented as an imperialist act which presents the rest of the world as how Europe desired. Until the Europeans moved with the high ambition of conquering the world, there was no need for map making. Till then "millions of Americans crossed the continent without maps, Genghis Khan and Charlemagne ruled without maps, Rome administered its empire without a map, pharaohs controlled Egypt without a map, the Bible was written without once referring to a map" (Wood). Since colonisation maps of the world were made based on the desire of the colonisers. Thus, map making by the Europeans was not to project the position and condition of the world to the readers/viewers whereas to present 'its' view of the world. The word 'discovery' itself is a dense one used by the British to present its ignorance about the existence of some lands, which later it claims as Britain had discovered such lands. The lands might have had names but by naming the continents, countries and places the British wanted to claim it as theirs. Not only were the places named by the British, even the natives of those places were 'discovered' and named by the British. Hence map making and naming played a major role in the process of conquering and controlling those lands and its people. Thus

> The geographical vocabulary is there (west-south-west), the activity of naming on behalf of Empire is highlighted (the mountain is given the name of King James), the possibility of expansion is retained (the road), the possibility of surveying the countryside is hinted at (the hill), and the wish for the stability of the white presence is also suggested (a memorial, a heap of stones) (Zbigniew: 42).

The maps were used as a source to construct the colonisers' ideology. Most of the places, especially places in North America and Australia were marked as empty land in the early maps (as terra-nullius – a Latin word meaning land belonging to no one) though the natives of those places had been living for centuries. Such kind of dark places invited investors or explorers to start their business there. In some cases, the explorers used the help of the native people in map making but mostly those people were silenced or projected as savages or cannibals. Thus, map making was like creating texts based on the interests of the British. Similarly,

> in one infamous incident, a whole mountain range called the Mountains of Kong supposedly found in West Africa in 1797 by explorer Mungo Park never existed at all, yet reappeared on maps through the 19th century. Part of the problem was that the maps were never the work of one cartographer, but rather a compilation of ideas and reports back … Other times, the land was a mystery as a competing coloniser used the suppression of information as a way to keep control (Meier).

Postcolonial critics see map making as a process of exploitation as it completely relied upon the European models of geography and maths. They decided where the countries have to be placed in the map based on their latitude and longitude. Consequently, they kept Europe as the centre of the map by leaving the other continents and countries to the periphery.

6. Centre/ Margin

The concept Centre/Margin is very important in postcolonial studies as this Binarism was used effectively by the British to colonise the other nations. The centre is the coloniser, the British with all positive qualities to civilise the others/marginalised/colonised. The British who literally projected themselves in the centre of the world (in maps as well as in ideology) took the burden of civilising the periphery/margin (colonised). Ironically, they maintained the difference more strongly. Thus, words like civilisation, knowledge and development were attributed to the centre and the margin always remained with the qualities of primitivism, savage and ignorance. The ideas about the margin were always constructed by the centre and it took more care to maintain those ideologies. The view of the centre is always subjective thus it maintains a central position by moving others to the periphery.

7. Colonial Discourse

The term 'colonial discourse' was first used by one of the key postcolonial scholars, Edward Said in his influential work *Orientalism* (1978). He has taken the idea of Foucault's discourse to project the colonial representations of the colonies by the coloniser. The term 'discourse' according to Foucault is about the construction of knowledge with respect to power relations. He believes that power constructs truth about something which becomes knowledge of the society. Thus, powerful people produce their wishes/views as truth later which becomes knowledge of the society.

This concept is adapted in postcolonial studies. Colonial Discourse presents the constructed knowledge/truth produced by the colonisers about the colonised. In order to conquer the lands and to colonise those natives they were in need of such constructed truths. In most of the cases the coloniser's population was comparatively less than the colonised. In some cases, millions of people were colonised and controlled by merely a thousand people. Thus, the conquering of nations happened not only through physical power but also through mental power. The colonisers came with the created vision to civilise, educate and to help the savages. Through repeated presentations of the same idea (the superior position of the coloniser and the inferior position of the colonised) they constructed the binary vision. Moreover, through literature and history the colonisers projected the colonised as savages, barbaric, uncivilised, beastly and ugly. Though such truths were created by the colonisers, they were accepted by the colonised and in a span of time the colonised started to look at themselves in the constructed images.

8. Creole/Creolisation

The etymology of the word 'creole' is from the Portuguese word 'Criolulu' meaning native. Originally it was used to refer to a form of language which is derived from pidgin. It denoted the languages spoken by the Creoles in the Caribbean islands and in West Africa. Successively it was used to denote people. Initially, it denoted a white (European) born and raised in a colony and later it included the natives and indigenous people. In the course of time the term 'creole' was used to denote different things. Edward Kamau Brathwaite, a Caribbean historian in his important work titled *Contradictory Omens: Cultural Diversity and Integration in the Caribbean* (1974) talks about the numerous meanings which are attributed to the word creole. He states,

> ... in Peru the word was used to refer to people of Spanish descent who were born in the New World. In Brazil, the term was applied to Negro slaves born locally. In Louisiana, the term was applied to the white franco-phone population, while in New Orleans it applied to mulattoes. In Sierra Leone, 'creole' refers to descendants of former New World slaves, Maroons and 'Black Poor' from Britain who were resettled along the coast and especially in Freetown, and who form a social elite distinct from the African population. In Trinidad, it refers principally to the black descendants of slaves to distinguish them from East Indian immigrants. When used with reference to other native groups, an adjectival prefix – French creole, Spanish creole – is used. In Jamaica, and the old settled

English colonies, the word was used in its original Spanish sense of criollo: born into, native, committed to the area of living, and it was used in relation to both white and black, free and slave.

The word 'Creolisation' denotes mixture of culture and tradition. After colonisation almost all the native cultures got exposed to the European culture and vice versa. Thus, both native cultures and the European cultures were mixed together. Hence creolisation reflects losing of pure culture on both sides. This could be seen more in the new settled colonies.

9. Decolonisation

The term 'decolonisation' refers to the process of dismantling colonial influences upon the colonised. During colonisation, the colonisers attempted to control the colonised not only physically but mentally too. Thus, it was easy for them to enable the colonised to consider everything associated with the coloniser as superior. Hence it led to the acceptance of the coloniser's culture, religion, language, education and lifestyle with great interest. They acknowledged the colonisers' language and education over theirs. Though some of them knew that the colonisers' education would leave them simply as a 'black white man' or 'brown white man', they happily accepted it.

Even after political independence (decolonisation) mental colonisation existed in almost all the decolonised colonies. The English language is still considered as the scientific language/language for development, which leaves the decolonised countries to consider the English language over theirs. In case of culture, almost all the decolonised countries feel privileged to follow the Western culture by thinking it as the superior one to accept. Arjun Appadurai's futuristic views of the world becoming a 'mono culture' presents loss of distinctive cultural practices. Many writers and thinkers like Fanon, Ngugi wa Thiong'o, Raja Rao and Chinua Achebe cry for the decolonisation of the mind. However, decolonisation though it means a simple political independence, which cannot be achieved in a day, whereas it is a complex one and it may take many decades or centuries to get it. Freedom to the physical space may be easy but altering the thinking process of the colonised may be a lengthy process.

10. Ethnography

Ethnography, a field of anthropology is seen as 'colonialism's twin' (Fardon: 6). It is a kind of social research where the ethnographer observes remote places, people, their society and practices. They try to be with them in order to make notes of the people's daily life, lifestyle and beliefs, which in a way led to an understanding of a social group. Ethnographers should observe the group in an objective way, whereas the British ethnographers observed the social groups in a subjective way that is with a purpose. Through their ethnographical records, they constructed the societies usually far away from Europe as below them/who need enlightenment or civilisation by paving the way for colonisation. The aim of such ethnographical works is stated by Richard Fardon thus:

> … the inversion of a self-image was generalised to some fictive collectively based on geography, skin colour, tribe or whatever. To counterpose to an enlightened Europe we produce an African heart of darkness; to our rational, controlled west corresponded an irrational and sensuous Orient; our progressive civilisation differed from the historical cul-de-sacs into which Oriental despots led their subjects; our maturity might be contrasted with the childhood of a darker humanity, but our youth and vigour distinguished us from the aged civilisations of east whose splendour was past… (6)

11. Hegemony

The term hegemony was used extensively by a Marxist Antonio Gramsci. He used the term to describe the success of the ruling class in showing off their interest for the society. Here domination does not happen through power, but with the concept of the society. Later this term was used in postcolonial studies to understand the ways hegemony works in controlling the colonised. The colonisers convinced the colonised to rule over them. The colonisers constructed a kind of an ideology that their culture, tradition, religion, language, education and belief as superior than the colonised. This mind set allowed the colonised to accept the rule of the coloniser. If it was done through military rule, the colonisers might have lost their population in a single war with the colonised. Thus, colonisation occurred through mind and not through military. Subsequently through the concept hegemony the colonisers ruled over the colonies.

12. Hybridity

It is one of the most sought-after terms in postcolonial studies. This term is basically used in Botany to refer to a cross-breeding of two species to form a third kind. In postcolonialism it is used to denote the emergence of new forms of language, culture and race. Initially the mixing of races was seen as a hazard by the Europeans and they considered the term hybridity as a threat. Moreover, they were dejected by the thought of losing the purity of races, which would lead to the dismissal of the construction of inferior and superior races. Thus, the Europeans were instructed about the greatness of their race and culture and those who have 'gone native' were criticised/condemned by society. The key thinkers in the realm of hybridity in postcolonial studies are Homi K. Bhabha, Robert Young, Gayatri Chakravorty Spivak. Hoogvelt comments on the term hybridity as, "... celebrated and privileged as a kind of superior cultural intelligence owing to the advantage of in-betweenness, the straddling of two cultures and the consequent ability to negotiate the difference" (158). The term hybridity is most often associated with Homi K. Bhabha. Bhabha states that in hybridity instead of pure form or multiple forms, in-between space happens which is called a 'Third Space'. The third space is an 'ambivalent' one where culture and its meaning have no 'primordial unity or fixity'. In the later days the term hybridity was simply used to denote cross cultural exchange than to emphasise the in-between space which carry the burden.

13. Mestizo

This term denotes the mixture of races/culture, especially the Spanish and the Portuguese with the Natives of America. As racial purity was the ultimatum of colonisation, the mixture of races was named and seen as low. The Spanish and the Portuguese colonised South America to establish their colonies first. There they ended up in mixing their races and culture with the natives. This cultural and racial mixture was termed Mestizo. This term is used widely to denote the new racial and cultural mixture in the Caribbean, American and Indian Ocean regions.

14. Miscegenation

Miscegenation means the sexual union of two races especially the coloniser and the colonised: the white and the black/brown. The colonisers were afraid of their racial mixture. As colonisation is based on the ideology of superiority/inferiority complexes of the coloniser/colonised, the colonisers were concerned about the skin colour level of the baby. "French colonisers, for example, developed no fewer than 128 differing degrees of pigmentation to distinguish between the children of mixed-race relations. Since the maintenance of absolute difference between Europeans and others, colonisers and colonised, was crucial to military and administrative control, miscegenation raised the constant spectre of ideological (and sometimes external) destabilisation of imperial power" (Ashcraft: 142)

15. Mimicry

It is one of the most important terms in Postcolonial Studies that presents the psychological impact from the side of colonised due to colonisation. Fanon in his work *Black Skin White Masks* talks about the ambivalent position of the colonised that is about their intention to imitate the coloniser. Even the colonisers wanted the colonised to mimic them but not to be the same. The term occupied a crucial place in Homi Bhabha's work. He states that "mimicry is at once resemblance and menace" (86, discussed in detail in chapter 5).

16. Negritude

It is a concept that celebrates the distinctiveness of African culture by rejecting the influence of the colonisers. It was developed by Aime Cesaire, Leopold Senghor and others. This concept aims to reject the colonial control over black culture and to unite the blacks in spite of their descendants across the globe. It also implies that all black people across the globe share distinctive characteristics. It retrieves the black cultural practices and thinking. Moreover it provides cultural pride to the black people's discovery of pride in their culture which will enable them to erase the inferiority complex. Though it has started as a cultural movement, it had its impact upon the psyche of the black too. The confidence over their culture and themselves changed the perception of the black about the world. The critics of the Negritude movement produced arts from their aesthetic and cultural standards of their own.

17. Neo-Colonialism

The term neo-colonialism was coined by Kwame Nkrumah, the first president of Ghana in 1965 in his popular work *Neo-Colonialism: The Last Stages of Imperialism.* The literal meaning of the term is new colonialism that denoted to happen in the countries that got independence from Europe then. The then decolonised countries were under the domination of the powerful countries. Thus, the term refers to any kind of control on the decolonised countries. In addition, the newly emerging powerful countries decided the global economy which further left those decolonised countries under economic dependence. The new ruling groups in the decolonised countries happened to be Euro-centred or trained by the colonial education, which led them to follow the footpaths of the colonisers. Thus, they often acted like the agents of the colonisers.

18. Worlding

This term is introduced in postcolonial studies by Spivak. It elaborates the way a colony is brought into the world map of geography and culture by the colonisers from their Euro-centric perspective. Spivak projects the way of overwriting the colonised places not only by the great authorities but even by simple soldiers. It proves that anybody from the imperial countries had power to 'discover' an already existing land or culture.

> If. . . we concentrated on documenting and theorising the itinerary of the consolidation of Europe as sovereign subject, indeed sovereign and subject, then we would produce an alternative historical narrative of the 'worlding' of what is today called 'the Third World.' (Spivak 1985: 128)

19. Worldliness

Edward Said used the term 'worldliness' in his work *The World, the Text and the Critic* from postcolonial perspective. According to him, a text should be read as a material of the world. Emergence or applications of fashionable theories should not narrow down a text. When a text is analysed based on some particular theories, the text will lose its real meaning. As most of the theories and critics are from the imperial nations, they read the texts from their subjective point of view, which they consider as the reality of the world. He complains that the specifications and literary criticisms move away from the worldly, political, economic, social and cultural realities of the world. Hence books should be read by understanding its worldliness.

CHAPTER 5

Key Thinkers

> "Has not the country become independent? Be sure, though, that they will direct our affairs from afar. This is because they have left behind them people who think as they do"
>
> — Tayeb Salih, *Season of Migration to the North*

Postcolonial Studies has achieved its success and popularity with the works of its key thinkers. Though the postcolonial thinkers/critics are huge in numbers this book presents the works of seven great thinkers of postcolonial studies: Aime Cesaire, Frantz Fanon, Chinua Achebe, Ngugi wa Thiong'o, Edward W. Said, Homi K. Bhabha and Gayatri C. Spivak. The writers selected here are from the countries with colonial history and they have experienced their (country/race) projected subordinate position in the imperial lands. These differences changed them as revolutionary at a point of time. All the select key thinkers understood the psychological impacts of colonisation and tried to project the imperialists' task of constructing the colonised in a negative light. The select works of the key thinkers are summarised with great detail in order to reach the understanding of the readers.

I. Aime Cesaire (1913-2008)

Aime Cesaire laid the foundation for Postcolonial Studies through his important concept Negritude. He is a unique postcolonial writer who produced both literary and critical works related to the theme of Anti-colonialism. Aime Ferdinand David Cesaire was born in Martinique, the French Caribbean. After his schooling from his native place, by getting a scholarship Cesaire moved to France in 1931. His exposure to Harlem Renaissance and the exile/subordinate condition of black communities sharpened his stance close to his community and his viewpoint against racism. Moreover, his acquaintance with Leopold Senghor and his friendship enabled Cesaire to understand the history and the civilisation of Africa and to understand his roots in Africa. Soon they started *L'Etudiant Noir*, a publication for the Black people from Africa. It is in this review, Cesaire first used the word Negritude in 1935. Later he married his fellow student Suzanne Roussi, along with her he started a journal titled *Tropiques*, which was dedicated for Black poetry. This influential work further developed the idea of Negritude.

Cesaire is considered as the founding father of Negritude, the Black consciousness movement. He claims that Negritude is "... the simple recognition of the fact that one is black, the acceptance of this fact and of our destiny as blacks, of our history and culture". In an interview he explains negritude as

> I would like to say that everyone has his own Negritude. There has been too much theorising about Negritude. I have tried not to overdo it, out of a sense of modesty. But if someone asks me what my conception of Negritude is, I answer that above all it is a concrete rather than an abstract coming to consciousness. What I have been telling you about-the atmosphere in which we lived, an atmosphere of assimilation in which Negro people were ashamed of themselves-has great importance. We lived in an atmosphere of rejection, and we developed an inferiority complex. I have always thought that the black man was searching for his identity. And it has seemed to me that if what we want is to establish this identity, then we must have a concrete consciousness of what we are – that is, of the first fact of our lives: that we are black; that we were black and have a history, a history that contains certain cultural elements of great value; and that Negroes were not, as you put it, born yesterday, because there have been beautiful and important black civilisations. At the time we began to write people could write a history of world civilisation without devoting a single chapter to Africa, as if Africa had made no contributions to the world. Therefore we affirmed that we were Negroes and that we were proud of it, and that we thought that Africa was not some sort of blank page in the history of humanity; in sum, we asserted

> that our Negro heritage was worthy of respect, and that this heritage was not relegated to the past, that its values were values that could still make an important contribution to the world (Cesaire, 1972: 91-92).

In 1939 he returned to Martinique with his family and in 1945 he started his political career. Since the 1950s he had been active in international forums for the liberation of the third world. In 2001 he retired from politics and died in the year 2008. His writings focused more on the themes slavery, freedom and language in the form of poetry. His works are considered to be the first type to write back against the Francophone, its colonial discrimination. Moreover, his works urge human dignity and cultural equality.

Cesaire's works, both literary and critical, accuse the colonisers who brought disaster to the colonised nations in the disguise of civilisation. Cesaire's first influential work *Cahier d'un retour au pays natal* published in 1939 and later with subsequent modifications published in 1947 and 1956 respectively. (in English: *Notebook of a Return to the Native Land* (1983)). It is a 1055 lines epic narrative poem first published in the magazine *Volontes*. The poem introduces the Black Consciousness Movement's basic feature: distinctiveness of Black cultural identity. During this time, he was greatly influenced by the technique of 'surrealism' and this poem contains many surrealistic images. According to him, "Surrealism was a logical instrument with which to smash the restrictive forms of a language which sanctified rationalised bourgeois values" (Cesaire, 1969: 23). The poem is based on his personal experience and transformation and is written in French. Regarding his choice of French language for his autobiographical poem, he states in an interview with Rene Despertre as,

> It was not something I wanted, but it happens that the language I used was the language I had learned at school. That didn't bother me in the slightest, it didn't in any way come between me and my existential rebellion and the outpouring of my innermost being. I bent the French language to my purposes.
>
> Nature and History have placed us at the crossroads of two worlds, of two cultures if not more. There is the African culture, which I see as being below the surface; and precisely because it is below the surface, overlooked, treated with contempt, it needed to be expressed, to be brought out alive into the light.
>
> But the other culture was the obvious one, the one we were conscious of from the books and from school, and which was also ours, an integral part of our individual and collective identity.

> And also I have tried to reconcile those two worlds, because that was what had to be done. On the other hand, I feel just as relaxed about claiming kinship with the African griot and the African epic as about claiming kinship with Rimbaud and Lautreamont-and through them with Sophocles and Aeschylus (Cesaire, 1972).

The poet tries to look into himself, the world around him, into his past to discover his identity. He feels connected with his African people and culture than the Europeans and their culture.

> My negritude is not a stone, its deafness hurled against the
> clamour of the day
> My negritude is not a leukoma[unetaie] of dead liquid over the
> earth's dead eye
> My negritude is neither tower nor cathedral
> It takes root in the red flesh of the soil
> It takes root in the ardent flesh of the sky
> It breaks through the opaque prostration [trouel'accablement]
> with its upright
> Patience.

Cesaire's famous play *UneTempête* (1969) (*A Tempest*, English) is a postcolonial rewriting of Shakespeare's *The Tempest*. This play is an adaptation of Shakespeare's drama and set in a Caribbean Island. In the play Cesaire focuses more on the manipulation of the colonisers who in reality colonised for their own economic development but presented it as civilisation of the uncivilised.

Cesaire uses all the characters of Shakespeare from the drama with addition of some new characters like Eshu, a Yoruba trickster God from Nigeria and made new rendering of the original cast. Through the casting of main characters, Prospero as a white master, Ariel as a mulatto (mixed black African and White European ancestry) and Caliban as a black slave, Cesaire projects the issues of race, power and psychology. Moreover, the play presents the mindset of the colonisers through the character of Prospero, the Europeans' attitude towards the colonised through Prospero's behaviour against Caliban and Ariel and the two types of behaviours of the colonised through Caliban and Ariel.

The play follows Shakespeare's play closely in action but emphasising the natives of the land, their culture and practices before the invasion of Prospero and his daughter Miranda. When Prospero enslaves the island, the reaction of Ariel and Caliban differ. Ariel follows non-violence by requesting Prospero to grant him independence, whereas Caliban revolts against Prospero. The attitudes of colonisers can be seen through the words of Prospero:

1. "You, a savage... a dumb animal, a beast. I educated, trained, dragged up from the bestiality that still clings to you" (Ceasire, 1991: 11). – This is about the objective of the civilisation mission of the Europeans and the education system.
2. "There is something you forgot, which is that what forced me to get rid of you was your lust. Good God, you tried to rape my daughter" (ibid: 13). – The desire of the coloniser to see the colonised as potential evil, unmannered, beastly is expressed here.
3. "If you keep grumbling you'll be whipped. And if you don't step lively, if you keep dragging your feet or try to strike or sabotage things, I'll beat you. Beating is the only language you really understand" (ibid: 14). – Like animals only beating/punishments can tame the colonised.

The other European characters Trinculo and Stephano desire to civilise the natives like the European colonisers. Their remark on Caliban is

1. "What kind of creature is this? Isn't it a Nindian?" (ibid: 40) – Not willing to accept them as humans.
2. I'll try to civilise him. Oh... not too much, of course. But enough so that he can be some use" (ibid: 40) –their aim is to civilise but not fully.
3. It's a miracle... He can talk! And what's more, he talks sense! O brave savage!" (ibid: 42).

The conversations and ideas of Caliban present the anti-colonial views of Cesaire. Through such dialogues, Cesaire attempts to neutralise the superiority (colonisers') and the inferiority (colonised) complexes. Caliban is brave and assertive who protests to use his own language over the colonisers and the control of the colonisers. "You think I'm ugly... well, I don't think you're so handsome yourself. With that big hooked nose, you look just like some old vulture. … An old vulture with a scrawny neck!" (ibid: 11).

Caliban's reaction to Ariel, who simply follows the footsteps of Prospero with the belief that soon he would enjoy freedom, is "What do you believe in, then? In cowardice? In giving up? In kneeling and grovelling? That's it, someone strikes you on the right cheek and you offer the left. Someone kicks you on the left buttock and you turn the right... that way there's no jealousy. Well, that's not Caliban's way... (ibid: 22). Through Caliban's character Cesaire tries to spread the seeds of pride in culture and to break the inferiority complexes of the colonised.

Cesaire's famous prose work "Discourssur le colonialism" (English: "Discourse on Colonialism"), the foundation book in postcolonial study was first published in 1950. With some changes the same work was again published in 1955 which attained huge popularity. The aftermath of World War II especially the projection of the U.S.A. and the Western Europe as the saviour of the world from the evil Nazis provoked Cesaire. People, who still colonise and slaughter people, calling the others (Nazis, who did the same) as evil and projecting themselves as the redeemers of evil, forced Cesaire to write this essay. This essay reveals the truth behind the European colonisation.

Cesaire begins the essay by giving two major problems faced by the European Civilisation: "the problem of the proletariat and the colonial problem". He sees European civilisation as "morally and spiritually indefensible" (75). The colonisers entered the colonies with a lie that is to civilise them. However, colonisation for the sake of civilisation was a hypocritical act of Europe "that cleverly misrepresents problems" (75). It projected "dishonest equations Christianity = civilisation, paganism = savagery" (75). Though colonisation was aimed to civilise the colonised, in reality it "decivilises" the colonisers. Cesaire addresses the coloniser's civilisation as sick civilisation.

> … no one colonises innocently, that no one colonises with impunity either; that a nation which colonises, that a civilisation which justifies colonisation – and therefore force – is already a sick civilisation, a civilisation that is morally diseased, that irresistibly, progressing from one consequence to another, one reputation to another… (79).

Though the coloniser came under the disguise of civilising and uplifting the colonised, in reality, "there is room only for forced labour, intimidation, pressure, the police, taxation, theft, rape, compulsory crops, contempt, mistrust, arrogance, self-complacency, swinishness; brainless elites, degraded masses" (81). Thus, colonisation has changed from civilisation to 'thingification'.

> Cesaire is of the view that colonisation has created destruction in every manner in the colonised countries. It changed the psyche of the colonised, "who have been taught to have an inferiority complex, to tremble, kneel, despair, and behave like flunkeys" (81). Not only the psyche, but the society, culture and the life source of the colonised, in short, the root of the colonised was disturbed. "...millions of men torn from their gods, their land, their habits, their life – from life, from the dance, from wisdom" (81). The coloniser has never seen the colonised as a human instead always prefer to see them as animals. Cesaire claims that this act of transferring humans (the colonised) into animals by the coloniser enabled them to ease their conscience. Cesaire states that, "... Europe is responsible before the human community for the highest heap of corpses in history" (82)

Cesaire points out that when Hitler killed many white people, it was seen as a barbaric act but the same act on the non-white by the Europeans was appreciated as a civilisation process by the Europeans. Cesaire claims that the act of Hitler revels,

> to the very distinguished, very humanistic, very Christian bourgeois of the 20th century that without his being aware of it, he has a Hitler inside him, that Hitler *inhabits* him, that Hitler is his *demon*, that if he rails against him, he is being inconsistent and that, at bottom, what he cannot forgive Hitler for is not *crime* in itself, *the crime against man*, it is not the *humiliation of man as such*, it is the crime against the white man, the humiliation of the white man,... (77).

Cesaire addresses European civilisation as bourgeois, which is the sole reason for the ruined nations across the globe. Then he states that the barbaric nature of Europe is now in the hands of America. He concludes the essay by warning the world, especially the decolonised countries that though America may look like a possible liberator, it is the 'modern barbarian' (88). "American domination – the only domination from which one never recovers. I mean from which one never recovers unscarred" (89). Moreover, he presents a future aim/objective for the decolonised countries. He does not believe in going back to the past, to the past culture/civilisation, instead he states that

> ... the problem is not to make a utopian and sterile attempt to repeat the past, but to go beyond. It is not a dead society that we want to revive. We leave that to those who go in for exoticism. Nor is it the present colonial society that we wish to prolong, the most putrid carrion that ever rotted under the sun. It is a new society that we must create, with the help of all our brother slaves, a society rich with all the productive power of modern times, warm with all the fraternity of olden days (86).

II. Frantz Fanon (1925-1961)

Frantz Fanon was born at Fort-de-France in the French colony of Martinique in 1925. His father was a descendants of slaves and his mother was half-French and in his native place all the blacks believed themselves as French. He had his education from the famous French postcolonialist Aime Cesaire. Cesaire's denouncement of colonial racism had a great impact on Fanon. As a youngster he joined the army and took part in many wars. While fighting against the Germans for France, Fanon experienced racial discrimination every day in France. "In France, he noticed that French women avoided black soldiers who were sacrificing their lives to liberate them" (Fanon, Frantz, 2008: VIII). Later with a scholarship he studied medicine and psychiatry in Lyon. During that period, he met Jose Duble who too shared his views against racism and colonialism, whom he married in 1952.

Fanon used psychoanalysis to study the impact of racism on the blacks especially on the individuals. Slowly he became involved in an anti-colonial struggle and he felt close to the Algerian subaltern community. Thus, he secretly supported the Algerian revolutionaries and started to identify himself as an Algerian. Later he was affected with leukaemia and died in the year 1961. After his death for nearly two decades Fanon was celebrated as a revolutionary writer and anti-colonial leader. His works promoted violence against discrimination and also analysed the impact of colonialism on the psyche of the colonised. Though he was severely criticised and rejected by the conservative writers for the advert of violence and forgotten for some period, since the 1990s with the arrival of Postcolonial Studies, a new interest has started growing towards Fanon.

During the 1960s and 1970s Fanon was very popular in academics and among the angry young men due to his work *The Wretched of the Earth*. When his fame got revived in the 1990s he was widely acclaimed for his first book *Black Skin, White Masks*. Being ahead of his time, Fanon was left in an unfriendly scholarly world. In the Foreword to the 2008th edition of *Black Skin, White Masks,* Ziauddin Sardar says, "Fanon was far ahead of his time. This is why he is disliked by some. This is why he is misunderstood by others" (xx). Consequently we have very few works on Fanon.

Fanon's two important works which are considered as the handbook in postcolonial studies are *Black Skin, White Masks* and *The*

Wretched of the Earth and both works are summarised here. His first book in French titled *Peau noire, masques Blancs* (1952; *Black Skin, White Masks*) was a much-acclaimed work in postcolonial studies. It was first published in French when he was 27. Later with the translation in English in 1967, it attained wide readership. It was the first book "to investigate the psychology of colonialism. It examines how colonialism is internationalised by the colonised, how an inferiority complex is inculcated, and how, through the mechanism of racism, black people end up emulating their oppressors" (Fanon, Frantz, 2008: x). This book is written from the perspective of the colonised and he used the pronoun 'he' to talk about human experiences. As a result, Fanon was criticised by feminists for his usage of the word 'man' as a general term to talk about human experiences. Homi K. Bhabha in the foreword to the 1986 edition of *Black Skin, White Masks* justifies Fanon for using the word 'man' thus,

> Fanon's use of the word "man" usually connotes a phenomenological quality of humanness, inclusive of man and woman and, for that very reason, ignores the question of gender difference. The problem stems from Fanon's desire to cite the question of sexual difference within the problematic of cultural difference – to give them a shared origin – which is suggestive, but often simplifies the question of sexuality.... I have therefore chosen to note the importance of the problem rather than to elide it in a facile charge of "sexism" (xxxvi-xxxvii).

Fanon tries to find an answer to the question "What does the black man want?" (Ibid: 1) through analysing the psyche of the black man. This search becomes the objective of the book that focuses to present the construction of black ideology/identity and its dangerous impact upon humans. Fanon cites Sir Alen Burns' words from his book *Colour Prejudice* (1948) regarding racial prejudice.

> It is laid down in the Bible that the separation of the white and black races will be continued in heaven as on earth, and those blacks who are admitted into the kingdom of Heaven will find themselves separately lodged in certain of those many mansions of Our Father that are mentioned in the New Testament... We are the chosen people – look at the colour of our skins. The others are black or yellow: That is because of their sins (Quoted in 18-19).

Fanon thinks that two ideologies became the fact (fate) of humans and they are, "... white men consider themselves superior to black men... Black men want to prove to white men, at all costs, the richness of their thought, the equal value of their intellect" (ibid: 3). Black men believe that, "For the black man there is only one destiny. And it is white" (ibid: 4). Fanon classifies the blacks based on their reactions to the white as two categories: the black who wants his people to turn as white and the black who preaches hatred towards the white.

The book consists of eight chapters. The first chapter titled "The Negro and Language" projects language as a powerful tool in colonising the mind of the colonised. Generally the colonised accept the colonisers' rules more willingly. The role of language in erasing one's culture and identity is projected by Fanon with reference to the French language in his hometown Antilles. Historically with the idea of French language as a tool to uplift the lifestyle and one's self, the Blacks in Antilles had been learning French. By burying their language and culture, the blacks tend to develop their inferiority complex more. The Blacks live like foreigners in their own place with "no culture, no civilisation, no long historical past" (10). By acquiring French education, the blacks try to become 'whiter'.

Moreover, the blacks who return from France, behave like newcomers who cannot understand the dialects of Antilles. Fanon elaborates this thus, "And the fact that the newly returned Negro adopts a language different from that of the group into which he was born is evidence of a dislocation, a separation. Prof. D. Westmann in *The African Today* (states that the ""'Negros' inferiority complex is particularly intensified among the most educated, who must struggle with it unceasingly'"" (14). The educated take pains to speak French like the French man, for which he is criticised in France as 'talking like a book' and in Antilles appreciated as talking like a white man.

The second chapter titled "The Woman of Colour and the White Man" deals with the relationship between the black woman and the European man. Fanon projects the psyche of the black women who prefer white men by rejecting the black men. He presents two types of black women thus, "the Negress and the mulatto. The first has only one possibility and one concern: to turn white. The second wants not only to turn white but also to slipping back" (38). The black women decide to fall in love only with white men due to their inferiority complex regarding their colour. They believe that winning a white man's heart will allow them to enter into the white world. On the other hand, the mulatto women do not need to be allowed by someone into the white world as they consider themselves as white. Mulatto women feel, "I do not like the Negro because he is savage. Not savage in a cannibal way, but lacking refinement" (41). Black men's love is seen as an insult by the white and the mulatto women.

For such proposal the black men could be punished legally. "Such an offence against principle should be punished by castration" (40). In case of the black women especially the educated black women show least interest to marry the black men. "I know a great number of girls from Martinique, students in France, who admitted to me with complete candour-completely white candour – that they would find it impossible to marry black men. …besides, they added, it is not that we deny that blacks have any good qualities, but you know it is so much better to be white" (33). Fanon concludes this chapter by stating the inferiority complex of the black is due to "neurotic orientation" (43) and he recommends that this poison has to be eliminated.

"The Man of Colour and The White Woman" is the title of the third chapter where the writer talks about the black man's desire to be white and his in between position. Fanon quotes from a novel about the educated blacks' condition as, "The Europeans in general and the French in particular, not satisfied with simply ignoring the Negroes of the colonies, repudiate the one whom they have shaped into their own image" (quoted in 46). The blacks especially the educated one finds difficulty in understanding their race. The inferiority complex of the blacks leads them towards the white. Fanon quotes, "mulattos and Negroes have only one thought from the moment they land in Europe: to gratify their appetite for white women" (50). At times the whites accept the educated black as "extreme brown" and not as "black", whereas the other times the sexual myth that is the black's quest for the white flesh is still green in their minds. Even when a white woman falls in love with the black, the black suffers with doubts. He doubts whether she loves him really or does she look at him objectively. Moreover, he doubts his own love. The black men, "tend to marry in Europe not so much out of love as for the satisfaction of being the master of a European woman; and a certain tang of proud revenge enters into this" (Quoted in 50). Fanon believes that a "healthy encounter between black and white" can resolve such doubts and revenges. He concludes this chapter by stating that the "restructuring of the world" can end this division.

The fourth chapter titled "The So-called Dependency Complex of Colonised People" talks about the origin, reason, and sources for the development of the dependency complex among the blacks. Fanon reviews Mannoni's work titled *Prospero and Caliban: Psychology of Colonisation* and states that it was a first kind of study to introduce two elements such as the colonisers and the colonised. Nevertheless, it has some limitations. Moreover, Fanon accepts that such works will be subjective and claims that his work is also subjective, as it conveys the misery of the black people, both, "physically and affectively" where subjective writing is only possible. Fanon states the purpose of Mannoni's work as, "...to prove the impossibility of explaining man outside the limits of his capacity for accepting or denying a given situation. Thus, the problem of colonisation includes not only the interrelations of objective historical conditions but also human attitudes towards these conditions" (62). In this chapter Fanon presents where he differs from Mannoni's thoughts and reasons for differences. (a) Mannoni believes that colonial exploitation and colonial racism are different from other forms of exploitations and racisms. He states, "European civilisation and its best representatives are not, for instance, responsible for colonial racism; that is the work of petty officials, small traders, and colonials who have toiled much without great success" (24). (b) Moreover, Mannoni claims France as the less racial country than the other European countries and America. (c) Mannoni states that one may feel inferior when one is part of the minority group living with the majority group.

Fanon disapproves of Mannoni's views and he replies thus; (a) Fanon mentions that colonial exploitation and colonial racism & the other forms of exploitation and racism are the same. He believes that all forms of exploitation could occur against humans. (b) Fanon rejects Mannoni's claim that France is the least racist country in the world. (c) Not only the minority community feels inferior but a majority community (blacks in South Africa) too feel inferior. "In Martinique there are two hundred whites who consider themselves superior to 300, 000 people of colour. In South Africa there are two million whites against almost thirteen million native people, and it has never occurred to a single black to consider himself superior to a member of the white minority" (68). Thus, an inferiority complex is not based on the number but "*It is the racist who creates his inferior*" (69).

Fanon is of the view that the arrival of the whites has changed the psyche of the native people. He states that the invasion of the Europeans happened in a different way.

When the question arises of understanding why the European, the foreigner, was called *vazaha*, which means *honourable stranger*; when it is a matter of understanding why shipwrecked Europeans were welcomed with open arms; why the European, the foreigner, was never thought of as an enemy, instead of explaining these things in terms of humanity, of good will, of courtesy, basic characteristics of what Cesaire calls " the old courtly civilisations," scholars tell us that it happened quite simply because, inscribed in "fateful hieroglyphics" – specifically, the unconscious – there exists something that makes the white man the awaited master (74).

Gradually colonisation created an inferiority complex to the colonised that leads to 'dependency behaviour'. Mannoni talks about the psychological transformation of the colonised. He describes Malagasy Psychology and the 'Prospero complex' where the racists view all the black men as rapists. Fanon concludes the chapter by commenting on Mannoni's work as, "it appears to me that Mannoni lacks the slightest basis on which to ground any conclusion applicable to the situation, the problems, or the potentialities of the Malagasy in the present" (81).

The fifth chapter titled "The Fact of Blackness" talks about the fact of objecthood experienced by the blacks. Being deprived out of past and future by the whites, the blacks stand in an ambiguous position. This chapter also discusses the construction of the image of the blacks and the in betweenness experienced by the blacks. When a black man stays along with other blacks, he cannot understand the black experience. Instead, when a black is with a white man, the black is exposed to an inferiority complex at any moment. (in Antilles the hierarchy of the people is based on race is as follows: white, mulatto, and black). The transformation experienced by a black in front of a white is stated from Fanon's experience thus, "An unfamiliar weight burdened me. The real world challenged my claims. In the white world the man of colour encounters difficulties in the development of his bodily schema. Consciousness of the body is solely a negating activity. It is a third person consciousness. The body is surrounded by an atmosphere of certain uncertainty" (83). Slowly the blacks were made to accept the views of the white especially about their objective position. The blacks are objectified by the whites through the repeated constructions of ideas like "The Negro is an animal, the Negro is bad, the Negro is mean, the Negro is ugly…" (86).

The humans were judged based on the colour and consequently the blacks were constantly made to accept their insults quietly. Regarding this Fanon quotes from Sir Alan Burns thus,

> As colour is the most obvious outward manifestation of race it has been made the criterion by which men are judged, irrespective of their social or educational attainments. The light-skinned races have come to despise all those of a darker colour, and the dark-skinned people will no longer accept without protest the inferior position to which they have been relegated (Quoted in 89).

All these differentiations are done with a purpose. The white man wants the world for himself and he does not want to share it with the other races. Hence, he constructed the blacks as inferior. However, all the information the whites mentioned about the black is a mere construction. Fanon states, "The white man was wrong, I was not a primitive, not even a half-man, I belonged to a race that had already been working in gold and silver two thousand years ago" (99). Nevertheless, such constructions enabled the whites to be superior and the blacks as inferior. The impact of colonisation transformed the psyche of the blacks. At present, after decolonisation the blacks live in an between position. "...without a Negro past, without a Negro future, it was impossible for me to live my Negrohood. Not yet white, no longer wholly black, I was damned" (106). Fanon concludes by stating the black's position as a kind of toy in the white's hand.

Fanon titles the sixth chapter as "The Negro and Psychopathology". He begins this part by stating the great psychoanalysts like Freud, Adler and Jung did not consider to analyse/ investigate the psyche of the black. Moreover, whatever analysis is done, the black is seen as an object which produces anxiety. Fanon calls it "Negro-phobogenesis" (117). Fanon begins the chapter by stating that family is an important source in psychoanalysis. He considers family as a miniature of a nation where every child follows his parents. A child from a normal family in Europe will grow up as a normal man. Whereas in a black family the opposite happens. A normal black child from a normal black family transforms as an abnormal child when he is exposed to the white world. The white family structure shapes the child for the society. In the case of the blacks, the grownup blacks reject family in order to be in the society. The black behaves normally until he has the white education/meets a white/leaves his hometown.

According to Fanon, growing up with different sources like "books, newspapers, schools and their texts, advertisements, films, radio... (118) constructs ideology about the racial behaviours. He further states magazines produced/written by the white man which are meant for the white children depict the blacks/the Indians as evil. Unfortunately, such books were read by the black children too, where the black children identify themselves with the white protagonists and traces danger from the blacks. This leads the black children into abnormality. Moreover, the impact of western education leaves the black children adopting the white attitude. In spite of a different geographical position and cultural practices, all the blacks were projected as a homogeneous group. Hence all the blacks are seen as a symbol of evil. "... the colour black – symbolises evil, sin, wretchedness, death, war, famine" (147). Most often the blacks unconsciously distrust their blackness by considering themselves as whites. At times they feel that, "one is a Negro to the degree to which one is wicked, sloppy, malicious, instinctual. Everything that is opposite of these Negro modes of behaviour is white. This must be recognised as the source of Negrophobia in the Antillean. In the collective unconscious, black = ugliness, sin, darkness, immorality" (148-149).

The next important issue is behavioural transformation undergone by the blacks when they encounter contact with the white world: from 'actional person' to other person. Fanon is of the view that the whites hate the blacks due to the "feeling of importance or of sexual inferiority" (122). The black is always associated with sexual power leading to the construction of negrophobia which is constituted on the biological level. "Negro brought forth biology, penis, strong, athletic, potent, boxer, Joe Louis, Jesse Owens, Senegalese, troops, savage, animal, devil, sin" (128). Fanon projects the white's attitude of superiority by stating that the whites take responsibility to construct ideology of others by doing some research on others. They never do research on themselves. In order to get away from the guilt feel for discriminating the black, the whites started to construct reasons for their activity as "Ever since slavery began, his Christian and democratic guilt as a slave-owner has led the southerner to describe the negro as an animal, an unchangeable African whose nature was determined as protoplasm by his "African" genes" (134).

Fanon rejects Jung's concept of collective unconsciousness. Jung states that collective unconsciousness is based on genes. Fanon states that collective unconsciousness is not based on genes but on the sums of prejudices, myths, collective attitude of a given group. He states that Jung got confused with instinct and habit. Fanon cites the example of Jews who have different collective unconsciousness based on their geographical locations such as Jews in Israel and Jews in the other countries. Thus, collective unconsciousness is cultural hence it can be acquired. The black ideology was imposed on both blacks and whites through "cultural imposition". Many critics think about removing the myth of blacks and they suggest that it could be "achieved only to the detriment of the cultural crystallisation" (157). Fanon concludes the chapter by stating that the blacks created/create a fear image among the whites and removing such an image completely is doubtful.

The seventh chapter titled "The Negro and Recognition" consists of two parts. The first part titled "A. The Negro and Adler" tries to apply Adler's psychology to the Antilleans. Fanon states that the black is always compared with someone on the basis of value, merit or intelligence. When this comparison is done, the blacks feel that they undergo a shameful experience. It is because of the fixed position/characterisation of the races. Incidents that occur out of curiosity/doubts of the subject/object, in the course of time becomes 1. The character, 2. The social structure, 3. The environment. Hence, it becomes impossible to come away from it. Fanon comments, "If we were strict in applying the conclusion of the Adlerian school, we should say that the Negro is seeking to protect himself against the inferiority that he feels historically".

In the second part of this chapter titled "B. The Negro and Hegel", Fanon talks about Hegel's concept of the existence of self-consciousness: that is, one's own human worth depends upon the other being or on the recognition by that other being. Fanon states that there is no open problem between the blacks and the whites but, "the White Master, *without conflict*, recognised the Negro slave. But the former slave wants to *make himself recognised*" (169). Fanon states that human reality is different from the natural reality. Though the white states that both white and black are equal, the blacks could feel the difference. The blacks expect the white to state their discrimination outwardly; hence they can indulge in a conflict or a riot. Fanon is of the view that the blacks in America through battle got some laws that support anti-discriminations. Whereas the blacks in France are still in the same condition. By stating this Fanon expects men to be yes to life, love and generosity and no to scorn, degradation, and exploitation of men.

The eighth chapter is the conclusion of his ideas titled "By Way of Conclusion". Fanon states that the past cannot guide someone in the present. The past glory of the black has nothing to change the present pitiable position. "I will not make myself the man of any past. I do not want to exalt the past at the expense of my present and of my future" (176). So, he requests one to come out of the past glory. Fanon talks about alienation as an intellectual character. When he talks about the educated blacks, he uses the term 'Intellectual Alienation' which he characterises as a quality of the middle-class society. An educated black becomes alienated when he tries to become white by moving away from his race. Moreover, the only destiny of a black man is to become white. The black is not bothered to 'pose the problem of black truth'. The black is not fighting for his rights or duties like 1. "to seek to know in what respect my race is superior or inferior to another race", 2. "to hope that in the white man there will be crystallisation of guilt towards the past of my race", (178). In the world where still dignity of a race is a question, "There is no Negro mission; there is no white burden" (178). The blacks should fight for the right of "demanding human behaviour from the other" (179). He concludes by praying to be a man who questions in order to make the world recognise the discrimination and to open the door of consciousness of equality.

Fanon's next influential work is *Les Damnés de la terre* (1961; *The Wretched of the Earth*) which also talks about the psychological impact of colonisation upon the colonised and their effort to end colonisation. He believes that liberation cannot be achieved without violence and this thought is presented throughout the book. In the Algerian war from 1954 to 1962 which was a cold war between the Algerians and the French, Fanon supported the Algerians, who fought for their independence. He made references to the Algerian war several times in this work. This book consists of five chapters where he talks about the tension and burden of the decolonised countries when they indulge in the process of functioning as a nation.

The first chapter titled "Violence" talks about the intrinsic role of violence in the process of colonisation and decolonisation. Initially the colonisers used violence as a main tool to colonise the fellow humans by forcing them to be slaves to them and later the colonised used violence to decolonise. Fanon states that "Decolonisation is always a violent phenomenon". The colonisers did not consider the colonised as fellow humans but as some 'species' who were inferior to them. The coloniser lived a comfortable and rich life, whereas the colonised lived-in hunger always. The colonisers divided the colonised into three groups. The first group consists of labourers who work for the benefit of the coloniser. The second group is the "colonial intellectual" (47) who gained the colonial knowledge. The colonisers "implanted in the minds of the colonised intellectual that the essential qualities remain eternal in spite of the blunders men may make: the essential qualities of the West, of course" (36). Thus, the colonised act as a spokes person of the colonisers. Fanon addressed the third group as 'lumpenproletariat', the term that was used by Karl Marx to mention the poorest class, who are outside the system. Along with them Fanon includes migrants, slum dwellers and criminals in this category and depicts them as the first to indulge in violence "the most spontaneously and radically revolutionary forces of a colonised people." (47). The colonisers never wanted to decolonise their colonies and on the other side the colonised wanted to be liberated from the colonisers. Slowly the colonised indulge in violence to receive freedom and consequently violence becomes unavoidable. Under the title "Violence in the International Context", Fanon talks about international political relationship between the newly independent and the former colonial nations. Fanon blames the colonisers who enriched themselves by looting sources and resources from the colonised countries. The European countries live a lavish life with the money looted from their colonies by leaving the colonies to face an economic struggle after decolonisation.

The second chapter "Spontaneity: Its Strength and Weakness" talks about the formation of political groups that consist of only the urban groups by the colonial intellectuals/elites. The urban parties are ignorant of the rural people and their issues but they decide the future though they are less than one per cent of the population. Fanon calls them the as 'Urban Proletariat' who are the most privileged people of the colonial society. The urban people and the rural people distrust each other. The urban elite people as well as the urban labourers did not bother about the problems of the rural people. Thus, the decolonised nation's 'Urban Proletariat' performs the role of the colonisers "some blacks can be whiter than whites, and that the prospect of a national flag or independence does not automatically result in certain segments of the population giving up their privileges and their interests".

The third chapter "The Pitfalls of National Consciousness" highlights the damages caused by the "national bourgeoisie" to the newly decolonised countries. The national bourgeoisie will be a decision-maker for the nation and they play their role by following the footpath of the colonisers. They oppress the poor rural people and maintain the hierarchical power. Fanon states the national bourgeoisie is the destructive thing to decolonised countries and offers a solution to the problem as "decentralisation in the extreme". He advises that all the groups irrespective of class differences should work in an integrated way towards the progress of the nation.

The fourth chapter "On Nation Culture" is an important chapter that advises the colonised intellectuals not to imitate the colonisers in politics as well as not to indulge or take pride in their past. Fanon complains that the native intellectuals in the decolonised nations, may be under the influence of European education, try to imitate the colonisers. He is of the view that the economic condition of the poor people remains the same both in the colonial period and in the decolonised period. All sorts of violence, struggle and suffering leave the decolonised countries similar to the colonial period. Fanon states as the Third World countries are different from the Western countries, the political condition also should be different and the native intellectuals should not follow the Western society. He recommends education about national consciousness should be given to everyone and moreover one set of people cannot decide for the entire nation. By moving the power/centre to the countryside a new nation can be built; a nation which is for people and not for politics.

Fanon states that the colonisers projected the colonised and their cultures as barbaric and uncivilised in order to colonise them. Thus, the colonisers "turn to the past of the oppressed people, and distorts, disfigures, and destroys it". Now in the decolonised nation the colonised intellectuals try to trace back their past and to project its glory. Thus doing so the black intellectuals create a separate art form for the blacks which is different from the rest. Fanon believes that the Negritude movement and the concept of black culture have some limitations in uniting all the blacks across the globe. Because the condition of blacks in America is different from the blacks in Africa and moreover they have different national cultures. For example black American writers like Richard Wright and Langston Hughes writings differ from Léopold Senghor from Kenya. The three stages undergone by the colonised writers are given by Fanon as 1. Works that project that the colonised have completely assimilated with the whites, 2.works where the characters move to their past culture in the precolonial period, 3. Works on the revolutionary theme, fight for people, national literature. He calls national literature "combat literature" as it creates national consciousness. This clarifies that nations exist due to people's struggle and not because of culture but in reality culture is the one that needs the nation for its existence. With regard to this, Fanon states, "If culture is the expression of national consciousness, I shall have no hesitation in saying, in the case in point, that national consciousness is the highest form of culture."

The fifth chapter titled "Colonial War and Mental Disorders" lists his case studies when he worked as a psychiatrist from 1954 to 1959 during the Algerian War. Before such wars, colonisation affected both the coloniser and the colonised psychologically and it was "a fertile purveyor for psychiatric hospitals". Due to the Algerian War, both the Algerians and the French soldiers suffered from 'psychotic reaction', a kind of psychological problem and due to it "The future of such patients is mortgaged". Fanon discusses the case studies in four sections. As a result of colonial racism, Algerians were considered to be born with criminal brains. Many scientific literature presented Africans as "born slackers, born liars, born robbers, and born criminals". Fanon quotes Dr. Carothers', an expert from the United Nations' World Health Organisation, comments about Africans as, "makes very little use of his [brain's] frontal lobes" and "All the particularities of African psychiatry can be put down to frontal [lobe] laziness". Fanon rejects such researches as they are based on power and biased in nature. He accepts that criminality exists in Algeria and he claims colonisation as the reason for it. "Algerian's criminality [is]... the direct product of the colonial situation". He believes that people use criminality to register their resistance and concludes that during the cold war time criminality by Algerians was reduced.

In the sixth chapter "Conclusion" Fanon calls "Comrades" to move away from Europe as "we have better things to do than follow in Europe's footsteps." He states "the European game has finally ended; we must find something different". He wants the decolonised nations "not to imitate Europe and let us tense our muscles and our brains in a new direction" and desires the third world countries to move in a new way and to create and discover new things by not imitating Europe anymore.

III. Chinua Achebe (1930-2013)

Chinua Achebe, who is celebrated as the Father of African Literature, was born at the Igbo (formerly spelled Ibo) town of Ogidi in Eastern Nigeria in 1930. His parents were the members of Protestant missionaries and at the same time followers of traditional practices. Hence at home he was raised with their traditional stories. He attended the Church Missionary School where he was taught in English since his eighth year. Thus he was good in his mother tongue as well as in English. He was a meritorious student who joined medicine in the first University College started in Nigeria. But later he changed his course to Literature and History and started writing creative works during this period. After completing his degree he joined the Nigerian Broadcasting Service, where he gained more experience both in expanding his societal knowledge as well as his writing skill. Later when he got an opportunity to get training from BBC, London, he shared the manuscript of his famous novel *Things Fall Apart* with a British writer and later the work was published in the year 1958. The novel was about the colonisation of Africa from the African point of view, which was later translated into more than fifty languages, was an immediate success. Later he was promoted as the Director of External Broadcasting. He along with his colleague wished to develop more national identity and unity by highlighting Nigerian culture to the people by creating Voices of Nigeria Network.

In 1966, in a political turmoil between the Igbo and non-Igbo groups, the non-Igbo defeated the Igbo group. Achebe was targeted for prosecution by the non-Igbo group as he was against the new regime. Hence he fled to Nsukka in Eastern Nigeria and worked as a senior research fellow at the University of Nigeria, Nsukka. Later he moved to London and America where he lectured in many universities and wrote most of his works. In 1976 he returned to the University of Nigeria and served there till his retirement in 1982. Achebe believed that art should deal with the problem of the society and it should have a purpose to the society. Achebe's works present the intersection of African tradition with modernity and the impact of colonisation upon African people. His other important novels are *No Longer at Ease* (1960 sequel to *Things Fall Apart*), *Arrow of God* (1964), *A Man of the People* (1966), and *Anthills of the Savannah* (1987).

His later works dealt with the political condition in the decolonised African countries especially about the failing leaderships. His critical work *The Trouble with Nigeria* (1983) was a critique of corrupt politics in his country, where he has mentioned that, "the

Nigerian problem is the unwillingness or inability of its leaders to rise to the responsibility and to the challenge of personal example which are the hallmarks of true leadership" (Ezenwa: 228). In the 1980s Achebe wrote important critical essays and lectured around the world. In 1900 due to an accident, Achebe became paralysed and spent the rest of his life in a wheelchair working as a professor for the next fifteen years in New York. Due to illness, Achebe died in 2013.

Apart from his novels, Achebe's famous critical work is `An Image of Africa: Racism in Conrad's Heart of Darkness', which led the readers to look at Conrad's work in a different perspective. The image of Conrad as an anti-colonialist was shattered and Achebe projected him as a 'thorough going racist'. Achebe in his reminiscences of his schooldays stated that he read Conrad's works with a different perspective and in the later days which was changed. He states that he could not see the Africa which is familiar to him in the words of Conrad,

> I did not see myself as an African in those books. I took sides with the white men against the savages. .. The savages arrayed against him were sinister and stupid, never anything higher than cunning. I hated their guts. But a time came when I reached the appropriate age and realised that these writers had pulled a fast one on me! I was not on Marlow's boat steaming up the Congo in the Heart of Darkness; rather, I was one of those unattractive beings jumping up and down on the riverbank, making horrid faces (Achebe, 2011: 87).

Later during his college days he studied Joyce Cary's *Mister Johnson* (1939), again about the colonial regime in Nigeria. The novel is about a Nigerian man who works under an abusive Englishman. The novel projected the Africans as savages. The Western projection/ construction of the colonised as primitive through literary works provoked Achebe. This planted a desire, to project his country based on his experience to the world, by being a writer. "Mister Johnson. .. was praised so much, and it was clear to me that this was a most superficial picture not only of the country, but even of the Nigerian character and so I thought if this was famous, then perhaps someone ought to try and look at this from the inside" (Achebe, 1972: 4).

Conrad's *Heart of Darkness* (1899) is celebrated as a modern classic, a trend setter in modern literature. Out of ten best literary works, definitely this work is included and prescribed in the college syllabus all around the world. Achebe wanted to show the reality of the work despite its merits. He accepts the artistic merit of the work and states,

> I never said at any point that you should stop attaching artistic merit to *Heart of Darkness*; if you want to you can. There are all kinds of sophisticated readings of *Heart of Darkness*, and there are some people who will not be persuaded there is anything wrong with it. But all that I'm really demanding, I'm not simply putting it, I'm demanding that my reading stands beside these other readings. .. Although he's writing good sentences, he's also writing about a people, and their life. And he says about these people that they are rudimentary souls. .. The Africans are the rudimentaries, and then on top are the good whites. Now I don't accept that, as a basis anything.
>
> (https://web.archive.org/web/20070707134706/http://www.upenn.edu/video/pvp/st-Series_Africana.html#3).

Achebe presents the Western colonial gaze of Africa and its people through his study of the novella. Critic Nicolas Tredell divides Conrad criticism "into two epochal phases: before and after Achebe" (71).

Two of Achebe's important essays are summarised here. The first is "An Image of Africa: Racism in Conrad's Heart of Darkness", Achebe begins the essay by stating the prejudiced view of the whites about Africa. Two of his personal experiences left him to encounter with the whites' perception of Africa; a land of superstitious belief and a land which cannot produce any knowledgeable source. A man whom Achebe met in a University in the U.S.A. said that he never thought of Africa as having any history or literature and on another occasion a young boy curiously asked Achebe about the superstitious beliefs of Africans. Achebe states that Americans also have some odd customs and superstitious beliefs but they expect to go to Africa to experience those things. He continues that one cannot neglect it simply by stating that it is due to ignorance but it is "that something more wilful than a mere lack of information was at work" (114). Hence the white's negligence cannot be ignored as inexperience but it is based on their desire, "to set Africa up as a foil to Europe, as a place to negations at once remote and vaguely familiar, in comparison with which Europe's own state of spiritual grace will be manifest" (114).

Achebe states that not only the common people but even scholars like Hugh Trevor-Roper, British historian and Regius Professor at Oxford, who due to his imperialistic nature, simply denied that Africa did not have history. Though the Western desires can be presented through the tools of social and biological sciences, Achebe likes to analyse one of the famous works of European fiction, Joseph Conrad's *Heart of Darkness,* to project the Western desire. Many Western writers' works were very obvious on the theme of colonial desire, whereas Conrad's style enabled it to be considered as a modern literature and not as an imperialist literary work.

Like all the imperialist writers, Conrad too projected the landscapes of Africa and Europe in a binary form. From the description of the rivers Congo and Thames one could get the construction of an imperialist idea. Achebe states that the Thames was actually resting peacefully

> ...at the decline of day after ages of good service done to the race that peopled its banks". But the actual story will take place on the river Congo, the very antithesis of the Thames. The river Congo is quite decidedly not a River Emirates. It has rendered no service and enjoys no old-age pension. We are told that "going up that river was like travelling back to the earliest beginning of the world (quoted in 114).

Not only about the geography of Africa but even about the African people Conrad has spoken in the same degrading manner. He has presented them as primitive and frenzy. He goes to the extent of mentioning African conversation as 'violent babble of uncouth sounds' and 'exchanged short grunting phrases' and does not accept it as speech. The European representatives who travelled in a steamer down the Congo described the land and Africans thus,

> We were wanderers on a prehistoric earth, on an earth that wore the aspect of an unknown planet... The earth seemed unearthly. We are accustomed to look upon the shackled form of a conquered monster, but there – there you could look at a thing monstrous and free. It was unearthly, and the men were – No; they were not inhuman. Well, you know, that was the worst of it – this suspicion of their not being inhuman. It would come slowly to one they howled and leaped, and spun, and made horrid faces; but what thrilled you was just the thought of their humanity – like yours – the thought of your remote kinship with this wild and passionate uproar. Ugly (116).

The stereotypical projection of an African woman character in the novel is another example to present Conrad's imperialist view. He used the African woman character for two reasons "first, she is in her place and so can win Conrad's special brand of approval; and second, she fulfils a structural requirement of the story: a savage counterpart to the refined, European woman who will step forth to end the story" (117).

Some critics, who are in favour of Conrad may say that the thought process given in the story is not Conrad's, whereas it is the protagonist of the story Marlow's. Marlow is presented as a person who believes in the English liberal tradition which required all the Englishmen to feel sad about the atrocities on the other people. Marlow indicated the pitiable condition of the Africans and atrocities in the Congo of King Leopold. This thought may present Marlow/Conrad as a good hearted person. But the fact that he was not even ready to consider the Africans as brothers or fellow humans indicates the true nature of Conrad/Marlow. In the below mentioned lines, "and the intimate profundity of that look he gave me when he received his hurt remains to this date in my memory – like a claim of distant kinship affirmed in a supreme moment" (quoted in 119), Conrad is very particular in the choice of words. He does not want to address the blacks as 'kins' but states that in the black's eyes Marlow could see the 'claim of distant kinship'. Here Achebe talks about Albert Schweitzer, who was celebrated for sacrificing his life for the Africans. Even Schweitzer like Conrad/Marlow was not ready to accept the Africans as fellow humans though he served them by sacrificing his life. Instead he addressed them as 'my junior brother'. Achebe explains that ignoring/forgetting some inventions/ talents of other racial people was a nature of the Europeans. He talks about the European travellers who omit or forget to mention certain things about the explored country. Marco Polo, the great traveller of all times, spent twenty years in China. On his return to Venice he forgot to mention the China Wall and about the art of printing in China. Hence most of the time the European travellers were blind.

Achebe states that Conrad's racist views were unnoticed as racism was viewed as normal. Thus the students of *Heart of Darkness* focus more on the solitude and the sickness of the European mind than on racism. Furthermore Achebe questions how can a novel that projects 'dehumanisation, which depersonalise a portion of the human race' be celebrated as a great work of art? Even the psychoanalytic critics who are/were interested in analysing Conrad's work could discuss the significance of hairstyle for pages but did not pay attention to the reasons for the uncivilised projection of blacks. Achebe is of the view that the Western psychoanalysts must feel it as normal to project the blacks in a primitive manner.

Achebe tries to prove that not only Conrad's works share racial views but Conrad himself as a racist. He quotes Conrad's experience of his first encounters with a black and later with a white. "A certain enormous buck nigger encountered in Haiti fixed my conception of blind, furious, unreasoning rage, as manifested in the human animal to the end of my days. Of the nigger I used to dream for years afterwards" (quoted in 120). And his first encounter with a white is described thus,

> [his] calves exposed to the public gaze… dazzled the beholder by the splendour of their marble-like condition and their rich tone of young ivory…. The light of a headlong, exalted satisfaction with the world of

> men… illumined his face… and triumphant eyes. In passing he cast a glance of kindly curiosity and a friendly gleam of big, sound, shiny teeth… his white calves twinkled sturdily (quoted in 121).

Achebe after analysing the novel, attitude of Conrad, Western writers and psychoanalysts towards the blacks, finds existence of two problems. Firstly fiction does not bother to please people about whom it is written. Hence some books presents "most vulgar fashion prejudices and insults from which a section of mankind has suffered untold agonies and atrocities in the past and continues to do so in many ways and many places today" (121) and that is how the humanity of the black people is in question. Secondly the challenges based on the grounds of actuality. Achebe questions how Conrad could be trusted especially about Africa and Africans when his biographers commented on him thus, "notoriously inaccurate in the rendering of his own history" (quoted in 122). When Conrad was projecting Africans as barbaric, at the other end of Europe, Europeans recognised the artistic intelligence of the Africans (especially the skill of Fang people from Africa) and they were considered as the great masters of the sculpture form.

Achebe states that Conrad did not originate the image of Africa in his book. Instead he presented the existing dominant image of Africa in other European works. Achebe gives reasons for such a dehumanised presentation of Africa as,

> …the west seems to suffer deep anxieties about the precariousness of its civilisation and to have a need for constant reassurance by comparison with Africa. If Europe, advancing in civilisation, could cast a backward glance periodically at Africa trapped in primordial barbarity it could say with faith and feeling: there go I but for the grace of God. Africa is to Europe as the picture is to Dorian Gray – a career onto whom the master uploads his physical and moral deformities so that he may go forward, erect and immaculate. Consequently Africa is something to be avoided just as the picture has to be hidden away to safeguard the man's jeopardous integrity (123).

Actually Achebe wanted to conclude this essay with the positive note that is with a wish to look at Africa as a nation and Africans as fellow humans. But when he remembers the continuous presentation of Africa as a dark continent, he could not conclude with a positive note. Thus in the concluding part Achebe believes that removing the racist view from the Europeans is not possible easily. He cites an article from a paper titled "The Christian Science Monitor". The article discusses the psychological and the learning problems faced by the children (migrants) who speak one language at home and some other language in school. The author uses the word 'language' to denote the language spoken at home by the Spanish and Italian migrant children, and uses the word 'dialects' to address the language spoken at home by the Indian and African migrant children. The imperialist writers use the language in their work as a tool to do inevitable violence which Achebe calls a, "reflex action caused by an instinctive desire of the writer". Though Conrad wanted to condemn the imperial exploitation, unknowingly he presented his racial views through writing. Thus even unknowingly the Europeans may spread their imperialistic views in their works especially through their languages.

The second selected essay, "The African Writer and the English Language" is centred on the post-colonial concept named appropriation. When many postcolonial writers rejected/ criticised the usage of the colonial language, some writers like Caliban in *The Tempest* wanted to use the master's language to curse them back. In this essay Achebe presents his acceptance of English as a tool to write back his African life to the world readers by following the methods of Caliban.

Achebe begins the essay by mentioning a conference titled "A Conference of African Writers of English Expression" happened in Africa in 1962. The conference attempted to define African literature with many questions like,

> Was it literature produced in Africa or about Africa? Could African literature be on any subject, or must it have an African theme? Should it embrace the whole continent of south of the Sahara, or just *black* Africa? And then the question of language. Should it be in indigenous African languages or should it include Arabic, English, French, Portuguese, Afrikaans, and so on? (27).

But they failed to define it satisfactorily. Later in another conference, African literature was defined as "Creative writing in which an African setting is authentically handled or to which experiences originating in Africa or integral" (27). This definition thus gives way to accept Conrad's *Heart of Darkness* as African literature and rejects Graham Green's *Heart of the Matter*. The first novel though written by a western writer, it was situated in Africa and about African people, whereas the latter though it discussed the similar experiences set in other black countries like West Indies was rejected as the story set in other locations. It suggests that African literature cannot be crammed into a small definition: it is not a single unit whereas, "a group of associated units – in fact the sum total of all the *national* and *ethnic* literatures of Africa" (27). Achebe states that in spite of their continuous attempts to define African literature, it cannot be homogenised; based on the geography, class, religion and ethnicity writings differ in Africa.

In the process of defining African literature, Achebe distinguishes national and ethnic literature: National literature as the one produced in English, the national language and Ethnic literature as the one written in the ethnic languages of Africa. Achebe claims that the African literature written in English as the reality of Africa. At the same time some may have different opinions and they may consider it as a controversial statement. For them Achebe clarifies that English should not be seen as evil like the other atrocities of racial arrogance. The geographical boundaries of Africa were created by the British. For their selfish benefits, the British united hundreds of autonomous communities into a big political unit named Nigeria. Moreover they introduced a common language, English. Similarly in the other parts of Africa, other languages like French and Arabic played the role of uniting different ethnic communities. Hence everyone in those newly united places started using a common language for communication. "Therefore those African writers who have chosen to write in English or French are not unpatriotic smart alecks with an eye on the main chance – outside their own countries. They are by-products of the same process that made the new nation-states of Africa".

Achebe shares his personal encounter with two African writers. With Joseph Kariuki of Kenya, who writes in English, Achebe could connect well though it was their first meeting, as Achebe was familiar with his works. With the other writer, Shadaan Robert of Tanganyika, who wrote in Swahili, Achebe could not communicate as he has not read his work. As Nigeria has many languages, learning all the languages is practically impossible. Thus the need for a common language is very strong. Achebe strengthens this idea by pointing out a Brazilian writer Jorge Amado, one of the important writers in the world literature because he wrote in English. He gives another example to prove that the works in the world language can convey truth to the people. Olauda Equiano widely known as Gustavus Vassa was from the Ibo community from Eastern Nigeria. He was sold as a slave in his youth and sent to America. After getting his freedom he moved to London and published his life story as a document in 1789. This work as it was written in a world language served as an evidence against the lies of the Europeans to justify the slave trade.

After projecting the importance and advantages of writing in a world language, he presents its disadvantages. The main problem in using a world language in a decolonised country is the impossibility of using the second language as effectively as the first. He quotes Obiwali's article "Dead End of African Literature", "...until these writers and their Western midwives accept the fact that any true African literature must be written in African languages, they would be merely pursuing a dead end, which can only lead to sterility, uncreativity and frustration". Here Achebe disapproves of the view that the western language leads to sterility in writing. Instead he believes that it creates new voices that share African experiences in worldwide language. He continues that the African writers can use English language effectively in creative writing and at the same time it is not necessary for them to write like a native speaker, whereas they can use it simply as a tool to share their experiences. "The African writer should aim to use English in a way that brings out his message best without altering the language to the extent that its value as a medium of international exchange will be lost. He should aim at fashioning an English which is at once universal and able to carry his peculiar experience". Achebe gives Amos Tutola's *The Feather Woman of the Jungle* as an example to indicate the usage of his limited second language knowledge in an amazing way. But some African writers think in their mother tongue and translate it into English, which actually lacks life. Hence the mechanical process of translation lacks natural flow of the work.

Achebe finally moves to an important complaint about the African writers who write in English: whether the African writers have to write in English by abandoning one's mother tongue, which is actually a betrayal. Based on his personal experience, he answers this complaint that he does not have other choices. He was taught in that language and he intended to use it. At the same time there will be more number of writers like Chief Fagunwa, who chose to write in his mother tongue for the development of the ethnic literature. He concludes the essay by comparing James Baldwin's experience of using English with his own experience. James Baldwin states,

> My quarrel with the English language has been that the language reflected none of my experience. But now I began to see the matter another way.... Perhaps the language was not my own because I had never attempted to use it, had only learned to imitate it. If this were so, then it might be made to bear the burden of my experience if I could find the stamina to challenge it, and me to test it (quoted in 30).

Achebe tells us that they both have different problems with the English language and Achebe wants the English language to carry the weight of his African experience. The English should be, "a new English, still in full communion with its ancestral home but altered to suit its new African surroundings (30)".

IV. Ngugi wa Thiong'o (1938)

Ngugi wa Thiong'o is a Kenyan writer, academician and social activist born in 1938 in colonial Africa. His original name was James Ngugi and changed it to Ngugi wa Thiong'o later in the 1960s when he renounced Christianity and English. He was born in a big peasant family where all the communication, activities and fun happened mainly in his mother tongue Gikuyu. His community was like other communities that considered language as part and parcel of their life. But the colonial education uprooted the children by forcing a foreign language on them. He attended colonial school and later Makerere University College (then a campus of London University) that tried to create distance from his Gikuyu language. During his adolescence he observed the Mau Mau war of independence from 1952 to 1963. This war had its impact on him which was set as a theme for his earlier works. His first play *The Black Hermit* was performed in Uganda in 1962 as a part of the celebration of Uganda's independence. His debut novel titled *Weep Not, Child* (1964) was the first novel in English written from East Africa.

Ngugi joined as a Lecturer at the English Department in the University of Nairobi in 1967. Then he was promoted as the Chair of the Department and continued teaching till 1977. During this period he was one of the members who wanted to change the name of the Department from English Literature to Literature in order to present African and Asian literatures at the centre. In 1977 along with the other members he started the Kamiriithu Educational and Cultural Centre, Limuru and wrote a play titled *Ngaahika Ndeenda* (*I Will Marry When I Want*). This controversial play was written in Gikuyu and performed in open space in front of the common people. It was a satire about the inequality and injustice shown by the then Kenyan government. This resulted in the ban of the drama and Ngugi was arrested and imprisoned for a year in a high security prison without being accused of any charge. In the prison he decided to write his creative writings in his mother tongue Gikuyu language by deserting English. At the same time in order to reach the world readers, he decided to continue writing the political and cultural essays in English. He wrote his first novel in Gikuyu language *Caitaani Mutharabalni* (*Devils on the Cross*) on toilet papers as papers were prohibited in the prison. After the imprisonment he lost his job in the University. He focused on his creative writing and travelled to London with regard to the publication of his work. Later by knowing the Kenyan government's plan to arrest him, he exiled in Britain (1982-1989) and in America (1989-2002) and was working as visiting professor in many universities. As his works were against the Kenyan government, his books were banned in Kenya from 1986 to 1996. All his writings focused on the injustice and oppression experienced by the poor people in Kenya under the colonial and neo-colonial Kenyan government. After spending 22 years in exile in 2004 he returned Kenya with his family but could spend only a month's time there. Due to the physical attack and life threat in Kenya he moved back to America. Presently he is a Distinguished Professor of English Literature at the University of California, Irvine.

Ngugi wa Thiong'o's *Decolonising the Mind: The Politics of Language in African Literature* is a very important work that discusses the politics behind the usage of English in Africa especially in Kenya. In 1977 he stopped writing creative works in English and continued only political and cultural essays in English and in this book he declared it as his last work in English. This book contains four of his developed papers, delivered earlier in many universities. All those papers are connected on the theme of language usage in African Literature and his recommendations. The aim of the book as given by Ngugi is that despite the differences of languages and classes all people should join together against the struggle by joining to "dream to change the world".

In the introduction of this work Ngugi states that this work is a part of the continuing debate about the destiny of Africa. In studies generally the African realities have been seen in terms of the tribes. What is seen as conflict between different religious groups or different cultural groups are seen as conflict between two tribal groups in the case of African countries. Moreover even the African literature is evaluated as a work with tribal theme/character. The main reason for such misrepresentation about Africa is the Western media. It actually deflects people from understanding the root cause of all the problems in Africa as imperialism. Not only the other countries, but even some Africans without doubting the divide and rule of the colonial origins became prey to the views of the Western media.

Ngugi presents two rival groups of African forces who affect the African realities. The first group is the follower of imperialist traditions, African neo-colonial bourgeoisie. Their dependence on economic and politics is reflected in African culture and they circulate the bourgeois ideology through academics. The second group consists of patriotic middle class people (working class, peasants, students and soldiers) who oppose the imperialist traditions. They believe that imperialism is not a slogan but in reality it has affected their lives for many centuries. The real situation of many African countries being mortgaged to IMF (International Ministry of Finance) proves that poor workers and peasants are the victims of imperialism. Ngugi calls America the present-day imperialist that punish the people who struggle for peace and democracy by death.

Exploitations by the imperialists still continue in the decolonised countries through cultural bombs which actually, "annihilate a people's belief in their names, in their languages, in their environment, in their heritage of struggle, in their unity, in their capacities and ultimately in themselves" (3). Consequently they look at their country as a waste land and distance themselves from it by being close to other cultures and languages. At times the imperialist ideology and the usage of other languages leave these people to doubt their cause. Slowly the neo-colonial bourgeoisie tend the other people to accept the slogan "Theft is holy", which is happening in many of the independent African nations.

The first chapter of the book titled "The Language of African Literature" talks about the usage of the native language to maintain its culture and life. This chapter consist of nine parts. Ngugi states that the languages of African literature could be discussed only within the context of social forces. On the one hand, imperialism in the form of colonial and neo-colonial governments continue to control economy, politics and cultures of Africa. On the other hand, the Africans try to liberate Africa from the imperial control. Yet always someone from the imperialist nations decides the fate of Africa. Ngugi cites two historical incidents that changed the fate of Africa. In 1884, in the Berlin Conference, the Western countries decided to transform the self-governing communities into colonies. Later in the recent conference held in London, Paris, Brussels and Lisbon, it was decided to transform the colonies into neo-colonies with boundaries. Presently Africa is divided based on the European languages as "English-speaking, French-speaking or Portuguese-speaking African countries" (5). The present situation is even the writers who are against the imperialist imposition are defined in terms of their imperial language usage.

Ngugi shares his personal experience in a conference titled, "A Conference of African Writers of English Expression", which admitted only the participants who have at least published two works in English. Thus the great writers in African languages were not permitted to the conference. But ironically the conference started with the discussion titled, 'What is African Literature'. The European languages are seen as a connector among the African people against the multiplicity of African languages. In literature the European languages are seen as the saviour of the African languages. In one of the African works written in English the Foreword goes thus, "However while rendering them into French he renews them with an art which, while it respects the genius of the French language, that language of gentleness and honesty, preserves at the same time all the – virtues of the negro – African languages" (quoted in 7). Some accept the view of Chinua Achebe, "fatalistic logic of the unassailable position of English in our literature" and some other writers state that they translate their African expressions, folklores and images which are completely African into the European languages. Ngugi questions why one should enrich other languages through their expressions from their mother tongue. Furthermore even if one continues to write in English/French will it be considered as 'good English or good French'. He uses Achebe's view, "I feel that the English language will be able to carry the weight of my African experience. But it will have to be a new English, still in full communion with its ancestral home but altered to suit new African surroundings" (quoted in 8) and Gabriel Okara's acceptance of English to create 'a Nigerian or west African English' to raise a point that, "a physical violence of the battlefield was followed by the psychological violence of the classroom" (9). Hence Ngugi believes that the psychological violence imposes English language as a vehicle to make them feel inferior. To illustrate this Ngugi shares his childhood experience, especially in relation to the usage of language.

Ngugi talks about his personal experience with his mother tongue and the English language. He was born in a bigger family with around 35 members. Their mother tongue was Gikuyu and it was used for communication. He remembers the evenings of storytelling around the fireside with his family members. The grownups narrated stories to the children and the following day the children would retell the stories while working in the fields. The stories were narrated in Gikuyu and most of them had animals as main characters, especially the hare, though small, it was full of wit and cunning. The children identified themselves with the hare as it struggled against big animals like the lion, leopard or hyena. The children personified the victory of the hare as their victories and it developed their confidence as the weak can outwit the strong. The children were also interested to observe the hostile natural elements which confront for animals' cooperation and sometimes their struggles amongst themselves. The children compared the animals struggle against nature/other animals with the real life struggles of the human. Stories with humans as the lead role had the central theme: togetherness is the ultimate for a community. Those stories had two sets of characters; humans with all positive characters and humans with all negative characters, who could eat other humans. Such stories cultivated moral values among the children.

Ngugi talks about good and bad storytelling. The good storytellers could narrate the same story interestingly many times with rich usage of different words and images with varying tones of voices. This kind of effective storytelling enabled the children to understand the value of words. He believes that language is not a mere connection of words but it is a powerful one. They enriched that power through language games like riddles and proverbs. It enabled them to understand the music of the language, also they could view the world with its images and symbols. The language they used in their homes and the community was the same.

Ngugi joined school and during the first four years of schooling he learnt the lessons in his mother tongue. He had a pleasant school experience. Later he joined a colonial school which broke the harmony of the language usage. The language used for education was not his cultural language. After the declaration of a State of Emergency over Kenya in 1952 all the schools were under District Education. Ngugi states since then English became more than a language in Kenya. Ngugi shares humiliating experiences faced by the children for communicating in Gikuyu in school. Students were punished with different types of penalties like (1) five strokes of a cane on their buttocks (2) made to carry a metal plate around the neck with inscriptions of 'I am stupid' or 'I am a donkey' (3) fined with unaffordable money. Every day teachers handed over a button to particular students to pass it to a student who speaks in the mother tongue. At the end of the day the students would give a list of students who had the button that day. This practice transformed the students as traitors to their own community. Moreover the attitude towards English language also got changed. Slowly the English language was seen as intelligence and ability leaving people to believe English as the main source for a child's progress.

Apart from the racial demarcation, the colonial education system followed a pyramid structure to reduce the number of educators in Africa. The primary school system was a broader one and in the college level the structure became very narrow. The students should clear 10 papers from Maths to Science in English language. A student who failed in a single paper though very brilliant, he could not continue his education. Ngugi remembers a boy who scored distinctions in all subjects except English, later became a turn boy in a bus company. On the other hand, Ngugi who passed with low marks got placed in one of the elitist institutions in colonial Kenya. Students in spite of their brilliance were denied admission in University colleges due to failure in the English language. Hence English was seen as the magic formula for higher education. Consequently Orature (Oral literature) in Kenyan languages has stopped.

In schools only the works of the English authors were prescribed by stopping the orature of African languages which moved the children further away from themselves and from their world. He believes that language paves the way to human experience, human culture and then the human perception of reality and distancing from the mother tongue breaks this chain.

Ngugi is of the view that language performs a dual task; as a source for communication and as a carrier of culture. He provides three aspects for language as communication: 1. Language as an expression/relation between human beings. 2. Language as speech that imitates the language of life. 3. Language as written signs – as a representative of visual symbols. Through these aspects communication becomes the integral part in the evolution of culture. Thus human experiences are passed to the next generation as culture through communication. "Language as culture is the collective memory bank of a people's experience in history. Culture is almost indistinguishable from the language that makes possible its genesis growth banking, articulation and indeed its transformation from one generation to the next" (15). Even for language as culture Ngugi provides three aspects: 1. Culture as a production and a reflection of human communication. 2. Culture as an image forming agent in a child's mind. Individuality of a human is based on that image and it is done by producing images of the world to humans. 3. Culture transmits the images of the world through language. Hence Ngugi states that culture and communication are the product of each other. "Communication creates culture: culture is a means of communication. Language carries culture and culture carries particularly through orature and literature; the entire body of values by which we come to perceive ourselves and our place in the world" (16).

Ngugi tries to find the impact of colonial imposition of their language upon the colonised children. He states that the aim of colonisation is to control people's wealth. Military conquest controlled society and wealth. For economic and political control, the colonised need to be controlled mentally. It, "involved two aspects of the same process: the destruction or the deliberate under valuing of a people's culture, their art, dances, religions, history, geography, education, orature and literature, and the conscious elevation of the language of the coloniser" (16). Through the imposition of a foreign language, the harmony of real life cannot be felt by the child. That child learns the written form of a foreign language and finds a gap between its spoken language at home and written language at school. Ngugi states that, "this resulted in the disassociation of the sensibility of that child from his natural and social environment, what we might call colonial alienation" (17). This alienation is intensified through the teaching of Europe-centred history, arts and literature. Hence the colonial child is exposed to an external culture but not to his/hers. The worst part of it is the colonial child is exposed to his/her world through the works of the colonisers. The colonised were presented as, "low-status, humiliation, corporal punishment, slow-footed intelligence and ability or downright stupidity, non-intelligibility and barbarism" (18) which was supported by the so-called genius from the racist groups to destruct the confidence of the colonised child. The lies created by the imperialists haunted the African children even in the later stages of life. Because "the negative image becomes internalised and it affects their cultural and even political choices in ordinary living" (8). This confusion led many to accept European language over their mother tongue. Ngugi cites example of African writers who considered a European language as their language and wished to pass it on to the next generation. He calls them bourgeoisie from colonial schools and universities. Leopold Sedar Senghor accepted French and claimed that French is better than the African languages. "In our language (i.e. African languages) the hollow that surrounds the words is by nature nearly that of sap and blood; French words send out thousands of rays like diamonds" (quoted in 19). Another person named Banda started The Kamuzu Academy to teach English to Malawi students and for that purpose he hired teachers with good communicational skill in English from Britain. Similarly, Chinua Achebe stated, "those of us who have inherited the English language may not be in a position to appreciate the value of the inheritance" (19) to show his gratitude to English. Thus the European language attained an unassailable position in Africa and Ngugi calls it the victory of imperialism which made the colonised to praise the system of domination. Ngugi quotes Obi Wali who presented the acceptance of European language that misrepresented African literature as, "the whole uncritical acceptance of English and French as the inevitable medium for educated African writing is misdirected, and has no chance of advancing African literature and culture" (24). Even when someone tried to write in the African languages, they were severely punished by the colonial government. Ngugi shares information about an African writer named Gakaara Wa Wanjau, who was imprisoned by the British for 10 years (1952-62) for writing his works in the Gikuyu language. Thus English was imposed on the Africans from schools to universities by expecting, "the African creator, deprived of the use of his language and cut off from his people, might turn out to be only the representative of a literary trend (and that not necessarily the least gratuitous) of the conquering nation" (25).

Ngugi divided the African writings in European languages into two categories: 1. Metropolitan bourgeoisies who wanted the imperialists to have a permanent alliance with them. 2. Nationalistic patriotic bourgeoisies who wanted independence. Ngugi talks about nationalistic writers who present Africa's present and past condition, culture and human complexity to the world through the European languages. They project the betrayal of hope in the post-independent period in a critical and cynical tone by using the African peasants' forms like proverbs, fables, stories, riddles and wise sayings. These works as they are written in the European languages, stays with the students and bourgeoisie by failing to reach the common people. Thus these writers oscillate between the peasants and the bourgeoisie as their works are about the peasants and in the form of peasants but reaches the bourgeoisie as they are in the European languages.

Moreover, these works present the peasants and workers talking in European languages in dramas and fiction which actually lack originality. He blames these writers who project their works as African literature by claiming that they write in Africanised English/French but it is easily recognised as English. He warns that if this class occupies superior position in the nation, "African language would have ceased to exist with independence" (22).

The sole reason for the existence of the African languages and heritage is the peasants. Even during the anti-colonial period, all the peasants united in spite of their language differences. They did not need a common language to be united. When a compulsion was imposed to accept a colonial language, they Africanised it. Unlike Senghor or Achebe, they created new African languages. Ngugi recommends that in future conferences on African literature should focus on the imperial problems of the African literature in African languages and the development of African sensibility.

Ngugi questions the difference between politicians who support imperialism and the writers who support European languages. Ngugi presents the irony that the European missionary made *The Bible* to be available to the Africans by translating it even into the less known African languages. But the African writers preferred to write in the European languages in order to reach the Africans. However, these writings belong to the section titles Afro-European literature, which means "literatures written by Africans in European languages in the era of imperialism" (27). The editors of Pelican Guides accepted the African literature in the European language as contribution to the 20th century English literature or French literature which leads to the creation of hybrid writing. Afro-European literary writers like Obi Wali rejects such a section by stating, " African literature can only be written in African languages, that is, the languages of the African peasantry and working class, the major alliance of classes in each of our nationalities and the agency for the coming inevitable revolutionary break with new colonialism" (27).

Ngugi has started writing his works in Gikuyu since 1977. In his own native language he wrote 2 plays, 1 novel and 3 books for children. Since then he was confronted with a question particularly in Europe about the reason for writing in Gikuyu language. His writing in the mother tongue was perceived as an abnormal act. The common practice in other cultures, i.e., writing in the mother tongue was criticised and questioned which indicates an imperialistic attitude. As a result, abnormal was perceived as normal and vice-versa. In reality Africa enriches Europe, whereas Africans were made to believe that Europe rescues them from poverty. Africa's resources like nature and humans developed Europe and America but in reality it is projected in the reverse manner.

Ngugi believes that his writing in Gikuyu is a part of the anti-imperialistic struggles of African, especially Kenyan people. In educational institutes the Kenyan languages were associated with negative aspects such as underdeveloped, humiliation and punishment. He does not want to see the future generation especially school children growing up in such an imperialistic tradition. He expects them to surpass the colonial alienation. Ngugi gives two interlinked forms of colonial alienation, (1) distancing themselves from the reality around (2) identification with what is most external to one's environment. This colonial alienation starts with disassociation of a language in an educational environment but used at home and society. He compares it with bodiless heads and headless bodies.

Ngugi visualises a future where he could see the restoration of harmony in language which enables the Kenyan children to be restored to their environment. He desires to see the Kenyan national languages having a literature which reflect the rhythms of the language as well as the natives' social nature and their struggle with nature. In such a harmonious situation one can learn other languages and could enjoy revolutionary elements in the other languages without any complex about his mother tongue, environment and himself. It will benefit the future generation of Kenya to live in harmony.

The writers of African languages should connect themselves with the peasants and working class people to defeat the imperialists. When they mirror the revolutionary ideas of the peasants in their works, there may be a threat for their lives/exile and they will not be celebrated as national writers. Ngugi, concludes this chapter by stating,

> ...a democratic participation of the people in the shaping of their own lives or in discussing their own lives in languages that allow for mutual comprehension is seen as being dangerous to the good government of a country and its institutions. African languages addressing themselves to the lives of the people become the enemy of a neo-colonial stage (30).

In this chapter Ngugi talks about the connectedness of language and culture to point out that imposition of a foreign language may affect the culture. Hence imposition of the European language in academics and later literary works produced as products of such education leave Africa as a country which is still mentally colonised.

He projects the vulnerable position of African languages and African language writers. He warns the future by elaborating the term colonial alienation.

The second chapter titled, "The Language of African Theatre" talks about the transformations of functions and roles of the African theatres in the pre-colonial, the colonial and the post-colonial period. Ngugi begins the chapter by describing the opening of the Kamiriithu Community Education and Cultural Centre in 1977. Kamiriithu is one of the villages in Limuru with different classes of people. The villagers in order to provide their cultural materials and activities for the new literates wanted to start the centre.

In pre-colonial Kenya, drama was an integral part of their life which was performed in an open space anywhere. Birth, growth and death of humans and nature were celebrated with ceremonies and rites. They used drama with multiple purposes; entertainment, moral instruction and to teach communal survival. The Ituika ceremony was an important ceremony that was held once in 25 years in Kenya. It was a symbolic ceremony where power was transformed from one generation to the next generation. The ceremony happened for around six months and new laws and regulations of the new governance were conveyed through songs, dances and mimes. During the colonial period the British destroyed the tradition of drama. With a purpose to spread Christianity, they banned ceremonies which were in the form of drama and in 1925 the Ituika ceremony was banned. The British missionaries and administrators destroyed the concept of open space performance and restricted it in the closed space like society hall and schools. The dramas aimed to promote Christianity and in schools Shakespeare's dramas were performed. These dramas often projected the Africans especially the peasants as stupid who act in a foolish way in the modern world.

After independence, mostly the same English literature based dramas were performed. The graduates were against the African stereotypes in the dramas and they produced counter Shakespeare and Shaw plays with their own scripts. In the 1960s and 70s, the Africans revolted against the domination of the British expatriate communities on the Kenyan theatres. In the 1970s, once the theatres came under the control of the Kenyan groups, they faced some transformation. The only difficulty felt by Ngugi was the usage of the English language in the theatres as most of the actors and directors had English education but enacted the lives of the peasants.

Ngugi felt that Kamiriithu theatre was an attempt to bring back the African theatre tradition. According to him, the neo-colonial theatres,

> ...practices education as a process of weakening people, of making them feel they cannot do this or that – oh, it must take such brains! – In other words education as a means of mystifying knowledge and hence reality. Education, far from giving people – the confidence in their ability and capacities to overcome obstacles or to become masters of the laws governing external nature as human beings, tends to make them feel their inadequacies, their weaknesses and their incapacities in the face of reality; and their inability to do anything about the conditions governing their lives (56).

On the other hand, Kamiriithu theatre enabled people to understand, "education as a process of demystifying knowledge and hence reality. People could see how the actors evolved from the time they could hardly move their legs or say their lines to a time when they could talk and move about the stage as if they were born repeating those lines or moving on that stage" (57). Here drama was based on the theme of peasants' lives and performed in open space in front of the common people. This drama was a result of collective work; the workers and the peasants shared their hardships in detail with Ngugi which he used as a source for this drama. He describes Kamiriithu as good theatre, "that which was on the side of the people, that which, without making mistakes and weaknesses gives people courage and urges them to higher resolves in their struggle for total liberation" (43). His play *Ngaahika Ndeenda (I Will Marry When I Want)* is based on the struggle for land and freedom. It depicted the transformation of Kenya from a British colony into a new colonial society with the imperialist interest of America and Japan. He preferred to use Gikuyu language, to project the rebellious theme in a more effective and natural way. The play was first enacted in front of the public in an open space on October 2, 1977. It was an immediate success as almost the entire audience could identify themselves with the characters in the drama. As the story was based on the repression and resistance against the new colonial government, it was banned on November 16, 1977. People involved in the drama were arrested and Ngugi was imprisoned.

In 1981, the Kamirrithu Centre was ready with another drama named Maitu Njugira, (*Mother Sing for Me*) based on the struggle Kenyan workers faced with confiscation of land and forced labour. The government refused license for this drama. Hence they performed it under the disguise of rehearsals with 10,000 audiences for 10 times. The provoked Kenyan government banned the activities of the Kamiriithu Centre and again all the people associated with the

Centre were imprisoned. Though, the Kamiriithu Centre existed for a short span, it had a great impact on the Kenyan people. It enabled them to understand the anti-people attitude of the Kenyan government.

The third chapter titled "The Language of African Fiction" deals with the form of fiction in pre-colonial, colonial and post-colonial African literature. Along with that Ngugi shared his personal experience of writing a novel in Gikuyu and the challenges he faced. His imprisonment in 1978 due to his production of drama in the Kamiriithu Centre, left him in deep thoughts about the African realities. He gives the transformations undergone from Orature of pre-colonial Kenya to the fiction form in decolonised Kenya. In the pre-colonial period, Kenyan oratures were filled with animal characters, half human, half beasts, nature and humans. As they were less interested in the productive force, their literature projected the life of people with the mixture of animal characters of different natures and heroic nature of kings who save their community. This literature was very close to life. During the colonial period, this closeness with life and nature was distanced by moving literature to constructed social order and capitalism. Ngugi presents the transformation of the African society through imperialism as,

> Capitalism introduced plenty and possibilities of the conquest of hunger: capitalism ensured poverty and mass starvation on a scale unknown before. Capitalism and the development of science and technology introduced the possibilities of the conquest of nature: Capitalism by its uncontrolled use and exploitation of natural, resources ensured the virtual dominance of nature over man by way of droughts and desertification. Capitalism introduced a new medical science to conquer diseases: capitalism through its selection prescription of medical care, at least in the colonies, ensured a disease-ridden population who now lacked help from the herbalists and psychiatrists whose practices had been condemned as devilry (66).

Thus they were distanced from their own tradition and culture. Later with the help of the printing press English and African language works, mostly The Bible messages were circulated. Those stories and even the animal tales were published with the morals connected to the White God. Later when the Africans started to write novels, they preferred the European language as all those writers were the product of colonial education.

Ngugi again highlights that the African languages exist due to the usage of it by the peasants and the working class people. He questions why the writers should not write in their language to reach their own people. His novel *Grain of Wheat* is about the peasants' struggle but written in a language that peasants cannot understand.

Hence Ngugi decided to write for the peasants in their language. He feels that challenges and struggles faced by the peasants are stronger than fiction, hence he decided to write about their day-to-day life. Moreover his reading of the Faust theme in literature, used by many writers enabled him to find similarity between a man selling his soul to the devil and a man selling his nation to the imperials.

Ngugi wrote the novel *Caitaani Muthorabaini (Devil on Cross),* in Gikuyu language when he was in prison. He shares his problems in using Gikuyu for fiction writing. He encountered confusion in distinguishing the long and short vowels as it led to different meanings. Adopting the African language to the style of fiction writing was the next problem. This novel was an immediate hit in the rural and urban areas and in a year the book was printed three times, which was a record in Kenya. The success of this book, he treasures as a motivation to the writers. He concludes by requesting the African writers to write in their mother tongue as it will develop African literature. The future of African fiction finds its form and character in its rich oral tradition of peasants and not in the imperialist tradition.

The fourth chapter titled "The Quest for Relevance" is a summing up of the discussions in the other chapters along with the relevance of teaching literature in schools and colleges. Ngugi finds teaching of literature involves two processes: 1. Choice of material, 2. Interpretation of material. During World War II, English occupied a dominant place in schools and colleges in Africa. The University of London established its overseas extension in many of the African cities and the students studied the British writers every day. Ngugi presents the British writers in three categories: 1. European writers, who presented the European experience of history 2. The liberal Europeans who presented Africa as the subject of their imaginary exploration 3. European writers producing racist literature, projecting the Africans in two types: one being good and the other being bad. The Africans who helped the European colonisers to colonise their country are presented as good, intelligent and handsome. The second type of Africans who resisted the foreign conquest are projected as bad with negative qualities, ugly, weak and cowardly. This projection was made with a purpose as such presentations will leave the readers to take the side of the good person that indirectly encourages the Africans to support colonisation. The irony is even after independence the same Eurocentric learning is given to the Kenyan students. As a result the African children were looking at the world in a way that was projected by the Europeans in the Eurocentric way.

> That Africa as a continent has been a victim of forces of colonial exploitation, oppression and human degradation. In the field of culture she was taught to look towards Europe as her teacher and the centre of man's civilisation, and herself as the pupil. In this event Western culture became the centre of Africa's process of learning, and Africa was relegated to the background. Africa uncritically imbibed values that were alien and had no immediate relevance to her people. Thus was the richness of Africa's cultural heritage degraded, and her people labelled as primitive and savage. The coloniser's values were placed in the limelight, and in the process, evolved a new African who denied his original image, and exhibited a considerable lack of confidence in his creative potential. (Quoted on page no. 100)

Ngugi is of the opinion that interpretation of literature is always subjective based on one's class and culture. Similarly the choice of materials, evolution of the material is also controlled by the nation and the class. Hence interpretations of history, politics and economy results in two contradictory ideas. One is identification with the thought process of the colonisers/neo-colonisers by accepting the interests of the imperialist. Such people praise colonisation and they believe that collaboration with the British imperialism brought them independence. They go to the level of accepting imperialist Europe as the beginning of Kenya's history and progress. The other is, resisting imperialism with the aim to have a democratic Kenya.

This chapter also presents brief information and outcome of the 'great Nairobi literature debate' by the literature teachers from universities and schools. The faculty members of English literature submitted a proposal to continue English literature by including writings from the Commonwealth countries and America. The main concern of the proposal was to know that even if African literature is included in English literature, will it occupy the central position or a periphery position. Ngugi along with two other teachers named Owuor Anyumba and Taban Lo Liyung firmly rejected English education by stating,

> We reject the primacy of English literature and cultures. The aim, in short, should be to orientate ourselves towards placing Kenya, East Africa, and then Africa in the centre. All other things are to be considered in their relevance to our situation and their contribution towards understanding ourselves (Quoted from 94).

They recommended the study of oral literature as it can give loyalty to indigenous values. In 1969, a new syllabus was accepted including African orature, African literature and the Third World literatures in English language. This syllabus reflected the African perspective to the students which enabled them to link with themselves. Regarding this Ngugi observes:

> The growth of the Literature Department at the University of Nairobi, a department which has produced students who can, by starting from their environment, freely link the rural and urban experiences of Kenyan and African literature to that of Garcia Marquez, Richard Wright, George Lamming, Balzac, Dickens, Shakespeare and Brecht is a far cry from those days in the fifties and sixties when they used to try and detect Jane Austen's characters in their villages. (Quoted from 95)

Another conference on "The Teaching of African Literature in Kenyan Schools" was attended by many delegates from the national and international level. The findings of the conference was,

> The present language and literature syllabuses are inadequate and irrelevant to the needs of the country. They are so organised that a Kenyan child knows himself through London and New York. Both should therefore be completely overhauled at all levels of our education system and particularly in schools (Quote from 97).

Hence they decided to havc thc centrality of oral literature and to teach African literature in order to enable the students to understand their culture and environment first. Moreover the committee recommended Pan-African consciousness. It wanted the African children to be exposed to the united African literature as its history, by introducing the works of Afro-Americans and the Caribbean's. It also recommended to include Swahili, a widely spoken African language, along with English in schools. Though the conference came up with many recommendations, Ngugi was doubtful about the government's implementation of them. The outcome of the conference was not about what authors are to be taught to break new colonialism but about changing the Africans to look at themselves based on the Afro-centric view than on the Eurocentric view.

Ngugi advises that educated people should be responsible for their society, because in the later years the simple men and women may question, 'how the educated left the country to be in poverty. There will be questions regarding the relevance of literature, art and culture, and to whom those works were produced.' He concludes this chapter by calling for the rediscovery of,

> It is a call for the rediscovery of the real language of humankind: the language of struggle. It is the universal language underlying all speech and words of our history. Struggle. Struggle makes history. Struggle makes us. In struggle is our history, our language and our being. That struggle begins wherever we are; in whatever we do: then we become part of those millions whom Martin Carter once saw sleeping not to dream but dreaming to change the world (Quoted from 108)

V. Edward Said (1935-2003)

Edward Said, known as a founder of the Postcolonial Studies, is a widely known intellectual and political activist of his time. He was born in a Christian family in Palestine. He attended Anglican school where he experienced problems with his identity. Regarding this he states,

> With an unexceptionally Arab family name like "Saïd", connected to an improbably British first name...I was an uncomfortably anomalous student all through my early years: a Palestinian going to school in Egypt, with an English first name, an American passport, and no certain identity, at all. To make matters worse, Arabic, my native language, and English, my school language, were inextricably mixed: I have never known which was my first language, and have felt fully at home in neither, although I dream in both. Every time I speak an English sentence, I find myself echoing it in Arabic, and vice versa (2002: 556-557).

After completing his graduation, Said received his PhD from Harvard University. He started his teaching career at Columbia University. His life was disturbed by the war between Arab and Israel. The Six-Day War between Israel and the Arab countries in 1967 was misrepresented by the U.S. media. Said felt that the reality was misrepresented by the Americans with the stereotypical presentations of the Middle East countries. Provoked, Said published "The Arab Portrayed" (1968) in order to orient the Americans about the historical and cultural realities of the Arabs. Consequently, such reading left him to describe the Palestinians as people without land. His readings of colonisation of Palestine led him to read about the imperialist discourse of the West. Said is of the view that the earlier Western scholarship to study 'the orient' was biased and aimed to construct 'the other' by Western cultural imperialist ideology. This anger led him to write numerous works in support of the Middle East countries. It enabled him to introspect himself with respect to his identity. "...he located himself in what he called an interstitial space, a space in between a Palestinian colonial past and an American imperial present, he found himself both empowered and obliged to speak out for Palestine, to be the voice of the marginalised and the dispossessed, and, crucially, to present Palestine to the American people" (Ashcraft and Ahluwalia: 6). Ironically, Said was criticised both by the Arabs as Westernised (and his works were banned in Palestine) and by the Americans as conservative. He is recognised worldwide with the publication of his magnum opus *Orientalism* which gave way for the postcolonial studies. This work expanded fields in anti-colonial and postcolonial studies. As it is a widely known and popular work, his other important work *Culture and Imperialism* is summarised in detail here.

Culture and Imperialism

Said begins the work by stating it as not just a sequel to *Orientalism* but it tries to do something more. The work *Orientalism* was limited to the Middle East and this work aims to describe the general relationship between the modern day West and its overseas territories. Also, *Orientalism* missed mentioning the decolonisation movements in the third world countries which this work will talk about. This work also tries to emphasise the world culture in a grand way. This book aims to present two factors: "a general worldwide pattern of imperial culture and a historical experience of resistance against empire" (xii) by looking at the role of culture in it. He states that imperialism and culture have to be studied together. For Said culture means two things: 1. Culture as a provider of pleasure which often exists in aesthetic form, 2. Source of identity. To explain the first meaning of culture he explores the formation of the 19th and the 20th century the modern Western empire's imperial attitudes, references and experiences through the cultural form of novels. Theses novels (ex: *Robinson Crusoe*) were written with 'the aesthetic object' that is to expand societies of Britain and France. Said believes that imperialism and the literary form of the novel are interlinked. The repeated style of works based on the theme colonial discourse presented general stereotypes of the colonised nations as 'the mysterious East' and Europe's justification of violence as 'they were not like us'.

Said emphasises in such colonial novels, narration is very crucial to attain their purpose. Narration is not a simple act of storytelling whereas it is a powerful act which decides who to rule and who to be ruled. Thus power to narrate is crucial in the formation of culture and imperialism. As nations become narratives, the colonial nations constructed images of the colonised by the explorers later became the colonial identity and history of the colonised. Similarly some narratives of emancipation and enlightenment enabled the colonised to fight for freedom. Thus narration is not a simple style to tell a story but to construct power.

The second type, culture as identity enabled the great 19th and 20th century writers of the West to associate themselves with their culture. Instead of condemning their nation's injustice of colonisation, they supported their nation's mission through their works. Charles Dickens *Great Expectations'* (1861) projected Magwitch as unacceptable as he returned from Australia. Dickens' novel constructed the ideology that,

> The prohibition placed on Magwitch's return is not only penal but imperial: subjects can be taken to places like Australia, but they cannot be allowed a 'return' to metropolitan space, which, as all Dickens' fiction testifies, is meticulously chartered, spoken for, inhabited by a hierarchy of metropolitan personages (xvii).

Dickens present almost all his characters to have association with the empire; to travel or to trade with the orient. The Western imperialists project the colonised nations as open to the interest of the travellers. Writers like Conrad, Kipling, Gide and Loti projected the empire as 'a central area of concern'. Said comments that Conrad cannot accept that the colonies of Europe too have cultures, histories and aspirations. He blindly neglected all the anti-imperialist independent movements as corrupt. Conrad might have felt that, "We Westerners will decide who is a good native or a bad one because all natives have sufficient existence by virtue of our recognition. We created them, we taught them to speak and think, and when they rebel they simply confirm our views of them as silly children, duped by some of their Western masters" (xx). Said presents Conrad as both anti-imperialist and imperialist. He states that, "Conrad both criticising and reproducing the imperial ideology of his time, to that extent we can characterise our own present attitudes: the projection, or the refusal, of the wish to dominate, the capacity to damn, or the energy to comprehend and engage with other societies, traditions, histories" (xxii).

In this work Said plans to read the individual works from the empires firstly based on its creative and interpretative imagination and secondly to present the imperialistic impacts in it. For this study he selects the empires of Britian, France and America as they were/are the biggest empires and moreover they used systematic methods/structures to spread their imperial culture. This book projects past and present and 'us' and 'them', as imperials made all the colonised as one. Similarly all the great metropolitans play the same strategy that is first to help and then to dominate the colonies.

Said states that the emergence of new political and intellectual consciousness as the second concern for writing this book. Now with the help of globalisation, the new powerful nations can give their empowered voices. The new power now challenges the core cultural thought of the empire which "had become the hallmark of imperialist cultures as well as those cultures trying to resist the encroachments of Europe" (xxviii). With the new empowered thinking, binary oppositions are erased. Yet the ideological presentation of identity is still based on the interests of various groups.

Said says that empire involved one culture with the other leaving no homogeneous culture. Hence "all cultures are involved in one another; none is single and pure, all are hybrid, heterogeneous, extraordinarily differentiated, and monolithic" (xxix). He invites the readers to explore history than to repress or to deny it. Moreover in the histories, minorities should be included with the main group. If the old idea or main group does not include the new group or the minority, instead of rejecting the new ideas they should be included by changing the old ideas.

Chapter 1: Overlapping Territories, Intertwined Histories

The first chapter titled "Overlapping Territories, Intertwined Histories" consists of five sub-headings. It states that there is no single culture or single history, whereas everything is intertwined.

1.1 Empire Geography and Culture

Said talks about the idea of imperialism, strategy of the empires and its construction of ideology and culture to colonise the desired lands. Moreover, he emphasises that texts played a key role in constructing such ideologies with examples. He begins this part by talking about the coexistence of past and present. By quoting T. S. Eliot, he presents the importance of history in arts by stating that art has a historical sense and art cannot stand alone without the help of history or time. Most of the time the past shapes the present. Said states that both the Western world and their formal colonies continue to apply the past cultural influences even in the present. Thus, he proves that past and present inform each other.

Said defines the term imperialism at the basic level as, "thinking about, settling on, controlling land that you do not possess, that is distant, that is lived on and owned by others" (5). Said believes that the global world is a consequence of imperial powers. Yet he is against the homogenisation of humans as it may lead to 'totalistic theories of human history'. He continues that historical experience is connected to geography. And border is not innocent only about the limited geographical territory but it is a discourse that talks about 'ideas about forms, about images and imagining'. Said states that the European world emerged as a new power. Unlike the other earlier powers like Rome, Spain and Baghdad, the Western imperialists occupied a larger landscape on earth.

In 1800 Western power claimed 55 per cent actually held approximately 35 per cent of the earth's surface, and that by 1878 the proportion was 67 per cent, a rate of increase of 83,000 square miles per year. By 1914, the annual rate had risen to an astonishing 240,000 square miles, and Europe held a grand total of roughly 85 per cent of the earth as colonies, protectorates, dependencies, dominance, and commonwealths (6).

Thus in the 19th century Britain and France were the two great empires. Said gives various strategies followed by some countries in their expansion of territories. Russia expanded its land by extending its borders whereas Britain and France expanded their colonies which were far from their geographical location. Mostly, thinkers wanted to look at imperialism as based on the political and economic conditions and scarce attention was paid to culture. Said was curious to focus on this by examining the set of cultural forms and feelings to dominate the distant places. In this work he aims to examine the way imperialism occurred by the recognisable cultural formation.

Imperialism is about, "the practice, the theory, the attitudes of a dominating metropolitan centre ruling a distant territory" (8) and even in the present when direct colonies do not exist, imperialism exists "in a kind of general cultural sphere as well as in specific political, ideological, economic, and social practices" (8). One cannot neglect imperialism and colonisation as a simple act of acquisition of land. Actually, it is much more than that as it happened with the ideological information of knowledge. Hence the imperial culture used words and concepts like "'inferior' or 'subject races', 'subordinate people', 'dependency', 'expansion', and 'authority' (8) repeatedly. The Western empire wanted to move their power relations with the colonies from 'a place of regular profit' to a place "to rule subordinate, inferior, or less advanced peoples" (10). The colonisers with a small number of members were able to control the large number of people in the colonies with the colonisers' will, self-confidence and at times even by arrogance. For example, in India in the 1930s merely around 2, 00, 000 British civil servants, soldiers and civilians controlled 30, 00, 000 Indians.

Though, after World War II the British and the French freed most of their colonies, the imperial past still existed in the form of "shared memories and as a highly conflictual texture of culture, ideology, and policy still exercises tremendous force". Hence, the hegemony of imperial ideology has to be studied very carefully as it is closely embedded in the culture. The ideas which helped for the subjugation of people and colonial territories should be read differently. Said calls to "misread both the culture's importance and its resonances in the empire, then and now" (12). He complains that at present the literary works are analysed based on specialisation in which the essence of the whole work is missing. Hence the connection between the fiction and the historical period is also missing. By giving the example of Charles Dickens' *Dombey and Son*, Said states that, "the way in which Dickens expresses Dombey's egoism recalls, mocks, yet ultimately depends on the tried and true discourses of imperial free trade, the British mercantile ethos, it sense of all but unlimited opportunities for commercial advancement abroad" (14).

Many critics including Raymond Williams believe that English is about England. But Said states that English is not about England but it gives constant refrences to the expansion of Europe. He is keen to present the role of texts in the formation of the empire. He believes that the connection between culture and imperialism is simple on one hand, and complex on the other hand. He wants to present both culture and imperialism in an integrated way than in a separate way.

1.2 Images of the Past, Pure and Impure

In the 20th century one could understand that cultures are human made structures of authority and participation. Almost all the cultures aspire to dominate. One cannot deny that culture is actually interested in accepting new elements, hence there is no pure culture. When the Greeks, the people of the ancient culture, could accept their culture as a hybrid one in the past, the Europeans are unwilling to acknowledge the same. The Europeans constructed their past to project its history with tradition and longevity. Even in the colonies during their freedom struggle the empire was constructing the image of their past in a glorious way. Such cultural attitudes of the Europeans exist even in the present. Both the former colonisers and the colonised countries have a different view about the past: some consider colonisation as an evil act and some accept it due to the problematic situation in the present. Similarly some wish to denounce the past and some others regret the ending of imperialism. Hence, at this juncture Said wants to do three things. 1. To concentrate on the source which encourages the 'rhetoric and politics of blame'. 2. By using the methods of comparative literature of imperialism, he wants to find out "how a post-imperial intellectual attitude might expand the overlapping community between metropolitan and formally colonised societies" (19). 3. By placing the intervened and overlapping histories aside by using the contrapuntal method he wants "to formulate an alternative both to a politics of blame and to the even more destructive politics of confrontation and hostility" (19). He concludes that these types of analysis may reduce 'the hostility between Western and non-Western cultures that leads to crisis".

1.3 Two Visions in Heart of Darkness

It is a known fact that power and wealth leads to imperialism. Presently though most of the former colonies are independent politically, they are still dependent in many ways on the European power. The independent former colonies are ruled by the nationalist bourgeoisie who follow the ideology of the departed masters.

Based on the 19th century geography, Said divides the world into two forces: empires (with rich cultural documents) and its colonies (animated and produced). The empires created plurality about both the colonisers and the colonised. In this part Said attempts to present, 1. How imperialism still lives in the recent cultural discussions, 2. How the imperial past lives in the arguments and the counter arguments, 3. Traces of the past in the present especially in the study of histories. He states that the residue of imperialism lies in the contemporary debates in the Western media about the independence of the former colonies of Europe. Most of the time the debates are manipulative as it only projects what is said but ignores to present how it is said, by who and where. The Westerners still believe that they have improvised the former colonies during colonisation. Hence, they expect appreciation for what they have done in the former colonies, but they have forgotten the colonial people,

> ...who for centuries endured summary justice, unending economic oppression, distortion of their social and intimate lives, and a recourseless submission that was the function of unchanging European superiority. Only to keep in mind the millions of Africans who were supplied to the slave trade is to acknowledge the unimaginable cost of maintaining that superiority (24).

Said captures the imperial attitudes in the 19th century by analysing Conrad's *Heart of Darkness* which is known for its complicated and rich narrative form. The narration is about Europe's mission in the dark world. Conrad wanted the readers to see, "how Kurtz's great looting adventure, Marlow's journey up the river, and the narrative itself all share a common theme: Europeans performing acts of imperial mastery and will in (or about) Africa" (25). Conrad is different from his contemporary writers. He, a Polish expatriate, an employee of the empire, knows about his mission. He projected the fact of Britain's transformation from the 'business of empire' to 'the empire of business'. The novel *Heart of Darkness* projects imperialist ideology aesthetically. A white man lives in a jungle and whose life is narrated by another white and the imperial ideology eliminated all the non-whites as unthinkable. Conrad used Marlow to present the imperialist view. Conrad understood that like imperialism even narration of the fiction has to be done by the white. Hence, he did not allow the African characters to speak but allowed Marlow to speak about them. Marlow's narrative enabled the readers to understand that one cannot escape the historical force of imperialism. Conrad's narrative style made two possible arguments about the postcolonial world. Firstly, to render the world as how the Western imperialists saw in the conventional way. Even after independence the former colonies exist as a locale to rule morally and intellectually by the imperialists. This discourse guides what never to be shared out and what to be shared as colonial experience. Secondly, the colonised countries like Africa, Asia and America as incapable of independence. Later, Said looks at Conrad's work as a piece of 'less imperialistic assertive possibility'. Conrad allowed Marlow to recreate Africa in England, an undefined and unclear world through his narration to the listeners. Said looks at Conrad differently and states that,

> Conrad sometimes seems to want to fold that world into the imperial metropolitan discourse represented by Marlow, but by virtue of his own dislocated subjectivity he resists the effort and succeeds in so doing, I have always believed, largely through formal devices. Conrad's self-consciously circular narrative forms draw attention to themselves as

> artificial constructions, encouraging us to sense the potential of a reality that seemed inaccessible to imperialism, just beyond its control… (32).

Said says that though Conrad's characters have European names, they think unlike the Europeans. He made his characters not to accept the imperial idea instead to worry about it. Moreover, "Conrad's way of demonstrating this discrepancy between the orthodox and his own views of empire is to keep drawing attention to how ideas and values are constructed (and deconstructed) through dislocations in the narrator's language (32). He allowed Kurtz and Marlow to talk about the imperial mastery especially about the Europeans over the Africans. Marlow even presents the reality of the empire. Being ahead of his time Conrad allowed his two white characters to present the darkness. Here "the darkness has an autonomy of its own, and can reinvade and reclaim what imperialism had taken for its own" (33). Yet Conrad had his limitations. Though he knew that imperialism means pure domination and land grabbing and criticised imperialism severely, he could not free the colonised people in the novel.

Imperial encounters have not stopped in the past but even in the present it continues. In the 1970s, important ideological transformation occurred. Thinkers like Jean-Francois Lyotard and Michael Foucault preferred to change the focus of cover from imperial to somewhere else. Lyotard wanted to focus "only with local issues, not with history but with problems to be solved, not with a grant reality but with games" (29). Faucault too thought that, "…since power was everywhere it was probably better to concentrate on the locale micro-physics of power that surround the individual. The self was therefore to be studied, cultivated, and, if necessary, refashioned and constituted" (29). Most of the decolonised countries, the new regimes were projected as barbaric. The Europeans claimed that those decolonised people deserve colonisation. Europe believes about the third world countries as 'atrocious nuisance, a culturally and politically inferior place', angered Salman Rushdie and Said. The Western journalists and critics separated Western and non-Western works and placed the non-Western works in spite of its differences in a homogenised manner and addressed it as 'terrorist, marginal, second-rate, or unimportant'. It is done with the interest to defend the Western spirit.

Both the 19th century imperialism and resistance in the native culture have confrontation. Most of the post-colonial writers with the past humiliation in mind, write about the new future that is the revised version of their nation's past. Said concludes this part by stating that writers like Rushdie, Derek Walcott, Aime Cesaire, Chinua Achebe, Pablo Neruda, and Brian Friel reread the colonial masterpieces to respond directly to them.

1.4 Discrepant Experiences

Said talks about the power of Western media in contradicting the image of the third world countries and the importance of comparative literature and contrapuntal perspective in understanding the discrepancies done by the empire to propagate the imperial desire.

Said recommends contrapuntal perspective to understand the connection between any two incidents. He explains the concept discrepant experiences by stating that when two experiences and views are culturally and ideologically close, one actually attempts to supress the other. Thus, "Far from seeking to reduce the significance of ideology, the exposure and dramatisation of discrepancy highlights its cultural importance; this enables us to appreciate its power and understand its continuing influence" (37). He explains this further by reading two works from the 1820s. (*Description del' Egypt* and *Aga'ib al Athar*). *Description* is a twenty-four-volume work about Napoleon's expedition to Egypt. *Aga'ib al Athar*is a personal experience of a French expedition written by a religious leader Abal al-Rahman al-Jabarti. Fourier, the author of the work *Description* justifies Napoleon's invasion to Egypt and he attempts to normalise the conquest while Jabarti's work presents the fear and trouble of conquests. Said read both works and states that, "the French expeditions was accompanied by a whole team of scientists whose job it was to survey Egypt as it had never been surveyed before – the result was gigantic *Description* itself – but Jabarti has eyes for, and only appreciates, the facts of power, whose meaning he senses as constituting a punishment Egypt" (38). Jabarti's work created anti-Western views on the readers from Egypt and the third world countries. On the other side, *Description* has done its role in the conquest of the orient in the past.

Imperial conquests did not happen only once but it was a continuous process, "...where the response to the silent and incorporated disparity between French and subjugated cultures took on a variety of forms" (39-40). Various studies like history, anthropology and cultural studies in Europe and America treat history as a Western super subject and presents other countries without history. The intellectuals created their own ideas and kept power on the side of the Western societies. The powerful Western countries could always take action against the decolonised countries. In the case of the U.S., war on Iraq indicates its right to safeguard remote countries with military invasion. All these power fights happen with the help of media which mould and manipulate the situation. On the other hand the lesser power nations with less rights could only claim for help. Since the 1967 war, Arabs were projected by the U.S. media thus, 'crude, reductionists, coarsely racialist'. Later due to President Bush's instructions in order to preserve the American way of life, media presented less information about the Arabs. According to Said, media is actually interested to deal with sensational news rather than the process of culture and society.

Said gives two examples to project the manipulative nature of media and media people. In the first incident when the students and the professors of Stanford University voted to change the syllabus by including more works from non-Europeans in 1989, Bernard Louis, a column writer for the *Wall Street Journal* stated that, "...if Western culture does indeed go a number of things would go with it and others would come in their place" (43) and along with that other subjects like "restoration of slavery, polygamy, and child marriage" (43) would follow soon. By stating this Louis is not only projecting the West as a supremacy in the world but also indicates the non-Western world as a violent one. The second incident occurred in 1986, where Prof. Ali Mazrui, a Kenyan Muslim, was a professor of Political Science at the University of Michigan, did a documentary titled *Africans* funded by the BBC. The documentary talked about Africa from an African point of view to the Western audience. Till then, the viewers had the Westerner's view of Africa. Prof. Ali Mazrui, stated that African history is made up of three elements as, "the native African experience, the experience of Islam, and the experience of imperialism" (44). Media person named John Corry, television correspondent of *The New York Times* attacked him by stating that he excluded certain information (example Israel was not mentioned in the documentary) and exaggerated the evils of Western imperialism. Said comments that this incident indicates that "non-Europeans should not represent their views of European and

American history as those histories impinged on the colonies; if they did, they had to be very firmly resisted" (44).

Said states that, the tension/conflict between those former colonies and the decolonised countries exists in a more dangerous way even after many years of independence. To explain this Said shares his experience of meeting an Arab Christian clergyman who came to America on an urgent and unpleasant mission. Since 1860s the Protestant community had been converting people in Syria, Lebanon and Palestine into Protestants. After 110 years, the Protestant missionary came to know that the Eastern Christians in those regions were constituted by the Greek Orthodox Church. Hence the Protestant community encouraged its followers to return to the Greek Orthodox Church and moreover it withdrew its financial support to the church and schools in those places. The young priest questions, "How do they expect us to efface our modern history, which is an autonomous one? How can they say that the mistake they made a century ago can be rectified today by a stroke of the pen in New York or London?" (46). Here the power politics and the imperial attitude is "the total disregard with which over a century of Arab Protestant experience was simply scratched off as if it had never happened" (46).

The modern intellectuals in the West develop dominant discourses which are exclusively based on the Western sources. Yet in the present, the Western and the decolonised countries' scholars are willing to have a fresh look at the collective histories. Thus we have a few books that deal with 'more complex genealogy of contemporary culture and ideology'. Said states that Gauri Vishwanathan's *The Masks of Conquest* is one such work where the writer has mentioned that the modern English studies was created for the colonised people and imposed on them in the 19th century. It was created for the "ideological pacification and reformation of a potentially rebellious Indian population" (48) and then it was imported to England with a different motive.

Said concludes this part by providing the problem that exists in comparative literature. The aim of comparative literature is to give perspectives beyond a nation. It actually originated during the period of European imperialism and is still linked to it. Hence its condition is still inactive in the modern world due to the influence of imperialism.

1.5 Connecting Empire to Secular Interpretation

Said talks about the careful creation of discourses by the imperials to differentiate the colonisers and the colonised. Such discourses can be brought to the notice of people through the new methods of reading followed by the postcolonial intellectuals. Further he talks about the successful usage of the methods like comparative literature and contrapuntal reading to bring the fact of imperialism to the world. Said explains contrapuntal reading as "reading a text with an understanding of what is involved when an author shows, for instance, that a colonial sugar plantation is seen as important to the process of maintaining a particular style of life" (78).

Said begins this part by continuing about the creation and the purpose of comparative literature. He refuses to describe comparative literature as criticism. From World War II to 1970 it was dominated by a style of scholarship. The present comparative critics provide romanticised history of France, England and Germany from 1795-1830. The scholars believed that history has to be studied differently from natural science as history is manmade. This idea of enlightenment has become a widespread concept in the European world. The Europeans did not understand the interrelatedness between scholarship and institutions of nationalism on purpose. They celebrated their own literature and society as classic by differentiating it from the occident. Hence they projected other literary works as inferior. The intellectuals believed that nationalism as a changing one and people will get out of shabby thoughts of boundary and xenophobia. These thinkers came up with the idea of transnational and trans-human perspective through comparative literature. Though comparative literature is about the interaction of world literatures, European, American and its Christian literatures always occupied the centre, not only due to their political power but also due to the constructed notion that these literatures should be studied. In the case of interaction of world literature, many Europeans were afraid of the emergence of other literatures. Auerbach in his famous essay "Philologie der *Weltliteratur*" expressed anguish and fear for the emergence of other languages and literatures. Auerbach's *Mimesis*, which he calls 'civilisational survival' presents the notion of the Western literature and its aim to celebrate the ideas of history with geography and politics.

Said wants the formerly colonised people to, "see that the contemporary global setting – overlapping territories, intertwined histories – was already prefigured and inscribed in the coincidences and convergences among geography, culture, and history" (56). The extraordinary privilege of a Western observer helped to retain the power in Western empire. He cites Gramsci's essay "Some Aspects of the Southern Question" to project the political cultural analysis of Italy by focussing on the 'territorial, spatial, geographical foundations of social life'. Gramsci mixes social history and actuality in the geographical terms. He divides Italy as south and north by giving different characterisations of the people living there. Gramsci wanted to connect the northern proletariat with the southern peasantry. He did it by introducing the northern culture to the southern culture, and he warns that it is a time-taking process. Said points out the connection between Gramsci and Gobetti and states that Gobetti's work represented the development of relationship between comparative literature and the imperial geography. This relationship is not coincidental or mechanical and this can be well understood from looking at the resistance movement in the colonised countries.

Western cultural forms were preferred as autonomous by the imperialists to maintain the context between the whites and the natives. Hence "imperialism as a process occurring as part of the metropolitan culture, which at times acknowledges, at other times obscures the sustained business of the empire itself" (59). Said states that one could arrive at the distinctive cultural topography in the course of analysing metropolitan cultures from their struggle for Empire. He names such study as 'Structure of attitude and reference'. Under this term he includes the works that are carefully plotted to create an ideology of Empire. Moreover, the term 'structure of attitude and reference' denotes the idea to rule some races by one race and that can expand its territory. The purpose of everything is to maintain the Empire and it was done so.

In British culture one could discover a desire to construct Britain as empowered, existed consistently for several centuries in their literary works. With this continuous references to rule, to dominate, Britain/Europe emerged powerful since the 17th century. With the development of British cultural identities, strategies like 'rule, control, profit and enhancement and suitability' too arose and later these strategies were followed by America to emerge as a new imperial power.

In the 20th century the continuous production and interpretation of the Western culture might have led the way for the political resistance in the colonised world. Hence different reading or interpretation is given to imperialism. Said observes that "history of such feels as comparative literature, English studies, cultural analysis, anthropology can be seen as affiliated with the empire" (59). Said gives a strategy of a study that the cultural archive of the Empire has to be read contrapuntally; the metropolitan history and the other histories. The resistant movement in the colonies paved the way for new readings and interpretations of the metropolitan cultural texts.

Culture is shown as a product of history, interpretations and politics which are primarily imperial. Said defines culture as,

> ...exonerated of any entanglements with power, representations are considered only as apolitical images to be parsed and construed as so many grammars of exchange, and the diverse of the present from the past is assumed to be complete. And yet, far from this separation of spheres being a neutral or accidental choice, its real meaning is as an act of complicity, the humanist's choice of a disguised, denuded systematically purged textual model over a more embattled model, whose principal features would inevitably coalesce around the continuing struggle over the question of empire itself (67).

Historians state that the age of Empire had started since 1879 but in reality, the cultural experiences of the Europeans reveal that it started much earlier. Said calls cultural experience as hybrid and adds that culture is also based on, "the *geographical* notation, the theoretical mapping and charting of territory that underlies Western fiction, historical writing, and philosophical discourse of the time" (69). He presents the cultural transformation of the Empire by reading John Stuart Mill's *Principles of Political Economy* and Jane Austen's *Mansfield Park* contrapuntally. Those two writers used the newly emerged genres such as novel and historical narratives successfully to present their subjectivity.

> In Mill we have the ruthless proprietary tones of the white master used to effacing the reality, work, and suffering of millions of slaves, transported across the middle passage, reduced only to an incorporated status 'for the benefit of the proprietors'. These colonies are, Mill says, to be considered as hardly anything more than a convenience, an attitude confirmed by Austen, who in *Mansfield Park* sublimates the agonies of Caribbean existence to a mere half-dozen passing references to Antigua (69-70).

Thus through such practice of writing the metropolis got the authority to rule the colonies. As discussed several times, those colonial discourses about the colonised as secondary to everything enabled the Empire to occupy the central position. Said states that this was explored by thinkers like Cesare, Fanon and Memmi. The present theoretical studies missed to read or understand, "determining, political horizon of modern Western culture, namely imperialism" (70). The new reading must focus on how to read than what to read. To present the cultural discourse, the scholars should follow a

> procedure entails reading the canon as a polyphonic accompaniment to the expansion of Europe, giving a revised direction and valence to such writers as Conrad and Kipling, who have always been read as sports, not as writers whose manifestly imperialist subject matter has a long subterranean or implicit and proleptic life in the earlier work of writers, say, Austen or Chateaubriand (71).

Said states that furthermore to project the relationship between Empire and culture, theoretical work must be formulated. He concludes this part by stating that past and present, culture and imperialism, and the coloniser and the colonised should be studied together to find the interdependence between these two.

Chapter 2: Consolidated Vision

2.1 Narrative and Social Space

In this part Said continues to elaborate the 'idea structure of attitude and reference' by analysing the British novels to project, (1) how the innocent act of narration is used to construct ideologies and (2) how geography is used to construct the hierarchy of the social space. The British novels played a crucial role in setting up Britain as an Empire. Said begins this part by stating that the 19th and the 20th century British culture was described elaborately in the British novels. The French imperialism was found only in art forms and it was missing in culture. Whereas, in British literature, the empire's functions were presented as code which was/is partially visible. (The imperial motive found in the American writing is actually rival to the European one). They projected the colonised as anonymous and Said refers to "Eric Wolf's somewhat self-congratulatory words, of 'people without history', people on whom the economy and polity sustained by Empire depend, but whose reality has not historically or culturally required attention" (75) to present the colonised people's reality. For the empire the colonies were a place of fortune enhancing one where the disgraced sons were sent to get good fortune.

Writers like, Martin Green, Molly Mahood, John McClure and in particular Patrick Brantlinger discussed the relationship between culture and empire and projected "the importance of certain historical conjunctures, the influence or persistence of ideas about imperialism – and they cover huge amounts of material" (76) in their works. William Appleman Williams states that the empire attained its development through the development of ideological construction with military, economy and politics. Many works projected the imperialist thought in a modern Western culture but it failed to change the view of people as the critics ignored imperialism in their study. Said cites Raymond Williams' work *Culture and Society,* that ignored imperial experience. Hence Said raises a question how the imperial idea could be ignored when a culture register and support it. But only the people from the colonial background could find the imperial theme which is absent for the readers from the European and American countries. Regarding the novels that promoted imperialism, Said raises questions such as (1) Did the Western writers of the 19th century, write their works with reference to the colonies (without mentioning the native people) only to their country audience? (2) Did they not expect those works to be read by those natives in future? By raising these questions, Said invites scholars from the former colonies to read the great colonial texts and cultures of modern and pre-modern Europe and America.

Said continues his recommendation for contrapuntal reading in this chapter too. He states that this reading must present both imperialism and resistance to imperialism, which enable people to understand the process of colonisation, its destruction and resistance from the colonies. He claims that imperialism as an art work where through the structure of narration, ideas, concepts and experiences are connected. Mostly, the experiences are not the direct experience of the writers. Thus the writers take ideas from texts and other people, mix it with their own imagination and experience. Said cites Conrad's *Heart of Darkness* as an example where the projection of Africa is, "a politicised, ideologically saturated Africa which to some intents and purposes was the imperialised place, with those many interests and ideas furiously at work in it, not just a photographic literary 'reflection' of it" (80). Thus literary works with imperial themes project the political setting of the empire by mixing imagination and reality.

Reading the canonical 19th and 20th century works with a new perspective may enable the readers to understand the extension of overseas domination consciousness in almost all literary texts. In *Heart of Darkness,* Conrad through Marlow's character contrasts colonisation of Roman from the colonisation of British: Marlow states that the Roman colonised through brutality and the British through efficiency. Moreover, he attributes salvation and redemption to the British imperials who saved the Africans from the Romans and the Belgians. By doing this, Conrad connects two different aspects of imperialism: one is conquering the land by power and the second is acting as a "justificatory regime of self-aggrandising". This explains that novel form and imperialism are interlinked. Said even goes to the extent of saying that without imperialism there is no novel form. He defines novel as,

> ...an incorporative, quasi-encyclopaedic cultural form. Packed into it or both a highly regulated plot mechanism and an entire system of social reference that depends on the existing institutions of bourgeois society, their authority and power. The novelistic hero and heroine exhibit the restlessness and energy characteristic of the enterprising bourgeoisie, and they are permitted adventures in which their experiences reveal to them the limits of what they can aspire to, where they can go, what they can become" (84).

Thus the novel form was used to project the ideology of the bourgeois society. These novelists locate their novels in a larger space than Britain. All the western critics who read the 18th century British novels find the relationship between novels and social space conveniently neglecting to look at from the perspectives of imperialism.

The English novels attained its eminent form by the 1840s to project the English society by giving an identity and presence. The ideological Britain was projected in the novels which is known to everyone and 'abroads' were unstudied, undocumented, vague and exotic. Thus novels constructed cultural affiliation in domestic ways. Moreover, the repeated projection of abroad as a place somewhere out waiting to be controlled by Britain and a free place to trade for Britain became a cultural view. Thus these novels continuously reinforced the power of Britain upon the overseas territories.

Said states that novels as a picture of reality projected England at the centre and its overseas territories at the margin in four ways. (1) The earlier narratives of the 18th and the 19th century have a kind of connectivity in projecting the empire. The earlier period works by

Jane Austen, Thackeray, Defoe, Scott and Dickens mentioned less information about Empire and the later works projected the Empire explicitly. Though they followed different kinds of projection, all these works "belong to the same cultural formation, the differences being those of inflection, emphasis, stress" (89). (2) These novels by keeping Britain as the centre of power and the world in relation to domination and subordination, raises the question of power. By consistently projecting Britain's overseas territories as an incident or as an unimportant part of the story and hiding the political agenda of Britain, these novels played a crucial role in the construction of discourse (for example, Kipling and Foster in *Kim* and *The Passage to India* respectively showed India without emphasising the resistance movement of the natives). (3) The illustrations of the overseas territories and Britain in the novels indicated the power of Britain. (4) Most of the time these novels made the readers feel the discrimination and subtle view more than the imperial vision which Said connects to the concept 'structure of attitude and reference'. All these four factors could be found only in the English novels as England as an empire colonised vast space and existed for a longer period.

Said calls the 19th century European novels as consolidated cultural form. Almost all the writers irrespective of their different themes, projected family as an important institution and connected to social power and governance. The idea of imperialism as normal is projected in the novel by three important authorities. They are (1) Author-projecting the process of society and institution of manners. (2) Narrators-projecting the discourses in recognisable manner. (3) Community-representation of family, nation and special location. Said talks about Lukacs study of the emergence of history in the European novels. Here history is used in narratives to the public (which actually meant only for kings and aristocrats in the earlier period). These novels conveyed the real history of nation in historical narratives. In the process of historicising the past, space was used for societal purposes. As imperialism occurs due to the possession of land, the social spaces such as territories, land and geographical domains are associated with imperialism and culture. Hence,

> ...imperialism and the culture associated with it affirm both the primacy of geography and an ideology about control of territory. The geographical sense makes projections – imaginative, cartographic, military, economic, historical, or in a general sense cultural. It also makes possible the construction of various kinds of knowledge, all of them in one way

or another dependent upon perceived character and destiny of a particular geography (93).

Said gives three points in relation to the projection of geography in the novels. (1) The obvious presentation of spatial differences as social discrimination are actually a continuous one in the 19th century novels. (2) In the novels the spatial 'hereness' that is anything from Britain is given a higher position. Hence along with family, property and nation 'hereness' is also addressed in the hierarchy of power. (3) The narrative fiction and history which are the domestic cultural enterprises present the power of the citizens of the Empire. Said concludes this part by stating that the western society through its repeated representation made its projection as the characterisation of its subordinates and it kept them inferior.

2.2 Jane Austen and Empire

Said brings this part with his constant view that European and American cultures prepare the idea of empire. Subsequently through 'narratives, political theory, or pictorial technique', west becomes an empire. This enabled the empire to assume the natives of their colonies as backward, savage and uncivilised. This assumption led Said to raise a question that why the rights to construct ideology are allowed for one and denied for the other. This complicated aspect is most often left as a casual one or as a serious act of blame and defensiveness. Here Said makes it clear that he does not accuse the European culture as a reason for the 19th century imperialism or Europe as a source for the problems of former colonies. But European culture was characterised continuously with its preferences to expand the imperial rule. After the 1880s, Europe's concern for imperialism got intensified. To understand it Said recommends to look at this concern of imperialism in the European works from the spatial point of view than from the temporal one. One could find the British writers even before the expansion of colonies, could situate their works in the larger world. For this the writers used the careful strategies of projecting "positive ideas of home, of a nation and its language, of proper order, good behaviour, moral values" (97). The problem with this positive projection is, it devalues other countries and in a way the writers did not oppose imperialistic process. Moreover, the empire got its power to flourish from the differentiation of 'our' and 'their'.

Said cites Raymond Williams' work *The Country and the City* to show that the imperial ideas were invented based on the geographical distinction. This work focuses on the projection of geographical transformation in England and about the relationship between culture and land. Said blames Williams that as usual he did not focus on the theme of colonisation. Many critics spoke about imperialism as an expansion of nationality and also about the rivalry between France and Britain with regard to expanding their territories.

Said decides to analyse Jane Austen's *Mansfield Park* (1814) with a dimension of expanding territories and the rivalry between France and Britain. Though it is a pre-imperial novel, it has more implications for imperialist expansion. Like other imperial novels *Mansfield Park* too presented small and large dislocations and relocations of places. According to Said, Austen places Fanny and Sir Thomas in a similar position in case of space. Fanny's entry into Mansfield Park and Sir Thomas' entry into Antigua are interrelated. Their departure promised them future and wealth. In Antigua Sir Thomas could fix "economical depression, slavery and competition with France" (104) and exhibited his power over the domination of land. Later when he returned to Mansfield Park, he immediately wanted to put things in order. During his absence, Bertram's family plan to play *Lover's Vows* by converting the arrangements of the rooms. But once he returned he stopped the play based on his protestant belief. Said states that this kind of fixing things at home and at colony (domestic and international) is synchronised well by Austen. Hence "She sees clearly that too hold and rule Mansfield Park is to hold and rule an imperial estate in close, not to say inevitable association with it. What assures the domestic tranquillity and attractive harmony of one is the productivity and regulated discipline of the other" (104). In the case of Fanny, she was brought as an ignorant maid to Mansfield Park where she was transformed as a member of the household. Her vision of home changed after her stay at Mansfield Park. When she visited her home Portsmouth, she felt upset about missing the aesthetic and emotional balance which she got at Mansfield Park. Hence, she could not feel at home in Portsmouth. Her movement from the smaller place to the larger place enabled her to have rights over Mansfield Park.

Austen's reference to Antigua has its significance. A casual reference to Antigua presents the importance of empire to home. Austen without projecting Sir Thomas' life in Antigua only refers to the place. Said states that Austen's awareness of empire is different from Conrad and Kipling's. She could see that expansion of territories was important to England. Her projection of Sir Thomas' property in Antigua, a sugar plantation estate with slave labour was actually a historical reality. The needs of Sir Thomas' family is met by the Caribbean sojourners in Antigua. Hence, action in 'out there' (colonies) is necessary for a comfortable life 'here' (Britain). Said quotes from John Stuart Mill's *Principles of Political Economy* to present the spirit of Austen.

> These are hardly to be looked upon as countries, carrying on an exchange of commodities with other countries, but more properly as outlying agriculture or manufacturing estates belonging to a larger community. Our West Indian colonies, for example, cannot be regarded as countries with a productive capital of their own... [but are rather] the place where England finds it convenient to carry on the production of sugar, coffee and a few other tropical commodities. All the capital employed is English capital; almost all the industry is carried on for English uses; there is little production of anything except for staple commodities, and these are send to England, not to be exchanged for things exported to the colony and consumed by its inhabitants, but to be sold in England for the benefit of proprietors there (108).

From *Mansfield Park*, the readers could understand that the geographical division is not natural but it is a politically changed one.

Said claims that *Mansfield Park* is the initial novel that projected the later English history. Later it was adopted/followed in many of the novels. Austen's

> 'Antigua' is therefore not just a slight but a definite way of marking the outer limits of what Williams calls domestic improvements, or a quick allusion to the mercantile venturesomeness of acquiring overseas dominations as a source for local fortunes, or one reference among many attesting to a historical sensibility suffused not just with manners and courtesies but with contests of ideas, struggles with Napoleonic France, awareness of seismic economic and social change during a revolutionary period in world history (112).

Mansfield Park should be seen as a work that experiences the historical changes in the society. The 18th and the 19th century British literary readers are familiar with the influence of classes in the Western society. But due to the expansion of colonies, the class system of Europe had undergone severe changes where new classes of settler planters replaced the old hierarchy. Abolition of the slave trade had its impact on the rich people who had estates in the overseas territories that resulted in power changes among the classes which reduced their power in the society. Moreover, aristocrats were less interested in Antigua but the minority group people saw the island as a place of wealth. Though this happened during Austen's period she cleverly left this information without mentioning it in the novel.

A century later, Lowell Ragatz's work *The Fall of the Planter Class in the British Caribbean 1763-1833*, presented the fact that the writers and the scholars even after knowing the facts involved with colonisation especially the construction of discourses, still continued to write in the same way. For example, Ragatz still projected the blacks as, "he stole, he lied, he was simple, suspicious, inefficient, irresponsible, lazy, superstitious and loose in his sexual relations" (113). Hence, writing itself is connected to the interest of the writers in the form of aesthetic work or historical writing. Said states that *Mansfield Park* cannot be ignored innocent as it is in the form of a novel (creative work) and as it does not have anything to do with history. It could be seen as a novel which is a part of the expression of the empire. It has presented the domestic imperialistic culture. The novel is based in England which actually relied on the Caribbean islands for the maintenance of its style. Said finds Jane Austen in a paradoxical situation as she has mentioned about the slave trade in the novel without condemning it. She might have improved Sir Thomas' wealth in other ways but she purposefully projected Antigua to improve wealth. Said continues to state that one cannot expect Austen to oppose slavery as she was not an abolitionist or a liberated slave. Said calls it as a rich work of 'aesthetic intellectual complexity'. Thus reading *Mansfield Park* is "the task to lose neither a true historical sense of the first, nor a full enjoyment or appreciation of the second, all the while seeing both together" (116).

2.3 The Cultural Integrity of Empire

Said projects the basic difference between the French and British imperialism. He states that unlike the British, the French produced limited literary and cultural concerns towards imperialism. Moreover, he suggests that the French literature and culture could be understood well when it is contrasted with the British literature. Though, France's imperial interest is not found in literary references, it is visible in its cultural discourses. For example, the French used Napolean as an iconic figure who was projected more as a romantic spirit abroad than as a conqueror. Writer Stendhal's characters are influenced by Napoleon. Though the novels did not project the career of Napoleon, one could feel the powerful Napoleonic ambience. Only after the mid-19th century commerce related colonisation started to exist in the French culture. Before this, French literature focused on travel and speculations about the other countries. Unlike the British works, the French works gave minimal projections of overseas territories.

The French imperials were culturally spreading due to Napoleonic overseas adventures and new sets of developments in science. Hence, the French social structure was more perfect than the British. The great institute of learning in France influenced arts and science disciplines. This enabled the French novelists to project the overseas territories as regulated discourses (as knowing of colonies) which was missing in British literature.

Overall the European culture wanted to project the non-European world into representations in order to master it and to hold it. Said cited the example of Philip Curtin's two-volume work *Image of Africa* to present Europe's view of Africa.

> The literature of [African] exploration and conquest is as vast and varied as those processes themselves. Yet with a few outstanding exceptions the records are built uniquely to a single domination attitude: they are the journals of men who look at Africa resolutely from the outside… the quality of their observation was circumscribed within a cramping limit, and they must be read today within this in mind. If they tried to understand the minds and actions of Africans they knew, it was by the way, and it was rare. Nearly all of them were convinced that they were faced by 'primeval man', by humanity as it had been before history began, by societies which lingered in the dawn of time… This point of view marched in step with Europe's overwhelming expansion of power and wealth, with its political strength and resilience and sophistication, with its belief in somehow being the elected continent of God (119-120).

The modern Western culture wanted to represent non-Europeans based on the Western knowledge. Writers like Jerome and Flaubert (mid-19th century) and Conrad and Kipling (late 19th century) used their narratives to state that the Europeans should rule the non-Europeans. Such works had its impact and it had gone to the extent of presenting the hierarchy of races as truth. These writings slowly become the constructed truth about the others. The non-Westerners were not given a chance to speak about themselves and simultaneously England was expanding its territories and economy.

Said looks at Carlyle's work *Past and Present* to provide two factors of colonisation: one is about 'energetic animadversions on revitalising Britain' and presented Britain in its full development and two is 'do nothing to animate quashee', and presented the blacks in a subhuman position. Carlyle's presentation has many similarities to Jane Austen and Mill's works especially in the projection of non-Westerners in a permanently subordinate position to the Europeans. Another important aspect in Carlyle's writing is his usage of language. He uses his language with generality and certainty to produce information about people, race and culture which were already familiar to his audience. Said compares Carlyle's style of writing with Thomas Macaulay and Ruskin, who believed in England's destiny to rule the world. Ruskin in his hortatory tone warns England to rule the world as it is the best. He combines this political idea with his aesthetic and moral philosophy. Said states that not only the selected writers, but any text of the 19th century would project the same ideology.

Until the second half of the 19th century, the European writers presented the imperial consciousness and its mission in their writings. Said believes that the imperial rule was implemented ideologically. To project this he gives a brief synthesis of modern studies in different fields which supported culture and imperialism. Said gives the strategies implicit in the imperial literature in five points. (1) The supremacy between the Western and the non-Western countries based on geography and culture enabled them to rule the others. (2) With the development of ethnography, the difference of codification of humans that is the construction of primitive race and civilised race have started. (3) Through the convergence of its geographical scope with its cultural discourse, the empire gains power. With this new power it starts

> ...to learn about other people, to codify and disseminate knowledge, to characterise, transport, install, and display instances of other cultures through exhibits, expeditions, photographs, paintings, surveys, schools, and above all to rule them. All this in turn produces what has been called 'a duty' to natives, the requirement in Africa and elsewhere to establish colonies for the 'benefit' of the natives or for the 'prestige' of the mother country. The rhetoric of *la mission civilisatrice* (130).

(4) The domination of the imperial power was very active and it was present in the metropolitan culture in many ways. Said states that the recent studies present the interrelatedness of imperial motive in the fields of "popular culture, fiction, and the rhetoric of history,

philosophy and geography" (130). This proves that domination always did not depend on the physical power but also on the implementation of the ideological vision. (5) It is seen as a period of creative power/greatness. The Western writers created discourses about orientalist and Africanist and such Western imperial images are "haunting, strangely attractive, compelling" (132).

2.4 The Empire at Work: Verdi's Aida

This part focuses on Verdi's *Aida*, a very famous opera that has survived as a popular work for more than a century. Said looks at the imperialistic views in the opera *Aida* that projected Egyptology.

Said begins this part by stating that the colonies were not only a place to exhibit the power of an empire but gave them the pleasure of surveying and ruling the place. His contrapuntal reading of imperial works enabled him to disapprove of the Western notions that its culture as an independent one with the worldly pursuits of power, privilege and authority. He states that the structure of attitude and reference existed even before the official existence of the empire that presents its culture as a hybrid one. Desire of Europe is understandable from the projection of the other non-European culture with the characteristics of "malleability and transportability of secondary or less culture". Said presents Verdi's *Aida*, a famous Egyptian opera that helped Europe to construct the orient as an 'exotic, distant and antique place'. *Aida* was Verdi's last public and political opera. Verdi's earlier operas got attention of the Italian audience directly as they were located in Italy. But *Aida* was filled with Egyptian characters and located in Egypt. Said comments about *Aida* thus,

> Aida, like the opera form itself, is a hybrid, radically impure work that belongs equally to the history of culture and the historical experience of overseas domination. It is a composite work, built around disparities and discrepancies that have been either ignored or unexplored, that can be recalled and mapped descriptively; they are interesting in and of themselves, and they make more sense of Aida's unevenness, its anomalies, its restrictions and silences, than analyses of the kind that focus on Italy and European culture exclusively (114).

In 1868 Verdi wrote a letter to his friend Camille du Locle, who visited Egypt to write about the colony, "the beauty and ugliness of a country which once had a greatness and a civilisation I had never been able to admire" (quoted in 115). Later he accepted a special opera for Khediev Ismail, to perform in Cairo. Verdi felt that he was doing something for Egypt on a national level despite knowing anything about modern Egypt. Hence, Verdi used Egyptologists historical version for his opera. In the form of art the Europeans have reconstructed Egypt. Napoleon's military expansion to Egypt was not only to present the power of France to the world but "also to put Egypt before Europe, in a sense to stage its antiquity, its wealth of associations, cultural importance, and unique aura for a European audience" (118). Egypt was reconstructed through drawings which Said prefers to call as 'Description'. The objective of such work was,

> The reproductions of the Description therefore are not descriptions but ascriptions. First the temples and palaces were reproduced in an orientation and perspective that staged the actuality of ancient Egypt as reflected through the imperial eye; then-since all of them were empty or lifeless--in the words of Ampere, they had to be made to speak, and hence the efficacy of Champollion's decipherment; then, finally, they could be dislodged from their context and transported to Europe for use there. This, as we shall see, was Mariette's contribution (118).

Such kind of representations happened in France between1798-1860. Scholars Kinney and Celile mention the importance of Western ethnography and exhibition about the orient for the 'presentational' and 'reconstructive' view about the orient.

> Ordering and characterisation ranked, rationalised, and objectified different societies. The resulting hierarchies portrayed a world where races, sexes, and nations occupied fixed places assigned to them by the exposition committees of host countries. The forms through which non-Western cultures were represented at the fairs were predicated upon the social arrangements already established in the "host" culture, France; thus it is important to describe the parameters for they set the patterns of national representation and provided the channels of cultural expression through which the knowledge produced by the expositions would be fashioned (quoted from 119-120).

Verdi and Auguste Moriette, a famous Egyptologist (as called by Said) worked together for the opera *Aida*. Like Verdi, Moriette too considered *Aida* as his work, as a creation of his brain. Moriette brought Egypt to Europe as it was 'excavated with complete abandon'. Though Verdi read materials related to ancient Egyptian religion, he allowed two changes to that information: (1) Converting some of the priests as priestess in order to project the oriental women during the exotic practices (in particular he projected "the dancing girls, slaves, concubines, and bathing harem beauties prevalent in mid-nineteenth-century European art" (121) as priestesses.) (2) Projecting the male priest as typical barbarians. Verdi and Auguste Moriette adapted whatever they have seen in 'Description' related to Egypt for the opera and produced *Aida* as 'orientalised Egypt'. In the story of opera, Verdi uses the historical background of Egypt from 1840-1860, when the Egyptian army defeated Ethiopian force. During the composition of the opera from 1870-71, imperial Europe has transformed Egypt as a dependent part of Europe. Later the British wanted Egypt to expand towards east Africa to block the French expansion but not on the south side as it might block their route to India and by 1880 Britain occupied Egypt.

As a concluding remark of this part Said gives five points as the method of subordination and victimisation of the colonised by the Europeans in the 19th century. They are (1) using the power – to observe (through voyages of discovery), rule and get profit from distant places (2) ideologically reducing the natives to a subordinate level that is ready to be ruled. (3) through 'civilising mission' giving salvation and redemption to the colonised (4) enabling the conquerors to accept violence as an act of correction (5) the native to be dislocated from their home countries and their histories to be re-written as preferred by the whites.

2.5 The Pleasures of Imperialism

Said looks at Kipling's *Kim* as a work of imperialism and analysed the novel in detail to present the pleasures of imperialism. Said compares Conrad and Kipling in the projection of the experiences of empire as their subject but differed in their style and tone. Conrad's works located in Africa, South Seas and South America whereas Kipling's works located in India, the largest colonial possession of Europe. From 1608-1947, India had its great impact on British life (especially the writers who wrote about India became very famous).

Kipling in spite of spending most of his life in India projected his superiority view in the novel *Kim*. Said states that *Kim* has to be read bearing two factors in mind (1) it is written by a writer who is from a country that has massive colonial power. Kipling projected it as uncontested empire. (2) Kipling can be seen as a historical being as he was experiencing the changing relationship between India and Britain since the 1857 mutiny. Even now many British intellectuals and historians believe that freeing India was a bad idea of Britain as it was bad for both the British as well as the natives. Kipling could not project the conflict between Kim's colonial service and loyalty to his

Indian friends. As he himself could not see any conflict, he believed that England ruled India due to India's best destiny and neglected the Indians' views about the British rule. Moreover, though Kipling had read and met Fanon and Gandhi, such meetings could not create any impact on his imperial view. For example, in an episode in *Kim*, an elderly Indian soldier who took part in the 'Mutiny' revealed the reason for the mutiny (which was based on the British ideological framework) as the bullets being greased with the fat of pig or cow which is against the religious belief of Hindu and Muslim soldiers in the Indian army. But Said states the real reason for the mutiny was resistance to the rule of the East India Company. In fact the mutiny had its great impact on both the Indians and the British. Due to it in 1857, the East India Company was replaced by a formal Government of India. The mutiny had changed the image of Britain from 'civilised' to 'cruel'. Kipling used an Indian, a loyal soldier of Britain to address the mutiny as his country's madness. Thus, Kipling projected his version of the mutiny through an Indian character. Regarding this Said states that,

> To reduce Indian resentment, Indian resistance (as it might have been called) to British insensitivity to "madness," to represent Indian actions as mainly the congenital choice of killing British women and children – these are not merely innocent reductions of the nationalist Indian case but tendentious ones (147-48).

In *Kim* all the Indian characters accepted the British rule and one particular character preferred the older style of colonial officials (like Kipling and his family) who lived among the natives than the officials (trained bureaucrats) who came to India after the mutiny. Thus, like other imperial works, *Kim* too projected the native people's acceptance of the colonial rule.

Kim could be seen as a novel with a male world and as an adventurous story. Kim's boyish enjoyment is actually a figurative idea of the political purpose of British control over India. Kipling purposefully made Kim to be in the companionship of a male Tibetan Lama to project the cultural motive of an adventurous story. By presenting Kim as the central character, Kipling wanted to present Indians as he liked. Said equates Victor Turner's term liminal with Kim's character. Turner explains the term luminal as some societies "require a mediating character who can knit them together into community, turn them into something more than a collection of administrative or legal structures" (140). Later Kipling allowed Kim to move from liminality to a dominant position of a sahib in colonial India. Said states the British control over India and Kim's travel across India happened because of imperialism. Kim could not speak several dialects (not languages) of Indian communities and he could mingle with everyone and at the same time maintain the difference.

The character Colonel Creighton is based on Kipling's experience and idea in/about India and Said gives the similarities between Kipling and his character Creighton. Said presents the purpose of the novel as surveillance over India and to present fascinating details about India. *Kim* is the overlap of political reality of British imperialism and aesthetic and psychological pleasure.

2.6 The Native Under Control

Said begins this part with an observation that the Europeans could not see themselves as imperialist but ironically the non-Europeans saw the Europeans as imperialist. Based on the ideology of imperialism, discrimination was imposed in the differentiations of two cultures. But some tactfully prevented the idea of seeing/observing culture as a part of imperialism. Reading of the major cultural texts provides the connection between these two. The careful observation of culture and imperialism may present various forms of its relationship.

Said presents the similarity in the writings of Conrad and Flaubert as, "Despite their differences both writers similarly emphasise characters whose capacity for isolating and surrounding themselves in structures they create takes the same form as the coloniser at the centre of an empire he rules" (163). Said views Conrad's *Heart of Darkness* as a task to restore Africa by historicising it and projecting its strangeness to European hegemony. His writing was similar to the two prominent historians of his age Sir Henry Maine and Sir Roderick Murchison. Said compares Marlow's projection of everything about Africa (which has no history worth telling) with the international Congo Association of King Leopold as the, "noblest and most self-sacrificing scheme for African development that has ever been or ever will be attempted" (quoted in 165). Moreover, the readers of *Heart of Darkness* were not bothered to ask about the natives and their conditions. Said rejects Chinua Achebe's criticism of Conrad (as a racist who dehumanised the Africans) as his later works *Nostromo* and *Victory* do not deal with Africa. But his projection of natives was always the same as his audiences were Europeans and through his fictions he tried to confirm the facts constructed about the natives. The European imperials through their constructions silenced the natives/colonised and constituted their identities. Said questions what if something resisted such constructed ideology of the Europeans about the natives. Said finds that European imperialism actually developed opposition by some people but still with other sets of people represented successful imperial culture. Said differentiates the explorers and imperialists based on their interests on impulsive power. In *Heart of Darkness,* Marlow's desire to fill the black spaces on the map is due to the culture of imperialism. Said explains that "the aim to civilise and bring light to dark places is both antithetical and logically equivalent to its effective end" (166) that is life and death of the natives are seen similarly. The imperialists divided all the natives/colonised from the white people.

The imperial consciousness projected the natives as people who require European presence either as a 'colonial implantation' or as a 'master discourse'. For example, Kipling's fiction projected India as dependent on Britain due to its own corruption and under development. In other kinds of works, the Europeans were projected as Lords to the indolent natives. Here it is the discourse of colonial capitalism, where the benefits of Europeans were hidden but projected as saviours of colonies. Said states that even thinkers like Marx and Engels projected the Africans as lazy by sharing the views of the French and the British government spokespersons. He gives reasons for such a constructed view by quoting Romila Thapar,

> Traditional Indian historical writing, with its emphasis on historical biographies and chronicles, was largely ignored. European writing on Indian history was an attempt to create a fresh historical tradition. The historiographical pattern of the Indian past which took shape during the colonial period in the eighteenth and nineteenth centuries was probably similar to the patterns which emerged in the histories of other colonial societies (quoted in 168).

Consequently through the imperial desire, the natives were transformed from a subservient position to inferior position. The colonisers by being an invisible scribe, presented the colonised, 'the other' as primitive.

2.7 Camus and the French Imperial Experience

According to Said all the empires were not the same. A famous French historian states that the French empire was energised by 'prestige'. Unlike the British, consistency and regular appeal justified France's territorial acquisitions. The Franco–Russian war of 1870 increased the French desire in expanding their territories. The French thinkers had visualised expansion and considered the imperial ideology as science. Hence, due to the interest of geographical expansion, between 1880-1895 the French colonial possession expanded from 1.0 to 9.5 million sq. / kms and 5 to 50 million native inhabitants. At the second International Congress of Geographical Science in 1875 it was decided that,

> "Providence has dictated to us the obligation of knowing the earth and making the conquest of it. This supreme command is one of the imperious duties inscribed on our intelligences and on our activities. Geography, that science which inspires such beautiful devotedness and in whose name so many victims have been sacrificed, has become the philosophy of the earth" (quoted in 169-170).

After 1880s fields like sociology, psychology, history and anthropology flourished due to colonial attention. This led the French to rule the colonised and they did not want to treat the colonised or the land as their entities. The imperial thinkers created the diversion of superior and inferior races. They made this racial difference as science by providing a reason to rule the inferiors. But Betts has rightly pointed out that, "imperialism did not occur by invitation but by force, and in the long run, all noble doctrines considered, was only successful so long as this ultima ratio was apparent" (quoted in 170).

In 1830, the French had colonised Algeria; first the natives were moved from their land and buildings, second the French occupied the natives' land and slowly the settler population increased by decreasing the native population. Said with the example of historians states the transformation experienced by the Algerian villagers like Bone and Mondovi. Mondovi was treated as a wine growing place of Bone. Albert Camus, a world famous French Algerian writer was born in Mondovi. He grew up as French in Algeria. Like Jane Austen, the facts of imperial actualities were dropped from his works by the readers. Camus is an imperialist but popularly known as a Universalist especially in the decolonised countries. Said states Camus narratives of resistance can be seen as a part of debate about culture and imperialism. O' Brien's comment about Camus thus, "No, other writer, not even Conrad, is more representative of the Western consciousness and conscience in relation to the non-Western world. The inner drama of his work is the development of this relation, under increasing pressure and in increasing anguish" (quoted in 173). Said claims like Conrad, Camus too represented Western dominance in the non-European world. Conrad in his essay "Geography and Some Explorers" celebrates the British explorers and states "putting my finger on a spot in the very middle of the then white heart of Africa, I declared that someday I would go there" (quoted in 173) which he made possible through his work *Heart of Darkness.* Both Conrad and O'Brien describes western imperialism through (1) penetrating into the geographical entity beyond the European frontier (2) specific presentation of Western consciousness with reference to the non-Western world.

Said presents methodological points with relation to Camus' work. (1) Camus uses Algeria as a locale for his narratives that actually referred to France, especially France under Nazi control. It raises a doubt that Camus' narratives are connected to imperial French narration. Moreover, his works were written during the French presence in Algeria (1940-50) and they refer and inflect the nature of French enterprise in Algeria.

The second methodology is based on the interpreter's region (Western or non-Western) its meaning changes. Camus paid more importance to Franco-Algerian affairs without bothering about the Algerian history. Thus, Camus' works were against Algerian independence. The third motto is about the presentation of detailed patience and insistence in Camus' work. In general the readers view Camus' work as a French novel about France. Moreover, his choice of Algerian locals was to give moral issues to the readers. His novels project the details of imperial conquests and the colonial period. Said's analysis of Camus'-fiction proved Algeria as a methodologically constructed geography of France and he clarifies that his analysis of Camus' work is neither to blame nor to vindicate.

Said reads Camus short story collection titled, *L'Exil et le Royaume*, that deals with people in exile. The stories make it clear that Camus believed that the Europeans achieved a good position in the overseas territory. He also warns that going native will result in the loss of identity. Moreover, he opposed the demands for the Algerian independence. His support for the imperialistic French rule is to be understood well from his views that,

> (As far as Algeria is concerned, national independence is a formula driven by nothing other than passion. There has never yet been an Algerian nation. The Jews, Turks, Greeks, Italians, or Berbers would be as entitled

> to claim the leadership of this potential nation. As things stand, the Arabs alone do not comprise the whole of Algeria. The size and duration of the French settlement, in particular, are enough to create a problem that cannot be compared to anything else in history. The French of Algeria are also natives, in the strong sense of the word. Moreover, a purely Arab Algeria could not achieve that economic independence without which political independence is nothing but an illusion. However inadequate the French effort has been, it is of such proportions that no other country would today agree to take over the responsibility.) (Quoted in 179).

Camus inherited the long tradition of colonial writings that is claiming Algeria by its geography. He actually mingles political context with geography in his works. His readers instead of looking at the imperial narratives appreciated his work by citing it as 'the human condition'.

In general France wanted to project itself as a superior colonial ruler than Britain. Hence, France repeated this ideology by 1930s that unlike Britain, France ranked its colonies without prejudice and racism. Imperial ideologies were constructed due to the French audience desire to see the French colonial rule as superior, the native resistance due to the European traditions' embracement; Camus' works incorporate such French discourses in Algeria. They projected the language of French imperial attitudes and geographical references. He present the various structures of French civil society that administrates the non-French. His works presents his hatred towards the Muslims by presenting the death of Arabs and as the decimated Muslim communities could not have any rights in the land.

Camus' works could be read contrapuntally with the Algerian writers. Letters and documents of Marshall Theodore Buge and Emir Kadel reveal the discriminations and cruelty of the French in the 1830s and 40s. Bugeaud and his officers talk about the atrocities of the French. The Arabs were prevented from doing agricultural work. General Changarnier, a French official, states that the French army troops got pleasant satisfaction through raiding the peaceful villages in Algeria. In spite of such cruel discriminations, the French fictions focused on "abuse of Algeria and the scandals deriving from shady financial schemes operated by unscrupulous individuals for whom the openness of the place permitted nearly every conceivable thing to be done if profit could be promised or expected" (182). Said calls the destruction of Algeria by the French as a systematic as well as constitutive of a new French policy. The French writers though they may differ in their French representation of Algeria, all their works were traced back to the geography of French colonial practice. Said quotes Laroui to present the reality of French colonisation.

> The history of Algeria from 1830 to 1870 is made up of pretences: the colonisers who allegedly wished to transform the Algerians into men like themselves, when in reality their only desire was to transform the soil of Algeria into French soil; the military, who supposedly respected the local traditions and way of life, whereas in reality their only interest was to govern with the least possible effort; the claim of Napoleon III that he was building an Arab kingdom, whereas his central ideas were the "Americanisation" of the French economy and the French colonisation of Algeria (quoted in 183).

Said states Camus in order to silence such Arab works might have diminished the presence of Arabs in his works. His works were actually to the French audience about colonialism. His feeling of loyalty towards French Algeria is presented as the human condition. Said concludes this part by making his observation of Camus writings thus, "… Camus's narratives have a negative vitality, in which the tragic human seriousness of the colonial effort achieves its last great clarification before ruin overtakes it. They express a waste and sadness we have still not completely understood or recovered from" (185).

2.8 A Note on Modernism

The coexistence of cultural texts and the global empires project the complex way of the undertaking of the empire. Such imperialist works were largely unopposed by the people at home (Europe). Not only the texts but the expansion of lands and compulsion on the natives to imperial services were also unopposed. When the imperial control over the colonies became inevitable, cultural discussions occurred frequently. Almost all the writings from the West (not only the novels but works in the form of travel narratives, colonial explorations, memoirs and experiences) celebrated the success of colonisation. All such works ended with optimistic conclusions like "Explorers find what they are looking for, adventurers return home safe and wealthier…" (187). Said again refers to Conrad as he presented 'the subtle cultural reinforcements and manifestations of empire'. In the writings of Conrad, Joyce, T. S. Eliot, Proust and Mann one could find the internal dynamics of Western society and culture by including the 'external pressure on culture from the *imperium*'.

The cultural texts of imperial enterprise initially stimulated the European readers. But later in the 20th century the same texts were used to present the vulnerability of Europe. To present such a new view, Said states that a new encyclopaedia with three features as necessary. The features are (1) circularity of structure inclusive and open at the same time (2) reformulation of the old works (3) irony of art form which was once a synthesis of the world's empire. Said concludes this chapter by stating that in the decolonised world the geography (spatiality) of the once colonised nations becomes a part of aesthetic work than of political domination challenges the empire and its culture.

Chapter 3: Resistance and Opposition

3.1 There are Two Sides

Said is of the view that under the concept influence, general history of ideas and study of cultures are collected. He cites T. S. Eliot's famous essay, 'Tradition and the Individual Talent', where Eliot gives the basic form of influence by discussing the relationship between a writer and his/her tradition. Said states that studying the relationship between the West and the other will not only provide the unequal relationship between these two, but most importantly it enables us to understand the formation and meaning of Western cultural practices. The power disparity between the West and the non-West could be understood well from the cultural forms like novels, historical accounts and ethnography. The cultural forms of a superior culture like literature and critical theory by interpreting the subordinate culture tries to put itself in a powerful position. Hence, the West depends on the non-West in order to emerge as a stronger one.

Gide's *L'Immoraliste* (1902) was cited as an example by Said to present the stereotypical projections of the Arabs and the Africans. This work follows the concept of 'structures of attitude and reference' by getting benefits from the overseas territories and by rejecting its independence. Gide used his work to construct North African stereotypical characters like Islamic Arabs and homosexuals. Gide's work and its imperialistic nature contributed much to the 20th century critical studies on the European attitudes towards Africa as 'Africanism or Africanist discourse'. Thus, African identity was produced by the imperialists as primitive, tribalism, etc… and such identity was spread by the European missionaries, anthropologists and historians. V. Y. Mudimbe's *The Invention of Africa* (1988) presents the history of African gnosis. Said states that until World War I, the cultural situation between the West and the colonies existed in the same pattern. Said wants to highlight the interacting experiences between the colonisers and the colonised at this specific period. It proves the connection between culture and imperialism as integral than as a discourse. The relationship between Western culture and the empire is similar to (1) rediscovery of Greece during the European renaissance (2) during the oriental renaissance, from the late 18th century to the middle of the 19th century, the cultural richness of the colonised nations were taken to the European culture. Thus, all the great epics, imaginary philosophies, languages of the colonised countries were appropriated by the Europeans. In the earlier period cultural exchange happened with a view of the commonwealth of the world. But in the modern period, cultural exchange happened with domination and forceful appropriation. Here someone loses and someone gains by leading the consciousness of inequality. Later when the anti-imperial nations started to emerge, they left the Westerners for the first time to confront themselves as the 'races accused of crimes of violence, crimes of suppression, crimes of conscience'. Similar kinds of revolt happened in the middle of the 19th century but in spite of such revolts, empire increased their colonies and profit. In the modern period though the resistance was different, it was not presented correctly by the empire in the imperial writing. This nationalistic resistance against imperialism could be seen as political movement than as an academic one. After World War II decolonisation happened suddenly and all the colonies of the British Empire were left free.

Said states culture actually prepares one society for the domination of another society and also prepares the society to modify the ideas of domination. Opposition to imperialism does not happen,

> unless the idea of empire and the cost of colonial rule are challenged publicly, unless the representations of imperialism begin to lose their justification and legitimacy, and, finally, unless the rebellious "natives" impress upon the metropolitan culture the independence and integrity of their own culture, free from colonial encroachment (200).

Said is of the view that on a particular cultural grounds the natives and the Europeans understood each other. To prove this point he cites E. M. Forster's *A Passage to India* that reflects his affection for the place. Said states that the crux of the novel as, "encounter between the English colonials--"well-developed bodies, fairly developed minds, and undeveloped hearts"-and India" (201). Forster's India was 'unapprehendable' and large. The British officials felt that any connection with Indians lead to disaster. Forster feels that Islam is somewhat closer to Western culture. Hence, the characters in the novel are closer to the Europeans than the Hindus. Forster's novel presents facts about the political condition especially about Indian nationalism in India. Said comments thus,

> Forster identifies the course of the narrative with a Britisher, Fielding, who can understand only that India is too vast and baffling, and that a Muslim like Aziz can be befriended only up to a point, since his antagonism to colonialism is so unacceptably silly. The sense that India and Britain are opposed nations (though their positions overlap), is played down, muffled, frittered away (203).

Kipling, on the other hand, directly acknowledges the political reality of India. His view is "Indians are a various lot, they need to be known and understood, British power has to reckon with Indians in India" (204). Forster shares Mill's view that the Indians are not ready for self-rule and the British should continue their rule in spite of the mistakes of the Indians. Consequently Forster used his work to project the attitudes and references of the British works.

Edward Thompson in his work *The Other Side of the Medal* (1926) presents the view of both the British and the Indians about each other. He states after the 1857 mutiny, the Indians had started to see the English as brutal and the British saw the Indians as barbaric, uncivilised and inhuman. Thompson looks at these two views as misrepresentation. He requests the British to express 'atonement and to recognise the Indians' wish for freedom. He states that the Indians, "want their self-respect given back to them. Make them free again, and enable them to look us and everyone in the eyes, and they will behave like free people and cease to lie" (quoted in 206). This powerful book is symptomatic. He accepts that culture played an important role in consolidating the cultural feelings. He obseves 'imperialism is a cultural affliction for the coloniser and colonised'. Said states that Thompson could understand the other side better than Forster, who still presented the colonised as subordinates.

French had a double consciousness about its colonies: pride and fear. In the 1930s some of the French ethnographic literatures discussed the native societies of the French colonies. Said presents

Malraux's *La Voie Royale* (1930) as an important work that presents the mix of learned attention and imperial enclosure. According to Said, Malraux's work presents the "inability of the Western humanistic conscience to confront the political challenge of the imperial domains" (208).When compared with Thompson, Paul Mus' work gives a clear picture of the political crisis between France and Indo-China. He recommends independence to Vietnam due to France's 'in alternative conquering'. For both Thompson and Mus, Europeans and Asians are bothered together.

3.2 Themes of Resistance Culture

Ideological resistance has started to reconstitute the shattered communities after the physical resistance against colonisation. The natives wanted to rediscover their suppressed past and moreover through the resistance movement they wanted to recover the established cultural forms of the empire. Said cites Africa as an example for it. Africa was designed and redesigned by the European explorers based on their desire. In the decolonising Africa, through resistance it has to remove those formed images of its imperial past. To present the projection of the non-European world by the European world, Said takes examples of literary works with quest or voyage motif that aimed to control places. The natives who could read and hear such constructed motif about them are re-experiencing the quest voyage. Two African writers' wrote back to Conrad's *Heart of Darkness*. One is Ngugi wa Thiogo's *The River Between*, re-projecting Africa which is different from Conrad's *Heart of Darkness*. The second work is Tayeb Salih's *Season of Migration to the North*, where he presents the Nile River rejuvenating its people. Instead of Conrad's British narrative style and European protagonists, Salih uses Arabic style and characters. Moreover, the voyage is from Sudan to Europe, northward into the heart of Europe.

Another important motif in the decolonising world literature is culture of resistance. Said states that *The Tempest* became inspirational for many such adventures and discoveries of new world stories. The reinterpretations of such stories cannot be simply rejected as 'simple-minded, vindictive or assaultive'. Moreover, it could not be simply seen as a part of a political movement but it makes clear that like the whites, re-seeing and re-thinking are common to the non-whites. For example, Aime Cesaire's *Une Tempete* is his connection with shape to represent the Caribbean: here his impulse is to discover their integral identity which is different from the constructed, derivate identity. The Cuban critic Roberto Fernandes Ret Amor states that for the Latin Americans and the Caribbean, Caliban is a symbol of hybridity than Ariel. Choice of Caliban enables them ideologically to decolonise and to restore their community and culture. George Lamming states that only Caliban can get his history and identity through his own effort.

Said proposes three choices of culture seeking after decolonisation: (1) Like Ariel, being a bourgeois native, not bothered their collaboration with the empire (Prospero). (2) Like Caliban accepting the past and aiming for the future development. (3) Like Caliban who sheds the sense of servitude and discovering the pre-colonial self. The anti-imperialist nationalism or the national consciousness may not replace old dispensation. The initial insight for national consciousness happens when one knows that they are prisoners in their own land. Regarding this Said quotes from W. E. B. Du Boise's *The Souls of Black Folk* (1903), "How does it feel to be a problem?... Why did God make me an outcast and a stranger in mine own house" (quoted in 215). In spite of this, Du Bois did not approve attack against the white or Western culture.

In the decolonising cultural resistance, Said finds emergence of three topics: (1) Insisting to see the community's history as whole and coherent. Through this an imprisoned nation can be restored by placing the national language in the central position. For the sustainability of language practice of national culture is important. (2) Understanding resistance as an alternative way of conceiving human history. It tries to write back to the metropolitan cultures by disrupting the European writing about the colonised, and replacing it with new powerful narratives. (3) Moving towards the integrative view of human community and human liberation by pulling away from separatist nationalism. Said looks at the fact of nationalism in all the non-European world against the European domination as "restoration of community, assertion of identity, emergence of new cultural practices – as a mobilised political force instigated and then advanced the struggle against Western domination" (218). He calls it the global reality against Western intrusion in the 20th century. After independence there is a need for new and imaginative re-conception of social culture. Said believes that the women's movement was central to the resistance movement as it was related to nationalist agitation. Said concludes this part by stressing the fact that decolonisation is a complex battle which cannot be homogenised.

3.3 Yeats and Decolonisation

William Butler Yeats is now considered as an important writer of modern English literature. He was Irish, but wrote his works in English. Along with the projection of British culture and literature in Ireland, he projected anti-imperial resistance, experiences and sufferings of the people under the British domination in Ireland. Like many other non-European writers, Yeats too belongs to the cultural domain that was dominated by the British.

Ireland's colonisation had started before the 1150s when Pope gave the land to Henry II of England. Since then Ireland was projected as a land with barbarians and degenerated race. The literary works of Edmund Spencer and David Hume had presented this idea largely in their works. Since Spencer's work on Ireland in 1596, Europeans had started to consider Irish as barbarians and primitives. In order to emerge as a powerful nation, Europe depended on the crucial role of its culture. Their cultural belief of Euro centralism enabled them to study the colonised, to classify them and to put them in a lower position. "This Eurocentric culture relentlessly codified and observed everything about the non-European or peripheral world, and so thoroughly and in so detailed a manner as to leave few items untouched, few cultures unstudied, few peoples and spots of land unclaimed" (222). Almost all the colonised countries had undergone the same kind of discrimination. To achieve this power of being an empire, the role of colonial schools (especially to spread the empire's idea about the colonised countries and their superiority) played a vital part. It enabled the native children of the colonies to know the history of Britain and France more than their own.

In almost all the colonised countries, resistance against imperialism had started under the context of nationalism. According to Said nationalism helps, "to identify the mobilising force that coalesced into resistance against an alien and occupying empire on the pan of peoples possessing a common history, religion, and language" (223). In countries like India, Ireland and Egypt the idea of nationalism was rooted in the freedom struggle. As imperialism primarily focused on the control of space, the natives wanted to get their geographical identity restored. Said gives three examples to project how imperialism on the theme of geography becomes specific. (1) Crosby's *Ecological Imperialism* focuses on the effect of imperialism in transforming the geography of the new land into images (what they have created about the colonies) or as new places. Said refers to Crosby's idea and states,

> ...wherever they went Europeans immediately began to change the local habitat; their conscious aim was to transform territories into images of what they had left behind. This process was never-ending, as a huge number of plants, animals, and crops as well as building methods gradually turned the colony into a new place, complete with new diseases, environmental imbalances, and traumatic dislocations for the overpowered natives (225).

The nationalist writers project this alienated version of their land through their works. Said states some territorial possessions exist for a longer period due to its profitable nature. Neil Smith in his *Uneven Development* presents the historical view of capitalism especially its role in the construction of "a particular kind of nature and space, an unequally developed landscape that integrates poverty with wealth, industrial urbanisation with agricultural diminishment" (225). This is possible due to imperialism which is justified by the cultural analogue of the late 19th century. Smith names his production of the natural world as 'a second nature'. According to the natives the outsiders for their own benefit have changed their space into something else. Hence the natives should discover their space (a third space) that could be seen in the works of Yeats' *The Rose*, Pablo Neruda's various poems depicting Chilean landscape, Cesaire's work on the Antilles, Faiz on Pakistan and Darwish's works on Palestine. (3) The imperialists wanted to transform the colonies to be familiar to them. When compared to the other colonies of Britain, Ireland had undergone several transformations. Due to the ordinance survey of 1824 in Ireland, the names of the natives were anglicised and it had its shuttering effect on the indigenous community. Mary Hammer gives its impact as, "immediate effect of defining the Irish as incompetent [and]... depress[ing their] national achievement" (quoted in 226). Said claims that the culture of resistance aims to reclaim, rename and re-inhabit the lands along with the redevelopment of native language.

Said states that Yeats was interested in expressing his predicament of sharing a colonial language.

> For Yeats the overlapping he knew existed of his Irish nationalism with the English cultural heritage, which both dominated and empowered him, was bound to cause tension, and one may speculate that it was the

> pressure of this urgently political and secular tension that caused him to try to resolve it on a "higher," that is, non-political level (227).

In his work *A Vision*, he wanted to elevate Ireland above the ground. His early poems discussed more about Irishness than about Ireland. His works promised (1) possibility of a new world with varying essences, (2) possibility of universalism (3) moving beyond nativism cannot be taken as abandoning. Said feels that nationality, nationalism and nativism are more constraining. In countries like Algeria and Kenya, the resistance movements against the imperial powers resulted in one party state that indulged in dictatorial rule. Here transformation of social consciousness did not happen. Said believes that nativism is not an alternate to imperialism. When there is a possibility for a generous and pluralistic vision of the world, the ideas of liberation starts. From 1939, Yeats writings projected this second movement that is 'liberation'. Thus, the transformation of social consciousness beyond national consciousness happened. Said clarifies that one cannot categorise Yeats as a negative Utopian writer. Thus, Yeats' mysticism and rejection of politics in the 1920s should be viewed by understanding that he is a poet from a decolonised country.

Said wants to project Yeats' poetry as a work of decolonisation and resistance. Like other poets Yeats too resisted imperialism. Said compares the resemblance between Pablo Neruda's 'El Pueblo' and Yeats' 'The Fisherman'. Both writers projected an anonymous man as the central figure of the poem who represents the expression of the people in their strength and loneliness. Said projects Yeats' Anglo-Irish conflict theme in poetry as the model for the 20th century wars of liberation. Yeats believes that decolonisation needs a balance between violence and exigent political and organisational process. Yeats posed and re-posed the provocative questions through his works like "Among School Children", "The Tower", "A Prayer for My Daughter", "Under Ben Bulben", and "The Circus Animals' Desertion". These works revealed the projection of the Irish as 'potato-eaters', 'bog-dwellers' and 'shanty people' through English literature for around eight centuries. Yeats through his poetry enabled his people to see their history. Thus, through his works he transforms from a personal one that is an individual type to be a national archetype. His works actually "stopped short of imagining full political liberation, but he gave us a major international achievement in cultural decolonisation nonetheless" (238).

3.4 The Voyage In and the Emergence of Opposition

Since 1950, European and American universities have been paying attention to African literature especially the works that present the independent African experiences. Yet African literature is seen as embedded in a political situation and a reason for it is understood as a history of imperialism. Said complaints that the contemporary scholars look at European cultural history and its literary works without noticing the presence of imperial attitudes, references and their authoritative centrality. However, some people from the empire itself opposed the dominant structure of Europe. End of slavery in 1840 could be taken as an example of the opposition from people. It proves that cultural and political resistance happened even within the empire. Though there was resistance against the cruelty of imperialism from some whites, even then it was with some limitations.

The anti-imperialist movements started by the nationalists were supported by the expatriate intellectuals. During the world wars, students from the colonised countries went to Britain and France. They expressed their anti-imperial views and those views and new ideas changed the European culture's structures of attitude and reference. These new views were addressed to the theme of modernism, decolonisation, cultural resistance and opposition to imperialism. These works challenged the imperial ideas as these writers write from the periphery in the imperial language to project their originality and creativity. Said cites Raymond Williams' *Culture* (1981) to present the historical transformation that happened between imperialism and anti-imperialism: (1) The anti-imperial intellectuals moved from the periphery to the centre for decolonisation. (2) Their works were concerned with the emergence of overlapping and interdependent experience, culture and tradition. To elaborate this idea, Said discusses four works that belong to the special historical moment. They are C. L. R. Jame's *The Black Fancobins* (1938), George Antonius' *The Arab Awakening*, Ranjit Guha's *A Rule of Property for Bengal* (1963) and S. H. Alatas' *The Myth of Lazy Native* (1977). The first two books were written during the anti-imperialist period. The second set of books were written during the postcolonial period.

The first work *The Black Fancobins* is about the black Caribbean insurrection in the 18th century where he forecasts the agonised unbroken history and unsettled Caribbean life. It bridges the cultural and political gap that existed between the history of the Caribbean and the history of Europe. James indicates the resistance movements in the colonies were not mentioned by historians. Though he presented the attitudes of the Western imperialism, he understood its cultural achievement. Antonius' *The Arab Awakening* is about the Arabs and he forecasted the contemporary projection of the Middle East on television and about the establishment of Israel in 1948 from the Arab point of view. Both works present the past events and through that depict the colonial reality which was ignored by Europe.

Ranjit Guha's *The Rule of Property for Bengal* is about the 1826 Act of Permanent Settlements for Bengal in an archaeological and deconstructive study. It explains "the British regulated rents and revenues in Bengal with unvarying precision – derived from a complex background of Physiocratic and Ideological thought in Europe that had been pressed into service in Bengal in the late eighteenth century by Philip Francis" (245). Moreover, he intends to dismantle the imperial historiography. *The Myth of the Lazy Native* which is about the Malaysians, aims to present the foundation for the postcolonial South Asian history and society and to demystify and deconstruct the imperialist view about the natives. This work establishes details about,

> ...how European colonialism created an object, in this case the lazy native, who performed a crucial function in the calculations and advocacies of what Alatas calls colonial capitalism. This native, subjected to stringent rules and an exacting discipline, was meant, in the words of Sinbaldo de Mas, a Spanish official who in 1843 was entrusted with keeping the Philippines as a Spanish colony, to be sustained "in an intellectual and moral state that despite their numerical superiority they may weigh less politically than a bar of gold"; this native was talked about, analysed, abused, and worked, fed with bad food and with opium, separated from his or her natural environment, covered with a discourse whose purpose was to keep him industrious and subordinate. Thus, says Alatas, "Gambling, opium, inhuman labour conditions, one-sided legislation, acquisition of tenancy rights belonging to the people, forced labour, were all in one way or another woven into the fabric of colonial ideology and given an aura of respectability. Those outside it were derided (245).

Said contrasts these two sets of writers: Jame and Antonius and Guha and Alatas. Jame and Antonius believed that the projection of the natives in the Caribbean and Arabs depend on the West. Though their works do not depict themselves standing outside the Western culture and tradition, they present the views of the non-Western colonial people. Jame stated in an interview that, "I think both of them. And fundamentally we are a people whose literacy and aesthetic past are rooted in Western European civilisation" (248). Similarly Antonius believes that Arab tradition should not have conflicted with Western tradition as Western tradition only paved the way to develop Arabic literature. On the other hand, the works of Guha and Alatas present the conflicts in the fields of economy, politics and culture due to Western imperialism on the colonies. In *The Myth of Lazy Narrative,* Alatas attacks his fellow writers in Malaysia who reproduced the thoughts of the colonial ideology. Thus both Guha and Alatas try to rescue the native history from the colonial history and to change the vulnerable position of the native societies in history.

The first set of works present the reality of the colonial society in great narration. As these works are meant also for the Western readers, they use alternative narrative by using the familiar stories from Europe which is not well known to the native readers. Said states that in some of the Arab writings, the narration moves from dependence and inferiority complex to independent state formation and partnership with the West. About Arab nationalism, Said comments that it, "is a complex of hope, betrayal, and bitter disappointment; the discourse of Arab nationalism today carries this complex along with it. The result is an unfulfilled and incomplete culture, expressing itself in a fragmented language of torment, angry insistence, often uncritical condemnation of outside (usually Western) enemies" (252). Regarding the aspect of postcolonial Arab states, some are retaining pan-Arab inflection and others are still dependent on the West in the case of political culture. Both these aspects are presented in Anotnio's work along with his preference of integral autonomy.

In the second set of works, both Guha and Alatas present the human adventure as irony. Guha reconstructs the British officials' ideology to make the British dominance permanent through the character of Francis. He believed that the British officials exercised their power in India through their ideologies. As usual the British took responsibility to solve the problems of India in order to become powerful. Alatas presents the British interest to get treasure and cheap labour from Malaysia. Added to that, along with extracting labour from the natives, Britain maintained the natives divided and constructed the natives with the image of being lazy. This myth of lazy natives was actually constructed by the British due to their desire for power and domination.

Said observes that these four works have politics behind as its pressure was constant for them. Hence, these works have to be read contrapuntally from the views of the metro political centre and the periphery. He believes that imperial domination, resistance movement and decolonisation cannot be studied separately. Thus, imperialism and the condition of all colonies have to be studied as interdependent histories. Almost all the postcolonial and liberation movements removed the monopoly discourse of the Eurocentric intellectuals. The four works discussed in this chapter paved the way for the coalition between the anti-imperial resistance in the peripheries and Europe and the U.S. oppositional culture.

3.5 Collaboration, Independence and Liberation

Said talks about the transformation of the national resistance movement to the liberation movement and the condition of the nationalist bourgeois position which again imitates the imperialists. He begins by talking about an interesting paper of Ronald Robinson titled, "Non-European Foundations of European Imperialism" presented in a seminar on *Imperialism* at Oxford in 1969–70. Robinson states, "Nor [without the voluntary or enforced cooperation of their governing elites and] without indigenous collaboration, when the time came for it, could Europeans have conquered and ruled their non-European empires. From the outset that rule was continuously resisted; just as continuously native mediation was needed to even resistance or hold it down" (262). Robinson cites that before 1882 Egypt allowed European penetration as Europe was perceived as advanced and modern. Similarly many individuals and classes collaborated with Europe with a desire to modernise themselves. A reason for the early movement to the West was to learn the habit of white men and to translate their works. Slowly the students of the east were exposed to the imperial hierarchy. Said presents the exchange of views by Afghani and Earnest Renan in *Revue de deux mondes* (1883). Renan projects Islam as lower than Judaism and Christianity. For this Afghani replies that Islam is better than Christianity and the West has developed itself by borrowing from the Muslims' scientific ideas. Afghani though he spoke for his community, he shares the same cultural framework of the West. This kind of elites though they take part in national independent movements, still maintain closeness with the colonial cover. Such kind of collaboration between the natives and the imperials grows cultural history across the world. In spite of this combined experiences, the 19th century imperial divide between the natives and the West still exist. Many colonial schools take responsibility to teach history, culture and science to the native children which reminded them to be dependent of the imperial authority. Said calls nationalism a culmination of this dependence that produced independence to the once colonised countries. The national struggle for freedom gave way for the national elites to replace the position of the colonisers. Said looks at Partha Chatterjee's observation regarding this situation as,

> Chatterjee makes the interesting point that by transforming nationalism into a new regional or state ideology, post-colonial countries subjected themselves to a global process of rationalisation based on external norms, a process governed in the post-war years of modernisation and development by the logic of a world system whose type is global capitalism, commanded at the top by the handful of leading industrial countries (265).

Said states that the 'national culture' joins with the culture of resistance to act against the discourses of imperialism. This national resistant movement produced the independence movement that later turned into a liberation struggle. Said refers to Fanon's *The Wretched of the Earth* where he states that national consciousness should change as social consciousness in order to get liberation from imperialism. Said believes that Fanon's work, "is a response to theoretical elaborations produced by the culture of late Western capitalism, received by the Third World native intellectual as a culture of oppression and colonial enslavement" (268). His work attempts to term the Western theoretical elaborations against these writers. Said analyses the work in detail and calls it a hybrid work as it is a combination of "... part essay, part imaginative story, part philosophical analysis, part psychological case history, part nationalist allegory, part visionary transcendence of history" (270). He finds the impact of Lukac's work *History of Class Consciousness* on Fanon's *The Wretched of the Earth.* He appreciates Fanon's brilliant analysis of liberationist tendency. Here Fanon points out that the nationalist leaders were exploited by the imperialists who maintain a gap with the peasants and the mass of people. Thus, the natives understand that the breaking of colonial oppression will bring another system of exploitation this time by the native elite. Said claims that Fanon was the first anti-imperialist theorist who realised nationalism that cleared imperialism, extend its hegemony through the nationalist bourgeoisie. Similar to Fanon, Ngugi, Achebe and Salih too wanted the humans to be liberated from imperialism. Hence they wanted to write their histories and culture in a new way. Yet some critics call Fanon a 'stupid enemy of the west' who encourages the oppressed to violence. Said believes that Fanon's work is beyond violence and like Fanon, Cabral's work is also misread by readers.

Cultural resistance to imperialism has taken the form of nativism to nationalism. Later many have started to criticise nationalism and its failure by stating that the non-Western world after decolonisation has become, "a nasty mix of tribal chieftains, despotic barbarians, and mindless fundamentalists" (276). Said believes that cultural opposition and resistance suggest an alternative method to reconceive human experience in non-Western terms. He addresses Fanon and Cabral as writers of liberation and not just writers of resistance or decolonisation. Said notices that the writers of liberation are not given commanding authority of their Western counterparts. One of the reasons for this is; many cultural theorists may pretend to accept the concept of universalism but in reality they accept the concept of inequality of races and subordination of cultures. Achebe claims that Western critics often criticise African writings for lagging behind universalism. He replies to them thus,

> Does it ever occur to these universalists to try out their game of changing names of characters and places in an American novel, say, a Philip Roth or an Updike, and slotting in African names just to see how it works? But of course it would not occur to them to doubt the universality of their own literature. In the nature of things the work of a Western writer is automatically informed by universality. It is only others who must strain to achieve it. So-and-so's work is universal: he has truly arrived! As though universality were some distant bend in the road which you may take if you travel out far enough in the direction of Europe or America, if you put adequate distance between yourself and your home (277).

Said cites the example of Foucault, Frankfurt school critical theory and other Western critics who did not have anything to say about anti-imperial resistance. Hence they might be part of connecting culture with imperialism for centuries. This unity was broken by the liberationists' anti-imperialists in three ways. (1) By giving a contrapuntal view of non-Western and Western experiences as they are both connected by imperialism. (2)Through imaginative vision that reconceives emancipatory theory. (3) Investing in migratory and anti-narrative energy and by not bothering about new authorities, or establishing new institutions. Though many British and French historians and journalists tried to write about the struggle between imperialism and the peripheries and about the intersection of imperialism with culture they could produce no neutrality. As they were from the side of the empire, they could not get away from it. Said again discusses C. L. R. James' *The Black Fancobins* and comments it is known for its imagination. He concludes this chapter by stating that works like James are needed with its audacity and generosity of spirit in the contemporary U.S. and Europe.

Chapter 4: Freedom from Domination in the Future

4.1 American Ascendency: The Public Space at War

Imperialism is not over immediately after decolonisation and its connection still exist in some countries like Algeria and India to France and Britain. Mass migration across the globe during decolonisation and cold wars had changed the world a lot. New sets of forces from the new super power nation, the U.S. has started to appear in the 1960s and 70s. The old terms or concepts which were used to describe the old form of imperialism cannot be used at present to describe the new imperialism. But both imperialisms followed the economic rift between the poor and the rich states. The Brandt report named *North-South: A Programme for Survival* (1980) states that the northern hemisphere uses the southern hemisphere for its own development and moreover the north controls the south. Though everyone knows about the greed and cruel nature of the north, no one can bring change. Hence, the gap between north and south got wider. Said agrees with Noam Chomsky's observation of the north in 1982,

> ...the "North-South" conflict will not subside, and new forms of domination will have to be devised to ensure that privileged segments of Western industrial society maintain substantial control over global resources, human and material, and benefit disproportionately from this control. Thus it comes as no surprise that the reconstitution of ideology in the United States finds echoes throughout the industrial world.... But it is an absolute requirement for the Western system of ideology that a vast gulf be established between the civilised West, with its traditional commitment to human dignity, liberty, and self-determination, and the barbaric brutality of those who for some reason perhaps defective genes--

> fail to appreciate the depth of this historic commitment, so well revealed by America's Asian wars, for example (quoted in 284).

Firstly, Said talks about the continuous ideological domination in terms of cultural that happened in the 19th century by the West. Later, he observes that the same theme is repeated by projecting and theorising the American power. This enables people to understand that now it is the period of American ascendancy. Said talks about the great personalities of America who took great part in constructing its foreign policy. The first person is Lippmann, a famous journalist, who spoke about the American global dominance without objection and its power upon the world. The second person is George Kennan, who believed that the U.S. would be the guardian of the Western civilisation. He believed in the American kind of informal imperialism and expected America to play the role once played by the British Empire. These two men though opposed America's involvement in the Vietnam War and hated the aggressive behaviour of America, they along with other forces shaped America's foreign policy. These authorities did not warn America to be an imperial power like the earlier ones but wanted to project it with the notion of 'world responsibilities'. Thus, after World War II, America's global interest has increased and its power is formulated by 'the foreign policy and intellectual elite'.

Richard Burnet in his work *The Roots of War* (1972) states, "The United States imposes the "international interest" by setting the ground rules for economic development and military deployment across the planet. Thus the United States sets rules for Soviet behaviour in Cuba, Brazilian behaviour in Brazil, Vietnamese behaviour in Vietnam" (quoted in 286). He is of the view that as a consequence of its powerful position, American military has intervened into the third world every year from 1945 to 1967. Said adds that after 1965, the U.S. has become more active especially during the Gulf War in 1991. He continues that the Americans dictate the law and peace of the world and Americans feel 'it is up to us' to right the wrongs of the world. Said quotes Kiernan's comment about Americans, "America loved to think that whatever it wanted, was just what the human race wanted" (quoted in 287). For many years the U.S. government has its direct intervention in the affairs of many countries in central and South America and Asia. Though it is obvious that the imperial control will face resistance from the past histories, the American inversion is accepted by many countries.

Americans unlike the West are considered as a new race of people who had a new and original relationship with nature. Such image was maintained from the 19th century literary works. Moreover, American cultural historians have done enough work to represent the domination as acceptable. Said cites Melville's *Moby Dick* as a representation of American world quest. From the 19th century America was extending its territory by taking places from the native people and by gaining hegemony over the North American continent and extending it to other countries.

J. Michael Dash's *Haiti and the United States: National Stereotypes and the Literary Imagination* presents the typical relationship between Haiti and the U.S.. After Haiti's independence in 1803, America started to pour its ideas there. This island was seen as inferior as the native people were black. Later in 1915, the U.S. occupied this island and agonised this place through its interventions.

The classic imperial hegemony depended on direct domination and cultural space for control but the modern imperial hegemony depends on the cultural authority for the control of information. As the US.. is a great holder of power, it emanates in various forms of cultural control to the other countries and through that it makes other cultures to be its subordinates. Now in the advanced world, media and information play a crucial role in imperial power. Many scholars found that America's media imperialism is exercised on the rest of the world as they are the owners of producing, circulating and representing the new items about other countries. Said narrates the strategy followed by the U.S. media to destroy other countries. First they will present some struggle and fearful foreign culture to their own people. Through this, they create a need for violence against those other cultures. This strategy was followed in the Gulf War. In the mid-1990s, journals and newspapers from America encouraged the attack on Iraq. The projection of the American media about Iraq is,

> as if an almost metaphysical intention to rout Iraq had sprung into being, not because Iraq's offence, though great, was cataclysmic, but because a small non-white country had disturbed or rankled a suddenly energised super-nation imbued with a fervour that could only be satisfied with compliance or subservience from "sheikhs," dictators, and camel-jockeys (295).

Said as he belongs to both these places felt this was a troubling thing. He states that the Arab world obviously fascinated the

Americans. For the Americans, media is an extension of their cultural context. For around a decade they projected Arabs/Muslims as terrorists like "as the Iraqi infraction seemed actually to grow before the collective eyes of the nation, Saddam became Hitler, the butcher of Baghdad, the madman (as described by Senator Alan Simpson) who was to be brought low" (295). With similar methodology all the old enmity with Palestinians, Arab nationalism and Islamic civilisations are settled by the American media. Said is of the opinion that again the entire situation is for colonisation. The third world countries are again controlled by America. What the British did in the 1920s (bombed Iraq for colonial resistance), America is doing now with the moralistic tone that actually hidden the truth behind the war. Said comments on America's presence in Iraq as due to its desire for its presence in the Gulf to have direct leverage on oil in order to affect Europe and Japan.

Said believes that the U.S. pretended as if it is acting in the interest of the United Nations especially in the case of the Gulf War. But the war was actually between George Bush and Sadam Hussein. In reality the U.S. has not officially supported any struggle for democracy, rights of women/minorities or for secularism. It has indulged in arms sale in Arab nations. Though America talks about multi-culturalism, it has never looked at the Gulf as a place with culture, society or even history. Moreover, American media did not cover the reality of the Gulf War but the least was covered and presented in the history.

4.2 Challenging Orthodoxy and Authority

Said is of the view that the other cultures are always viewed through the perspective of pathology or therapy by the imperial culture. Books and scholarships from London and New York are attracted towards the "frame of acceptance" about the postcolonial countries. Said states that the non-Westerners are unfortunate in every way. Till 1991, people from the dominant country paid less attention to Iraq as a society or as it has history or culture and with the similar view all the decolonised countries were interpreted. The demythifying cultural constructs happen in the writings of the imperial works. Works like Lukacs, Frederic Jameson, Foucault, Derrida, Sartre, Adorno and Benjamin re-project the cultural hegemony. Said feels surprised to find most of the liberational theoretical concepts emerge from the West than from the decolonised countries. Said introduces two terms which became famous after the 1980s: terrorism and fundamentalism.

Among English-speaking new communities those who have various languages still have many deformations. Schiller in his work *Culture, Inc.* describes how all the departments of culture are invaded by or enclosed with corporation. Its consequence is: the international media has ideologically inspired the notions of what the imagined communities aspire to do. Though the western news agency or the category postmodern unite the whole world, it keeps the separation somehow between the postcolonials and the imperials. The institutional versions of history of many countries especially the once – colonised nations are freezed by the colonisers for the later official identities. Said cites the names of great thinkers from the post-colonial countries who through their writings projected how, by whom and for what they all were projected/constructed by the power, and pleaded the reader not to accept the constructed political identity. This kind of identities need to be investigated. Said is of the opinion that identity need not to be with uniqueness or privileged states, whereas literary works have to be read based on its differences. A literary or critical work begins from its political, social and cultural situation. Hence, all these works from all around the world need not to be homogenised. After World War II, due to the non-European nationalists' struggle, a different topology has started to emerge in the new academic fields: (1) To look at the politics of what they study (2) should discuss slavery, colonialism and racism with reference to their circumstances. Similarly mimicry or emulation cannot be acceptable with regard to the non-Western literatures.

When the literary experiences overlap with one another in spite of its national boundaries, a new type of connection exists. Here exile is not seen only as border crossing but the loss and sadness are also registered and acknowledged. Said suggests that as a reader of literature, one should deal with the literature of peripheries by attending the literature of metropolitan centres too. Only then one can get a full view of literature. Thus, he recommends contrapuntal analysis by rejecting national or separatists' works. "... we must take into account all sorts of spatial or geographical and rhetorical practices--inflections, limits, constraints, intrusions, inclusions, prohibitions--all of them tending to elucidate a complex and uneven topography" (318).

In human history, earlier there were identities of force and idea from one culture to another culture. Now it happens exclusively from America to the rest of the world. Hence other cultures have been fragmented, reduced from their original/true cultural identity. Said blames the division and specialisation or separatist knowledge as these may disable/disempower the original insights. William Bennett with Allen Bloom and his followers called the multiculturalism of new knowledge as barbaric threat to the western civilisation. The Westerners have projected cultural study as the recovery of western heritage that is free from the non-Western world. American electronic media and its print culture maintain America's perspective of the non-Western world. Said confirms that the notion of the public and projection of the media about the non-Western world are the same. A 30 second sound bites introduces foreign societies to the American students. The Americans are keen to know whether a foreigner is a pro/anti American. The media presentations will report to the public about what is good for America.

Said adds another element to America, i.e., hegemony. He states that its act of pressure and constraints on other countries and culture exposes its imperial identity. Said refers to Jameson's description of consumer culture with relation to America, its "central features are a new relationship with the past based on pastiche and nostalgia, a new and eclectic randomness in the cultural artefact, a reorganisation of space, and characteristics of multinational capital" (323). In America marginalisation means an important position usually associated with, "what are considered euphemistically as "alternative" modes, alternative states, peoples, cultures, alternative theaters, presses, newspapers, artists, scholars, and styles, which may later become central or at least fashionable" (324). Centrality means identity, power and its balance between extremes. This centrality allows to produce semi-official narratives that project America as a force for good in the world that fight against obstacles forced by foreign conspiracies. Thus, attacks on Vietnam and Iran were projected against terrorist fundamentalists. All the capsule histories were written as novels or published in media: these official narratives actually have power to "interdict, marginalise, and criminalise alternative versions of the same history-in Vietnam, Iran, the Middle East, Africa, Central America, Eastern Europe" (324). These other cultures, without acceptable narratives to rely on and without any permission to elaborate, stand silenced.

Said observes the third world as a place that had faced several political problems since colonisation. Now, after decolonisation, only a few countries have parliamentary or democratic system. All the third world countries have problems and challenges like giving up the traditional belief and possibilities of inheriting all societies' belief and cultural practices. Said concludes with the optimistic view of the third world nations thus by quoting, "the emergence and diffusion of a feeling of hope and power, of the belief that what exists does not have to exist, that people can improve their lot if they try [and]... rationalism... the spread of the presumption that planning, organisation and the use of scientific knowledge will resolve the social problem" (quoted in 325).

4.3 Movement and Migration

Said talks about the new patterns of domination in the era of mass societies. Paul Virilio gives reasons for it in the present as, "it is a polity based on speed, instant communication, distant reach, constant emergency, insecurity induced by mounting crises…" (326). America with the help of media carry its war and the rebellious people pay huge price for their resistance against the power. Said talks about the plights of the refugees, 'boat people', 'undocumented immigrants', guest workers and these people are forgotten in the present world. Their cry has not reached the attention/appeal of people. A reason for it is their problems are disseminated by the mass media. The U.S. and Europe maintain distance between insulting/rejecting other cultures or religion and self-praising theirs. They maintained their 'cultural literacy' by prescribing what should be read by leaving 'how' they should be read. The other cultures' affirmations were maintained by professionals and experts. After the dismissal of great thinkers in the 1980s, critical theories entered into a new period of uncertainty.

Now the world is bothered about safeguarding personal freedom and environment. Said is of the view that presently a new critical consciousness is needed which could be achieved through revised attitude to education. He wanted the students to be taught about their identity, history, tradition along with others' identity, tradition and history. The contemporary world due to the postcolonial and imperial conflicts, has left many people as homeless. There are more number of refugees, migrants, exiles and displaced people at present due to the formation of new boundaries. He states that the hybrid-counter energies are not based on domination but on collective human existence. It invites, "mixed genres, unexpected combinations of tradition and novelty, political experiences based on communities of effort and interpretation (in the broadest sense of the word) father than classes or corporations of possession, appropriation, and power" (335).

Said quotes Victor Hugo,

> The person who finds his homeland sweet is still a tender beginner; he to whom every soil is as his native one is already strong; but he is perfect to whom the entire world is as a foreign place. The tender soul has fixed his love on one spot in the world; the strong person has extended his love to all places; the perfect man has extinguished his (quoted in 335).

and states that only a person who follows it can be a historian who can grasp human experience with all its diversity and particularity. Due to imperialism, today no one is culturally 'one' thing, everyone has several identities like Indian, woman, Muslim, etc. Imperialism has consolidated the mixtures of culture and identities. Everyone has their culture, history but attached to it and insisting its distinctiveness is due to the fear or prejudices of the people. Hence, Said advises/pleads all humans to think in terms of everyone. "It is more rewarding-and more difficult-to think concretely and sympathetically, contrapuntally, about others than only about "us." But this also means not trying to rule others, not trying to classify them or put them in hierarchies, above all, not constantly reiterating how "our" culture or country is number one" (336).

VI. Homi K. Bhabha (1949)

Homi Bhabha was born in Mumbai, India in 1949. He is an influential figure in the Postcolonial Studies. His challenging concepts such as hybridity, mimicry, differences and ambivalence are central to postcolonial theory. His concepts present the resistance nature of the colonised. Bhabha rejects the concept that colonialism is about something in the past, and believes that histories and cultures intrude on the present. He presents the hidden gaps and anxieties that existed in the colonial situation. Huddart believes that the originality of Bhabha's ideas lies in his two approaches. He states,

> First, it provides a conceptual vocabulary for the reading of colonial and postcolonial texts, beginning with those of British India in the nineteenth century... Second, through its conceptual vocabulary Bhabha's work demonstrates that the West is troubled by its 'doubles', in particular the East. These doubles force the West to explain its own identity and to justify its rational self-image. Western civilisation is not unique, nor simply Western, and its 'superiority' is not something that can be confidently asserted when other civilisations are so similar. So, on the one hand, Bhabha examines colonial history; on the other, he rethinks the present moment, when colonialism seems a thing of the past (1-2).

Bhabha was born in a Parsi family. He had his education in India; completed his schooling and college in Mumbai and completed his D Phil from Christ Church, Oxford University. He started his career as a professor at the University of Sussex and then moved to other universities in the U.K. and the U.S. One could find the influence of post-structural and psychoanalytical theories in Bhabha's work. He stated in one of his interviews that he was greatly influenced by the works of Edward Said. As mentioned earlier, his work differs from Said and he projected the ambivalent and hybrid condition of the colonised. In 2012 he was honoured by the Padma Bhushan by the Government of India. He is academically very active especially in the field of Postcolonialism and Cultural Studies.

Bhabha's concepts changes the thinking of the postcolonial critics and the most influential concept of Bhabha in postcolonial theory is 'Hybridity'. He borrowed this term from botany to present the hybrid condition of the cultures of the coloniser and the colonised. By this concept he breaks the concept of purity and superiority. He shifts 'the noisy command of colonial authority' and 'the silent repression of native traditions' to 'the colonial hybrid'. He believes that cultures always be contact of other culture that leads to culture mixedness and they cannot be pure. This concept 'hybridity' is usually associated with ambivalence and sly civility. He explains it as,

> [C]olonial hybridity is not a problem of genealogy or identity between two different cultures which can then be resolved as an issue of cultural relativism. Hybridity is a problematic of colonial representation and individuation that reverses the effects of the colonialist disavowal, so that other 'denied' knowledges enter upon the dominant discourse and estrange the basis of its authority – its rules of recognition. Again, it must be stressed, it is not simply the content of disavowed knowledges – be they forms of cultural otherness or traditions of colonialist treachery – that return to be acknowledged as counter-authorities. For the resolution of conflicts between authorities, civil discourse always maintains an adjudicative procedure. What is irremediably estranging in the presence of the hybrid – in the revaluation of the symbol of national authority as the sign of colonial difference – is that the difference of cultures can no longer be identified or evaluated as objects of epistemological or moral contemplation: cultural differences are not simply there to be seen or appropriated. (114)

Two of his important essays from his famous book *The Location of Culture* are summarised in this part which elaborates his other important concepts. "The Other Question: Stereotype, Discrimination and the Discourse of Colonialism" gives important concepts and their definition such as, fixity, colonial discourse, ambivalence, stereotype, racial discourse analysis. Furthermore, Bhabha elaborates where Said's concept of colonial discourse fails and he presents an alternation by giving the concepts of stereotype and ambivalence.

Bhabha begins the essay by stating that in colonial discourse 'fixity' is an important feature in the ideological construction of otherness; Fixity based on cultural/historical/racial difference is a mode of representation. Bhabha moves his colonial discourse analysis from ready recognition of images as positive or negative to understand the 'process of subjectification' through the discourse of stereotypes. He recommends to dismiss the stereotypical images than to displace them as the effective usage of domination and dependence construct 'colonial identification subject (both coloniser and colonised)'. At the same time, he does not want to deconstruct 'colonial discourse' to present its misconception or self-reflexivity: he believes that the productivity of colonial power lies in its construction of its truth than in representation. It enables to understand the 'productive ambivalence of the object and desire and derision'. Such reading reveals the boundaries of colonial discourse.

Bhabha believes that colonial discourse needs 'articulation of forms of difference' to the construction of the colonial subject and to exercise its power. That is, the colonisers need the colonised in order to differentiate them from the others. Such articulation enables them towards domination and power through the construction of theoretical space and political space. It results in differences of racial and cultural 'hierarchisation'. In the colonial discourse analysis, Bhabha looks at the 'mode of representation of othernesses' and discusses the way how racial/cultural/historical otherness had been constructed in the theoretical texts that aimed to present the 'difference' or 'contradiction'. While constructing colonial discourse, Bhabha explores a concept 'ambivalence' which is central to the stereotypes. He defines ambivalence as a force that "gives the colonial stereotype its currency: ensures its repeatability in changing historical and discursive conjunctures; informs its strategies of individuation and marginalisation; produces that effect of probabilistic truth and predictability which, for the stereotype, must always be in excess of what can be empirically proved or logically construed" (66). He is of the view that to recognise stereotype as an ambivalence (a mode of knowledge and power), it needs to challenge the relationship between discourse and politics through theoretical or political response.

Bhabha reads Stephen Heath's analysis of Welles' movie *A Touch of Evil* with attention to the structure of Mexican and the U.S. border which is given with the notion of 'limited being'. Heath's projection of contradiction and diverse sites to construct the national/cultural difference as impure/mixed/foreign is clearly revealed. Heath has read the problems of the Mexican/the U.S. border exclusively under the sign of sexuality and 'feminist focus'. This work presents America as a land of law and morality, whereas Mexico as a land of desire and immorality. Bhabha quotes from the work,

> Vargas is the position of desire, its admission and its prohibition. Not surprisingly he has two names: the name of desire is Mexican, Miguel. . . that of the Law American – Mike. .. The film uses the border, the play between American and Mexican. . . at the same time it seeks to hold that play finally in the opposition of purity and mixture which in turn is a version of Law and desire (quoted in 68).

Bhabha refers to the works of Robert Stem and Louise Spence's "Colonial Racism and Representation" to present their limitation as they rely upon the stereotypes as a point of identification, though the work aims to give anti-colonial objectives. He comments that their works attempt to present the same stereotypical representations in a passive way but which has its effect on politics. Bhabha states that his idea of a

> stereotype differs from them. According to him stereotype is, "a complex, ambivalent, contradictory mode of representation, as anxious as it is assertive, and demands not only that we extend our critical and political objectives but that we change the object of analysis itself" (70).

Bhabha elaborates colonial discourse as an 'apparatus of power' in this part. It starts with the recognition/disavowal of differences. The important function of colonial discourse is production of knowledge; it creates space for subjects and construct knowledge about the stereotypes of colonised and coloniser. Thus, colonial discourse is constructed by the colonised to justify colonisation and to establish systems and administrations. Along with the power play, colonial discourse is crucial to construct the colonised as 'the other'. Bhabha states that, "It resembles a form of dreams, images, fantasies, myths, obsessions and requirements" (71). He comments that Edward Said's examination of European discourses constructed orient as a 'unified racial, geographical, political and cultural zone of the world'. Said presents the centre of Orientalism as a continuous projection of division: one side it is discovery, practice and learning and on the other side is images, dreams, fantasies, obsessions, myths and requirements.

For Bhabha, Said's orientalist discourse emerged with 'alternity and ambivalence' and it was with Binarism. He considers that Said used Binarism initially to see

> ...opposition between these two discursive scenes, finally allows them to be correlated as a congruent system of representation that is unified through a political–ideological intention which, in his words, enables Europe to advance securely and unmetaphorically upon the Orient (71).

Said believes that Europe's imaginative writings, fantasy and ideas became the content of orientalism. Moreover, the division of manifest and latent orientalism led the effectiveness of the concept discourse to be undermined by 'the polarities of intentionality'. Bhabha believes that Said's use of Foucault's concept of power/knowledge create a problem here. He observes that Said has rightly stated that orientalism as misrepresentation of the orient. But Said fails to look closely on the notion of power/knowledge instead he readily accepted the view. Bhabha states that if colonial discourse is viewed with the attribution of ambivalence to power/knowledge, it can present the negative stereotypes of the colonised. Those stereotypes are seen as the "signal points of identification and alienation, scenes of fear and desire in colonial texts" (72) and leads to colonial fantasy.

Bhabha finds an under developed passage in *Orientalism* that articulates the question of power and desire. Knowledge and power led to the construction of colonial discourse, which is brought out with reference to Foucault's concept of apparatus. "Foucault insisted that the relation of knowledge and power within the apparatus are always a strategic response to an urgent need at a given historical moment" (73). Bhabha applies Freud's concept of fetishism to read discourses. Here Bhabha talks about the reading of stereotypes in terms of fetishism. Myths about racial purity and cultural priority normalises the colonial stereotypes. Similarly, fetishism reactivates the fantasy (anxiety of castration) and normalisation of the differences. Bhabha states that there are two types of justification with regard to fetishism in colonial discourse; structural and functional. Said believes in the structural link but for Bhabha functional link is more relevant because

> ...fetishism is always a 'play' or vacillation between the archaic affirmation of wholeness/similarity – in Freud's terms: 'All men have penises'; in ours: 'All men have the same skin/race/culture' – and the anxiety associated with lack and difference – again, for Freud 'Some do not have penises'; for us 'Some do not have the same skin/race/culture.' Within discourse, the fetish represents the simultaneous play between metaphor as substitution (masking absence and difference) and metonymy (which contiguously registers the perceived lack) (74).

According to Bhabha, stereotype is a false representation of a given reality: he elaborates it as "a simplification because it is an arrested, fixated form of representation that, in denying the play of difference (which the negation through the other permits), constitutes a problem for the representation of the subject in significations of psychic and social relations" (75). He refers to Fanon's positioning of the stereotype as a sign of 'negative differences'.

Bhabha refers to two incidents mentioned by Fanon in *Black Skins, White Masks*. On one occasion, a white girl fixes the identity of the black as cruel, ugly, and terrific and on another occasion a black boy gets confused with racial and cultural stereotypes (white heroes and black demons) in Children's Literature. The boy gets confused with his identity and he might consider white as positive by moving away from himself. Regarding this Bhabha states that,

> In the act of disavowal and fixation the colonial subject is returned to the narcissism of the Imaginary and its identification of an ideal ego that is white and whole. For what these primal scenes illustrate is that looking/hearing/reading as sites of subjectification in colonial discourse are evidence of the importance of the visual and auditory imaginary for the histories of societies (76).

Next, Bhabha presents the problematic of 'seeing' and 'being seen'. The pleasure of seeing keeps the object in 'imaginary position'. Here Bhabha uses Lacanian 'Imaginary' to present the transformation happens in the subject, when it assumes 'discrete' images of the object. The problem here is the subject recognises itself and simultaneously alienates which leads to confrontation. According to Bhabha, stereotypes are constituted by two forms of identifications namely 'narcissism and aggressivity'.

Racial discourse leads to discrimination as a political effect with respect to race and skin. According to Bhabha, in the stereotypical racial discourse, "There is a tie-up between the metaphoric or masking function of the fetish and the narcissistic object-choice and an opposing alliance between the metonymic figuring of lack and the aggressive phase of the Imaginary" (77). He believes in stereotypes, that signify the cultural and racial differences and in that skin colour plays a major role. Here colour gives knowledge about the colonised. Bhabha refers Paul Abbot, who is of the opinion that stereotypes are attributed with recognition, which is spontaneous and visible. Here skin is seen as a natural identity to present the cultural/political sign. Hence in colonial discourse one could find the binding of knowledge & fantasy and power & pleasure.

The stereotypes which are 'impossible' objects are produced repeatedly by racial discourse and colonial fantasy. Now Bhabha defines stereotypes as

> ...not the setting up of a false image which becomes the scapegoat of discriminatory practices. It is a much more ambivalent text of projection and introjection, metaphoric and metonymic strategies, displacement, over-determination, guilt, aggressivity; the masking and splitting of 'official' and phantasmatic acknowledges to construct the positionalities and oppositionalities of racist discourse... (81).

For Bhabha colonial fantasy is an ambivalence. For Example, "The black is both savage (cannibal) and yet the most obedient and dignified of servants (the bearer of food); he is the embodiment of rampant sexuality and yet innocent as a child; he is mystical, primitive, simple-minded and yet the most worldly and accomplished liar, and manipulator of social forces" (82). Thus, colonial fantasy does not separate need and desire which leads to ambivalence.

Racist stereotype discourse by continuously trapping the colonised in the 'circle of interpretations' forms a notion that political control on these natives as appropriate. Consequently, it justifies the white to rule; either under the moralist ideology of 'civilising mission' or 'the White Man's Burden'. With these strategies, colonised societies were marginalised and the colonial government could rule these people from the distance. Bhabha concludes this essay by quoting Fanon,

> ...this behaviour [of the coloniser] betrays a determination to objectify, to confine, to imprison, to harden. Phrases such as 'I know them', 'that's the way they are', show this maximum the other question 119 objectification successfully achieved.... There is on the one hand a culture in which qualities of dynamism, of growth, of depth can be recognised. As against this, [in colonial cultures] we find characteristics, curiosities, things, never a structure (quoted in 83-84).

The second essay titled "Of Mimicry and Man: The Ambivalence of Colonial Discourse" begins with quotations from Lacan and Sir Edward Cust with regard to mimicry. For Lacan, "Mimicry reveals something in so far as it is distinct from what might be called an itself that is behind. The effect of mimicry is camouflage" (85). The British Constitution yet still the colonies have to be in colonial dependence because independence to the colony is mockery. Bhabha states that mimicry is the result of the strategies of colonial power and knowledge. He looks at mimicry as a form of 'ironic' compromise and defines colonial mimicry as "the desire for a reformed, recognisable Other, as a subject of a difference that is almost the same, but not quite" (86). He calls mimicry a discourse which continuously produces slippages, excesses and differences. Hence mimicry is,

> ...the sign of a double articulation; a complex strategy of reform, regulation and discipline, which 'appropriates' the Other as it visualises power. Mimicry is also the sign of the inappropriate, however, a difference or recalcitrance which coheres the dominant strategic function of colonial power, intensifies surveillance, and poses an imminent threat to both 'normalised' knowledges and disciplinary powers (86).

Bhabha feels the effect of mimicry on coloniser as both profound and disturbing. The reforming mission of the coloniser is threatened by the 'double' (imitation) by the colonised. He places colonial imitation between mimicry and mockery. The ambivalence of mimicry fixes colonial subject as 'practical' (incomplete and virtual). When colonial appropriation depends on the inappropriate object, it turns mimicry as resemblance and menace.

Bhabha refers to the work of Charles Grant's "Observations on the State of Society Among the Asiatic Subjects of Great Britain" (1792) as the one which superseded Mill's *History of India.* Grant wanted to implement 'a reform of manners' to the Indians but it led him to fear about Indians' interest for liberty. "Grant paradoxically implies that it is the 'partial' diffusion of Christianity, and the 'partial' influence of moral improvements which will construct a particularly appropriate form of colonial subjectivity" (87). It left the British to imitate the British manners and to remain under their control. Bhabha states that Macaulay's *Minutes* is based on the influence of Grant's work; it is a mockery of oriental learning under the pretention of reforming colonial subjects. With the European educational methods in India, Macaulay wanted to produce 'mimic mam' raised through English education. Bhabha believes that mimicry 'repeats' than 're-present' something. Though some writers wanted to be authentic through mimicry (repetition), it results in partial representation.

Double vision presents the ambivalence of colonial discourse and disrupts its authority. According to Bhabha, a double vision is a result of 'partial representation/recognition of the colonial objects.' It is,

> ...the figures of a doubling, the part-objects of a metonymy of colonial desire which alienates the modality and normality of those dominant discourses in which they emerge as 'inappropriate' colonial subjects. A desire that, through the repetition of partial presence, which is the basis of mimicry, articulates those disturbances of cultural, racial and historical difference that menace the narcissistic demand of colonial authority. It is a desire that reverses 'in part' the colonial appropriation by now producing a partial vision of the coloniser's presence; a gaze of otherness, that shares the acuity of the genealogical gaze which, as Foucault describes it, liberates marginal elements and shatters the unity of man's being through which he extends his sovereignty (88-89).

Mimicry is a colonial discourse that indicates 'almost the same but not quite'. Here, the desire of mimicry is actually 'an interdictory desire' which Bhabha calls as 'metonymy of presence'. In mimicry, identity and meaning are rearticulated along metonymy and it leads to resemblance. Thus, resemblance is considered as the most terrifying thing to behold by the colonisers. Here mimicry emerges as a problematic of colonial subjection.

> Mimicry, as the metonymy of presence is, indeed, such an erratic, eccentric strategy of authority in colonial discourse. Mimicry does not merely destroy narcissistic authority through the repetitious slippage of difference and desire. It is the process of the fixation of the colonial as a form of cross-classificatory, discriminatory knowledge within an interdictory discourse, and therefore necessarily raises the question of the authorisation of colonial representations; a question of authority that goes beyond the subject's lack of priority (castration) to a historical crisis in the conceptuality of colonial man as an object of regulatory power, as the subject of racial, cultural, national representation (90).

Bhabha states that at this point colonial discourse splits into two parts; 1. Consider the reality, 2. Disapprove the reality. It replaces with a desire to repeat/rearticulate the reality which is known as 'mimicry'.

Bhabha states that if desire is used as discipline, then the repetition of guilt and justification can make them 'normalise' and 'enlighten' the colonised. This leads the colonial authority to turn from, "a difference that is almost nothing but not quite – to menace – a difference that is almost total but not quite" (91). Thus, by colonial power history prevents a part that projects, "the twin figures of narcissism and paranoia that repeat furiously, uncontrollably" (91).

VII. Gayatri Chakravorthy Spivak (1942)

Gayatri Chakravorthy Spivak is known as an Indian scholar, postcolonial and feminist critic and it is difficult to fix her name under a single category of specialisation. She was born in Calcutta (Kolkata), India in 1942. She had her schooling and college education in Calcutta. In 1961, Spivak joined Cornell University, New York for her higher studies. Due to the financial difficulty, she joined the newly opened Comparative Literature Department in the same university under the guidance of Paul de Man. Her initial research work was on W.B. Yeats. Later in 1967, she read the work of Derrida titled *De la grammatology* and translated it which became very popular. Then onwards she became very famous and held many positions in many universities. Spivak is known for her famous essay "Can the Subaltern Speak" (1988) and for the translation of fiction of a Bengali author, Mahasweta Devi. She has received various awards and honorary doctorates from many universities across the globe.

Spivak, like Said and Bhabha, challenged the literary convention of the English societies and some of the dominant ideas of the contemporary society. She rejects the ideas that the European world as more civilised and the postcolonial period as more progressive than the colonial period. She is of the view that the anti-colonial movement emerged with a bourgeois character could be seen as a replica of the colonisers. Both the bourgeois ideology of the postcolonial rulers and the present-day imperialist America leave the third world women in the subaltern position. She questions why the protest of the majority of Indians (peasants and women) is hidden in the history of the freedom struggle. Spivak developed the Subaltern studies further and argues that problems and challenges faced by the 'Third World women' are unique and a complex one which cannot be understood by the Western critics. According to her the word subaltern,

> It refers to those who don't give orders; they only receive orders. That comes from Antonio Gramsci, who made the word current. He was looking at people who were not in fact working-class folks or victims of capitalism. He was looking at people who were outside that logic because he was himself from Sardinia, which was outside of the High Italy of the north. But "subaltern" also means those who do not have access to the structures of citizenship. I'm now talking about India today, where the largest sector of the electorate is the rural landless illiterate. They may vote but they have no access to the structures of citizenship. So that's a subaltern (Paulson)

When the Western critics write about the 'Third World women', they write from their own understanding which leave the 'Third World women' in silence and also in a subaltern position. Two of her works that contributed to the emergence of new postcolonial views are summarised here.

Spivak's *A Critique of Postcolonial Reason: Towards a History of the Vanishing Present* was published in 1999. The objective of the work is given in the preface to track the figure of Native informant through various practices like philosophy, literature, history and culture in four chapters. Spivak believes that the native informant's position is still vulnerable. The *Encyclopedia of Life Support Systems* projected by UNESCO defines the Aboriginal period in the history of humans as "timescale of the *far past*... associated with inactive approaches in which there is no concern for environmental degradation and sustainability "(ix). Provoked by such comment, Spivak through this work tries to present the movement from colonial discourse studies to transnational cultural studies. In general, the main stream studies teach to ignore other streams of studies; but now these sub streams make the main stream to deconstruct itself. The first chapter of this work titled 'Philosophy' applies deconstructive reading of Kant, Hegel and Marx. Postcolonial studies is not just about the colonial discourse study but it is more than that. Spivak suggests to consider the third world as displacement of the old colonies and neo-colonialism as displacement of colonialism. Furthermore, the new north and south division and the narration of great thinkers are based on the aspect of financialisation of the world. At this point Spivak would like to look at the works of Kant, Hegel and Marx from the perspective of 'remote discursive precursors than as repositories of ideas'. She believes that imperialism maintain the clean image of the mainstream though it is discursive. She used Lacanian term 'foreclosure' to denote 'the pre-emergence of narrative as ethical instantiation' (the word 'foreclosure' means 'to rule out or prevent something from being considered as a possibility in the future'). In this work Spivak dockets the meanings associated with the word 'the native informant', which is known 'as the name of Man'; this term carries the meaning of affecting the being of human. Freud used this thought in his work *The Un-ease (Unbehagen) of Civilisation* to state that "this kind of rejection of affect served and serve as the energetic and successful defence of the civilising mission" (5). According to Spivak, the word 'native informant' denotes 'a name for that mark of expulsion from the name of Man' or mark crossing out the impossibility of the ethical relation'. In ethnography the native informant is a black whose cultural history could be written only by the West. The natives too accept that only the Europeans could describe them. Moreover the Europeans needed the natives to construct images about them. Spivak presents the three important European thinkers and their dependence upon these natives as,

> In Kant he is needed as the example for the heteronomy of the determinant, to set off the autonomy of the reflexive judgment, which allows freedom for the rational will; in Hegel as evidence for the spirit's movement from the unconscious to consciousness; in Marx as that which bestows normativity upon the narrative of the modes of production (6).

In general the critics of imperialism call these writers/thinkers 'motivated imperialists'. Here Spivak's deconstructive reading of Kant and Hegel is summarised.

A deconstructive reading of such work will acknowledge 'the determination as well as the imperialism and also check whether such texts could be used to see that construction of 'other'. Foucault's historical fable (Spivak uses this term) presents the emergence of French and British power at the end of the 18th century. End of the 18th century presented 'scientific fabrication' of the representation of the self and the world that helped for domination and exploitation through the establishment of colony and empire. Interestingly, the German cultural self-representation is different from the western European context. It differs from Europe in establishing its identity and kinship. In all works central identities are negotiated and re-negotiated by great narratives.

Philosophy is seen as the merging filed of science and truth. Germany used 'universal' narratives to mix with European subjects in works like "Kant's cosmopolitheia, Hegel's itinerary of the Idea, Marx's socialist homeopathy-neither inaugurated nor consolidated a specifically scholarly control of the matter of imperialism" (8-9). Spivak calls the works of Kant, Hegel and Marx as the source texts for the European ethno-political self-representation because in their works 'the other' always remains in the same objective position.

In the first part Spivak rereads Kant's work. Spivak perceives philosophical texts as being filled with "empirical and anthropological" ideas that provide morals and also serve as historical narratives. Kant too produced such kind of narrative works by not giving an opportunity to the natives to narrate. His work *The Critic of Judgement* presents the connection between aesthetic judgement and theoretical reasons. Here she states that 'the subject represents an object for cognition'. He believes that nature needs culture to judge something but this judgment is not culture produced one. He states "Without development of moral ideas, that which we, prepared by culture, call sublime presents itself to man in the raw [dem rohen Menschen] merely as terrible" (12-13). Here the word roben means uneducated; it may indicate child/woman/poor/savage or primitive. Those who follow culture occupy superior position. The raw man, who is assumed as not having any culture, must be corrected through culture and moreover he has not achieved a subjective position too. Kant believes that "This gap between the subject as such and the not-yet-subject can be bridged under propitious circumstances by culture" (14).

Spivak wants to present the deconstructive reading of philosophy which is similar to the deconstruction of Derrida's (anthropologising philosophy) and Paul de Man's (analysis of Rousseau). Paul de Man discloses a lie which is established as a corrected version of truth. She does the same in Kant and found out the "the presupposition of the nascent axiomatics of imperialism that gives the tropological deconstruction the lie" (19) which was clearly seen in the last part of the book *The Critic of Judgement.* In the last chapter, Kant gives the thoughts purpose human life as to have desire. He states that,

> [to] suppose [man] to be the final purpose of creation, in order to have a rational ground for holding that nature must harmonise with his happiness if it is. .. an absolute whole according to principles of purposes. .. is only the capacity of desire [*Begehrungsvermiigen*-generally translated "faculty of desire']. ... It is that worth which he alone can give to himself and which consists in. .. how and according to what principles he acts, and that not as a link in nature's chain but in the *freedom* of his faculty of desire. That is, a good will is that whereby alone his being [*Dasein*] can have an absolute worth and in reference to which the being of the world can have a *final purpose* (293).

Spivak states that desire and goodwill are different; desire is an inbuilt characteristic of the mind and goodwill is a 'deliberate or characterological property'. By using this difference, she explains how that one is presented as the other.

Kant believes God is presented as law of moral beings that enabled the discourse of desire to turn as faith. Thus the moral law is seen as real as it cannot be seen with contradictions and moreover it leads to principle in life. Kant gives limitations to reasons with an expectation to remain a lack always. According to him until human cannot cognise himself, he can be moral. Hence, subject of reason do not have cognitive power. He feels that the New Hollander (the Australian aborigine or the inhabitants of Tierrade Fuego) could be turned into humans (subjects) through the supplement of reasons. Though Kant's text cannot develop this idea but it has presented it. When Kant's work is read under the deconstructive way, that is the possibility of production of the native, this book is, "lodged in the fact that, for the real needs of imperialism, the in-choate in-fans ab-original para-subject cannot be theorised as functionally completely frozen in a world where teleology is schematised into geo-graphy (writing the world)" (30). If the duty of the philosopher is to help humans, especially to resolve the contradiction between 'what can be known and what must be thought', then Kant differs in it. His work instead of projecting initiation into humanity, presented initiation into culture and civil legislation. Kant, who is celebrated as the philosopher of bourgeois society presented the geo-political differentiated subject. Spivak quotes Manfred Riedel's comment about Kant as, "Kant tacitly re-introduces empirical concepts into the normative approach" (31) to cover the norm and the fact of civil society and citizen. For him the culture of other societies, have its own limitations and their moral reasons 'boundlessness' result in 'uncultivated reasons'. Hence, he believes that the other civilisations produce 'senseless supplements'. He believes Christian monotheism as 'wondrous' as it is philosophy, and philosophical supplement: hence it is not necessary to consider Christianity specifically as a religion but people can accept it as philosophy. Kant projects his philosophy in terms of implicit cultural differences. Practically man should be accepted as, 'noumenon as its subject as such' though cultural difference did not come here, the raw man is reduced from the normal man as he cannot conceptualise man as noumenon. A civil society is placed within the developed culture. This will consider the inequality of races as the natural tendencies of human race and imperialism is presented as a social mission. Spivak clarifies that she does not want to diagnose the hidden 'beliefs' of Kant; instead she has given the deconstructive view of the text. She concludes a deconstructive study of Kant by quoting Gananath Obeysekere, who stated that Kant, "was no crook; indubitably, as he embarked on his great voyages of discovery, he was the great civiliser, a Prospera of the Enlightenment" (37).

In the second part Spivak attempts to re-read Hegel's comment on *Srimadbhagavadgita.* Spivak begins this part by giving difference between time and timing as the word time gives various meanings. Kant believed that one could not think or act without time. Freud calls the real lived time as the time that is produced by the 'machinery of the mental theatre'. On one hand considering time as timing that is sequential process enables one to group life as well as to understand the historical events. On the other hand, the real law of motion is denoted as time. According to Spivak, time if often mis-caught by the process of timing. She observes this in the text of Hegel on *Srimad Bhagavad Gita* and *Srimad Bhagavad Gita* itself.

In deconstructive study, according to the readers' interest, a text is deconstructed. Here Spivak is interested in deconstructing the opposition between Hegel and *The Gita* on the track of the native informant. Spivak is willing to re-read Hegel by following perspectives on Indian poetry by concentrating on some paragraphs from `Lectures on the Aesthetic'. Hegel gives three movements in the work of art: form, content and meaning. Here the true meaning is towards 'self-knowledge'. Spivak thinks that Hegel's narrative about the development of art form is not 'an epistemology' but 'an epistemography' (how knowledge becomes being). In epistemography, somehow both the sign (spirit) and meaning (knowledge) are made to fit. But this epistemography does not accept the spirit of the sorts from Persia, India and Egypt. In Indian art, shape and meaning are considered separate. According to Hegel, unlike the other proper art, Indian art gives only the external representation, which stops it from giving the contradiction between shape and meaning. Spivak quotes Hegel's view thus,

> The contradiction "is supposed to produce a genuine unification. .. yet," in Indian art, "from one side it is driven into the opposite one, and out of this is pushed back again into the first; without rest it is just thrown hither and thither, and in the oscillation and fermentation of this striving for a solution thinks it has already found appeasement" ...Therefore, "the Indian knows no reconciliation and identity with Brahma [the so-called Hindu conception of the Absolute] in the sense of the human spirit's reaching knowledge of this unity (42).

Spivak attempts to present time as law that manipulates history as 'timing in the interest of culture, political explanations' in the work of Hegelian and Hindu contexts. Hegel by quoting Krishna's speech from the *The Gita*, states that the spirit in the tone is monotonous. His conclusion of alternative reading "to gain enough sense of the *Gita* and its place within a historical narrative to realise that the *Gita* itself can also be read as another dynamic account of the quenching of the question of historical verification" (44). *The Gita* is from the epic *Mahabharata*, is structured in the form of a dialogue between the human prince Arjuna and the divine charioteer Krishna. Spivak proposes to give a dialectic reading to *The Gita*, to present the play of law and history that requires 'impossible anachronistic absence of ideological motivation' to prove India as the inhabitant of 'pre-conscious' of the Hegelian symbolic.

Hegel wanted India to be in 'a way' to prove his ideas about India. He projected that the Indians cannot move history and stated that "(This passage the English translator had no mind to translate word for word because it is all too wanting in decency and shame.). .. Schlegel has not translated this part of the episode" (48). It proves that the normality of such constructions are normal in imperialism. Based on this interpretations, Spivak questions, "is it mean-spirited, unduly polemical, and ultimately mistaken to fix on these time-bound details? (49). She feels that to criticise something from within and to differentiate that from itself, the imperialist need time bound bits. The attempt taken by Hegel to dismiss this great epic as static and monotonous is due to his imperialistic nature.

Partha Chatterjee presents the existence of culture in two spheres: the material and the spiritual. In material sphere, the Western civilisation is powerful and in the spiritual sphere, the Eastern civilisation is powerful. Spivak states that based on Chatterjee's concept *The Gita* occupies an important place in spiritual and cultural sphere. The colonial and the postcolonial subjects did not experience the perception of the negative informant. She metonymically names a concept as 'Hegel' that denotes the displacement of what one has and she believes that Hegel as refracted into the colonial subjects. Spivak uses three sources, Aurobindo Ghose's *Essays on the Gita* (1916), Sarvepalli Radhakrishnan's *The Hindu View of Life* (1927) and S. G. Sardesai and Dilip Bose's *Marxism and the Bhagavad Gita* (1982) to analyse the 'Hegel' concept. In these works, *The Gita* is divided as materials and spiritual. Spivak finds that the colonised/nationalist subjects act as an agent of Hinduism and refine the religion to its Universalist lineaments. Now they consider *The Gita* as a script of Aryan philosophy that considers cast division as the secret of freedom. In the newly independent nation, confusions exist in religion, culture and ideology with regard to the national identity. Now along with the earlier universalisation, typical fundamentalism and nativism is added to *The Gita*. The U.S. pedagogy aims to put the 'third world' in the chain of displacement. Its ultimate aim is not to produce the historical Indians but to celebrate the hybridity. Slowly it makes the natives to forget that there was not 'historically' authentic native point of view to reclaim Indian's place in the narrative of world history. Moreover, writings from the metropolis and the former colonies try to present positive negotiations of imperialism. It results in the production of the native informant who is actually the evidence of the European knowledge of culture. Thus, the field work ethnography is transformed as anthropology. It transforms timing (the lived time) into time (the graph of law). Spivak urges the readers to have their own perspective about the native informant than by simply following the information given in the text.

The second work summarised here is Spivak's famous essay "Three Women's Texts and a Critic of Imperialism" (1985). She is of the view that the 19th century British literature projected imperialism as the social mission of England as well as considered it as a part of cultural 'representation of England to the English'. Thus literature played a major role in the production of cultural representation. Spivak complains that presently these two facts are neglected while reading the 19th century British literature which leads to the existence of the imperialist's ideas in the modern forms. Spivak is of the opinion that if these facts are remembered while reading the British literature, then the third world could produce the literary history of 'worlding'. Third world is considered as a distant and an exploited culture waiting to be interpreted/recovered in English translation. Spivak states that it is unfortunate that feminist criticism re-presents/reproduces the 'axioms of imperialism'. "If, in the context of colonial production, the subaltern has no history and cannot speak, the subaltern as female is even more deeply in shadow". They establish the feminist norms by looking at/reading the female subjects in the 18th and the 19th century literature. But the first world feminist deliberately present 'information-retrieved approach' to the third world with 'self-conscious rectitude'. Spivak believes that though the first world feminists talk for the freedom of all, they themselves dominate over the third world women. Through this essay she deconstructs the writings of three women's texts. She attempts to re-read (1) *Jane Eyre* with the operation of Worlding, (2) Wide *Sargasso Sea* as reinscription of *Jane Eyre* and (3) deconstruct *Frankenstein.* She clarifies that her objective is to re-read the works and not the authors.

In the age of imperialism, the feminist individualism constituted the subject not only as individual but also as an individualist which is based on child bearing and soul making. Here child bearing is based on (domestic-society) 'compassionate love' and soul making is seen as an imperialistic project based on civil society through 'social mission'. The female individualist tries to articulate herself in such a situation and moreover the native female is excluded actually from this norm. Spivak again classifies that she does not want to accuse anyone through this study. Instead, she looks at the projection of Caliban and Ariel characters from the postcolonial point of view: the first half of the 19th century works tried to produce Ariel. She prefers Caliban's honour of place in the rebellious rank.

Elizabeth Fox-Genovese, while talking about women's history in one of her articles, presents female access to individualism as the historical moment of feminism in the West. Spivak uses this work to read *Jane Eyre* and highlights the marginalisation and privatisation of *Jane Eyre.* Furthermore, she presents the family, counter family of Jane Eyre and finally Jane's move from the counter family to the family in law.

Spivak considers that Bertha Mason, a white creole was produced by the axiomatic of imperialism. Through Bertha Mason, Bronte presented the human/animal frontier. Jane's projection of Bertha ('beast or human being, one could not... tell') and Rochester's speech to Jane are used to project Bertha as 'not-yet human other'. Spivak does not want to doubt the ideology of Terry Eagleton, Sandra Gilbert and Susan Gubar. Terry Eagleton observes Jane's move from counter family to family in law as in terms of 'ambiguous class position of a governess' and Sandra Gilbert and Susan Gubar see Bertha as 'Jane's dark double'.

Spivak claims that the 19th century feminists projected soul making as an important theme. Bertha is seen as an object of the 'categorical imperative'. Spivak uses 'Kant as a metonym for the ethical moment of the 18th century Europe. Kant's terminology 'categorical imperative' was conceived as the universal moral law. The transformative power of philosophy later justified the imperialist project, "makes the heathen into a human so that he can be treated as an end in himself" (151). Spivak traces out the allegorical language and the similarity to *The Pilgrim's Progress* in the concluding part of the novel (especially the decision of St. John River's to stay in Calcutta). She complains that Eagleton and Gilbert and Gubar did not pay attention to this aspect in the story. She is of the view that the project of imperialism is presented through the words of St. John Rivers, "my hopes are being numbered in the band who have merged all ambitions in the glorious one of battering their race-of carrying knowledge into the realms of ignorance – of substituting peace for war-freedom for bondage – religion for superstition – the hope of heaven for the fear of hell" (Quoted in 152). It is projected that St. John River sacrifices his life by preaching in Calcutta. But in reality due to Jane's rejection, in order to escape from his failure, he moves to Calcutta in the disguise of enlightening people.

In *Jane Eyre*, the character of Bertha was used to "render indeterminate the boundary between human and animal" and projected her as less enlightened. Jean Rhys, from the Caribbean islands of Dominica, in her childhood days read *Jane Eyre* and moved by the character Bertha Mason which motivated her to write Bertha's life. Thus, the novel *Wide Sargasso Sea* with the central character of Antoinette (Bertha) was published in 1965. In *Jane Eyre*, Jane hears a snatching, snarling sound and finds Richard Mason bleeding and both are used to project Bertha's wild nature. In *Wide Sargasso Sea*, a minor character Grace Poole is allowed to give reason for the wild behaviour of Bertha. Bertha was not happy with the word 'legally'. The law created by the British provokes her and leads to her violent reaction. Moreover, Rochester violently renames Antoinette as Bertha (it explains the politics behind naming as an act of possession); here Antoinette personal and human identity is changed by the politics of imperial. She suffers between the English imperialists and the black natives.

Spivak is of the view that Bertha is seen as the suppressed self of Jane. In *Wide Sargasso Sea*, Rhys uses the thematic of Narcissus to present Antoinette and her identity. Spivak observes that in Ovid's *Metamorphoses*, Narcissus' madness was established when he took his other as himself. In the case of Antoinette, she sees her in mirror and in that reflection she could see herself as 'the other' that is Bronte's Bertha (Western representation of herself). Antoinette/Bertha states that she knows the purpose of her stay in London was to transform the 'self' to 'the other' and to kill herself by giving Jane a chance to become 'the feminist individualist heroine of British fiction'. Spivak reads this as an "allegory of the general epistemic violence of imperialism, the construction of a self-emulating colonial subject for the glorification of social mission of the coloniser" (154). Spivak mentions that many critics have commented that the novel *Wide Sargasso Sea* treated Rochestr's character with sympathy. Rhys presents Rochester as a victim of the patriarchal inheritance law. He was forced to move to the colonies to buy an heiress. Spivak is of the view that Rhys uses the theme of Oedipus in the case of Rochester. Rhys projected the suppressed letter of Rochester addressed to his father in order to highlight the practice followed by the whites to increase their wealth especially in the case of the second sons.

> Dear father. The thirty thousand pounds have been paid to me without question or condition. No provision made for her (that must be seen too)… I will never be a disgrace to you or to my dear brother the son you love. No begging letters, no mean requests. None of the furtive shabby manoeuvres of a younger son. I have sold my soul or you have sold it, and after all is it such a bad bargain? The girl is thought to be beautiful, she is beautiful. And yet … (quoted in 154).

Spivak claims that just like Charlotte Bronte, Jean Rhys too presented Christophine's character with its own flaws. Christophine, Antoinette's black servant character in *Wide Sargasso Sea*, carries its own discourse. She is from Martinique, who is considered as a good servant and she is allowed to be a 'speaking subject' in the novel. She was given as a wedding present to Antoinette's mother by her father. Spivak finds that Rhys used Christophine to do some crucial work. She was the only one who challenged Rochester but still Rhys does not project the oppressed (Christophine) as heroic. In front of the forces of law and order, the oppressed understood their power as nothing. Spivak finds out that in *Wide Sargasso Sea*, the native is left out like the Creole (Bertha) who was left out in *Jane Eyre*. Rhys showed her interest in rewriting the story from the point of view of a white Creole by leaving the native in a subordinate position. Before the conclusion of the story, Christophine was just driven out of the story without any justification which is similar to Bertha's disappearance in *Jane Eyre*. This reading leads Spivak to state that,

> Attempts to construct the 'Third World Women' as a signifier remind us that the hegemonic definition of literature is itself caught within the history of imperialism. A full literary reinscription cannot easily flourish in the imperialist fracture or discontinuity, covered over by an alien legal system masquerading as Law as such, an alien ideology established as only Truth, and a set of human sciences busy establishing the 'native' as self-consolidating Other (157).

Consequently, Spivak rejects Rhys' *Wide Sargasso Sea* by stating that it was written with the imperial rules.

Spivak looks at Mary Shelley's *Frankenstein* in the concluding part of the essay. She calls this work a 'text of nascent feminism that reminds cryptic'. Barbara Johnson claims this work as 'the service of feminist autobiography'. George Levine looks at this work as 'creative imagination and the nature of the hero'. Spivak prefers to read this work based on the 'sense of English cultural identity' and finds existence of imperialist sentiments in *Frankenstein.* She claims that discourse of imperialism exists in a powerful way in the novel. According to her this work is not about individualism of male and female but it is about the dark side of imperialism which came under the disguise of social mission. Shelley's work tries to

> …tame the monster, to humanise him by bringing him within the circuit of law". But through this novel she proves that the other cannot be transformed to 'self' as it has its own properties. "At the end of the text, the monster having confessed his guilt towards his maker and ostensibly intending to immolate himself, is borne away on an ice raft. We do not see the conflagration of his funeral pile – the self-immolation is not consummated in the text: he too cannot be contained by the text. In terms of narrative logic, he is 'lost in darkness and distance' (quoted in 162).

These three novels are echoing the imperialistic act of that period by politicising/manipulating the natives through law. In *Jane Eyre*, Bertha is made to self-immolate to give way for Jane. In *Wide Sargasso Sea*, though Rhys gave voice for the Creoles, wrote the novel bound to the norms of the European novels. In *Frankenstein*, the monster named after the title of the work is the representation of the colonised. Spivak concludes this essay with her remark that,

> The power of that suggestion remains unclear if we remain insufficiently knowledgeable about the history of the legal manipulation of widow-sacrifice in the entitlement of the British government in India. I would hope that an informed critique of imperialism, granted some attention from readers in the First World, will at least expand the frontiers of the politics of reading (163).

Along with the above mentioned thinkers, still more thinkers contributed hugely to the development of the postcolonial studies. Thinkers like Aijaz Ahmad, Kwame Anthony Appiah, Bill Ashcroft, Amilcar Cabral, Partha Chatterjee, Rey Chow, Gareth Griffiths, Ranajit Guha, Bob Hodge, Abdul Jan Mohamed, Ania Loomba, Trinh T. Minh-ha, Vijay Mishra, Chandra Talpade Mohanty, Arun

Mukherjee, Benita Parry, Kumkum Sangari, Jenny Sharpe, Stephen Slemon, Aruna Srivastava, Sara Suleri, Gauri Viswanathan, Helen Tiffin through their works analysed and projected various aspects of postcolonial studies. As introducing them and their contributions may end in writing an endless work, this work has just named them.

CHAPTER 6

Post-Postcolonial Studies

Many critics believe that the term 'Postcolonial' has been over-used in last three to four decades and its theoretical paradigm as exhausted due to its over usage. They believe that it needs to undergo some changes now or it has to be stopped from usage. Some have started addressing Postcolonial as post-postcolonial in order to include the new issues faced in the contemporary world. Ania Loomba mentions in her work *Postcolonial Studies and Beyond* states "it is important to go beyond a certain kind of postcolonial studies in order to engage with the imperial formations and ideologies associated with globalisation". Critics like Aijaz Ahmad, Benita Parry and Arif Dirlik have tried to change postcolonial studies to engage with the present changes like globalisation, cosmopolitanism, climate change, habitual destruction and their consequences in the present-day life. Presently critics are of the view to shift the postcolonial focus from culture to politics and materialism. Some of the fields for the future research in postcolonial studies are given below.

1. The terror attacks on the former colonies and the present-day imperial nations (Europe and America) & the association of terror and the Middle East countries could be analysed in detail. Elleke Boehmer and Stephen Morton's *Terror and the Postcolonial* (2010) looks at the subject of terror as both an expression of globalisation and a postcolonial product. Discourse of terrorism by projecting a historical relationship between imperialism and the discourse of terrorism can be undertaken.
2. Imperial nations fear for the immigrants from the decolonised countries (especially for people who follow Islam) actually led to the construction of discourses about immigrants. Thus researches about discourses on immigrants can be undertaken.

3. Migration and Diaspora studies take postcolonial studies on a new route. Hence border studies, transnational studies, globalisation could be placed under postcolonial studies.
4. Postcolonial studies and globalisation lead to the development of urbanisation and metropolises, where the power relation and position changes which results in cosmopolitanism.
5. Postcolonial Studies and climate change are buzzing topics at present. Imperialism and colonialism had exploited the natural resources of the world that led to climate change. The expansion of Empire and the misuse of the colonies resulted in damaging the eco system. Presently eco-criticism and postcolonial studies attempt to record the damages produced by the colonisers.
6. In continuation of the above mentioned area of research, a new discourse is found in the treatment of poor people from the decolonised countries as 'unwanted people' with regard to climate change. The concept Anthropocene describes a new geological time period, "the most recent period in Earth's history when human activity started to have a significant impact on the planet's climate and ecosystems" (https://www.nationalgeographic.org/encyclopedia/anthropocene/). Though all the humans should act united to save the planet, some deprived decolonised countries are left out as unwanted people to face tragedy and the rich countries lead a comfortable and safe life. One evidence for such mistreatment of people from a poor country is Lawrence Summers, former president of the World Bank (1991-1993), approving to export the toxic waste and garbage produced by rich nations to poor countries in Africa. People from poor countries are treated as unwanted people by the rich countries. Such people's lives under the new imperialist nation could be studied in future. Clara de Massol states, "'Disposable' communities are excluded from dominant narratives, and while global warming instigates ecological catastrophes, neoliberal and postcolonial structures reinforce the disposability of certain communities". Moreover "Postcolonial narratives are crucial in understanding the cultural significance and the physical implications of anthropogenic climate change". Massol recommends, "We

need to formulate an epistemological strategy that conciliates the socio-environmental injustice and postcolonial discourse associated with climate change with a vision of humans as a geological force".

Bibliography

Achebe, Chinua. "The African Writer and the English Language." *Transition.* 18 (1965): 27-30.

.... "An Image of Africa: Racism in Conrad's 'Heart of Darkness'". *Postcolonial Criticism.* Gilbert, Brat Moore et al. London. Routledge. 2013. 112- 125.

Andrews, Edward E. "Christian Missions and Colonial Empires Reconsidered: A Black Evangelist in West Africa, 1766–1816". *Journal of Church and State*, 51:4, 2009, 663-691, https://doi.org/10.1093/jcs/csp090

Ashcroft, Bill, Gareth Griffiths, and Helen Tiffin, Eds. *The Empire Writes Back: Theory and Practice in Post-Colonial Literatures.* London: Routledge, 1989.

.... *Post-Colonial Studies: The Key Concepts.* 3nd Edition. London: Routledge, 2013.

Ashcroft, Bill and Pal Ahluwalia. *Edward Said.* New York: Routledge, 2001. Online.

Ayyildiz, Nilay Erden. *British Children's Adventure Novels in the Web of Colonialism.* Cambridge Scholars Publishing: U.K. 2018

Ballantyne, R. M. *The Coral Island.* ed. J. S. Bratton Oxford: Oxford University Press, 1990.

Brathwaite, E.K. *Contradictory Omens: Cultural Diversity and Integration in the Caribbean.* Mona, Jamaica: Savacou Publications, 1974.

Bhabha, Homi.K. *The Location of Culture.* London: Routledge. 1994.

Bhatt, Sujatha. "A Different History". https://poetryarchive.org/poem/different-history/

Boehmer, Elleke. 2005. *Colonial and Postcolonial Literature.* New York. Oxford University Press.

Boehmer, Elleke and Stephen Morton (eds). *Terror and the Postcolonial.* Wiley-Blackwell, 2010.

Brown, Judith. M. & William Roger Louis (eds). *The Twentieth Century: The Oxford History of the British Empire.* Oxford: Oxford University Press, 1998.

Bryden, Diana. "Common Wealth or Common Poverty? The New Literatures in English and the New Discourse of Marginality". *Kunapipi.*1.1 (1989): 6-15.

Cameron, Verney Lovett. *Three sailor boys, or, Adrift in the Pacific.* London: Thomas Nelson, 1907.

Cesaire, Aime. *Return to My Native Land.* Trans. John Berger & Anna Bostock, Great Britain: Penguin Books, 1969.

.... *Discourse on Colonialism.* Trans. Joan Pinkham. New York: Monthly Review Press, 1972.

.... *The Collected Poetry*, Trans. Clayton Eshleman and Annette Smith (Bakerly: University of California Press, 1983.

.... *A Tempest*, Trans. Richard Miller, New York: Ubu Repertory Theater, 1991.

Chatterjee, Partha. *The Nation and its Fragments: Colonial and Postcolonial Histories.* Princeton: Princeton University Press, 1993.

Chaudhury, Sarbani. "Introduction to *The Tempest*". *Longman Study Edition.* New Delhi: Dorling Kindersley, 2009.

Chinweizu, C. A. *The East and the Rest of US*. Lagos: Nok Publishers (Nigeria) Ltd. 1978.

Conklin, Alice. L.A *Mission to Civilise: The Republican Idea of Empire in France and West Africa, 1895-1930*. Stanford, Calif.: Stanford UP.1997.

Conrad, J., 1902. *Heart of Darkness*. Penguin Modern Classics, 1982.

Crafford, F.S. *Jan Smuts: A Biography*. Montana: Kessinger Pub Co. (2005).

David Cody, "The growth of the British Empire", *Victorian Web*, (Paragraph 4) http://www.victorianweb.org/history/empire/Empire.html. Accessed on 26/05/2020.

Defoe, Daniel. *Robinson Crusoe*. New York. WW Norton & Company, 1994.

Dennis Duerden and Cosmo Pieterse, eds, *African Writers Talking: A Collection of Interviews*. London: Heinemann, 1972.

Dryden, John.1675. *Aureng-Zebe*. University of Nebraska Press. 1971.

Ezenwa-Ohaeto. *Chinua Achebe: A Biography*. Bloomington: Indiana Univ. Press, 1997.

Fardon, Richard. (ed.) *Localizing Strategies: Regional Traditions of Ethnographic Writing.* Edinburgh: Scottish Academic Press. 1990.

Fanon, F. *The Wretched of the Earth*, Trans. Constance Farrington, New York: Grove Press, 1963.

.... *Black Skin White Masks*, Trans. Charles Lam Markmann. London: Pluto Press, 2008.

Foucault, Michel. *Power/Knowledge*. C. Gordon(ed). New York: Pantheon Books, 1980.

Freud, Sigmund. 1930. *Civilization and Its Discontents. (Das Unbehagen in der Kultur)* London: Penguin, 2002.

Gandhi, Leela. *Postcolonial Theory: A Critical Introduction*. Edinburgh UP, 1998.

Gilbert, Helen; Tompkins, Joanne. *Post-Colonial Drama: Theory, Practice, Politics.* London: Routledge. 1996.

Gilbert, Brat Moore et al. *Postcolonial Criticism*. London. Routledge. 2013.

Gilley, Bruce (2017). "The Case of Colonialism". *Third World Quarterly*. DOI: 10.1080/01436597.2017.1369037

Go, Julian. *Postcolonial Thought and Social Theory*. Oxford University Press, 2016.

Guha, Ranajit. *Subaltern Studies Reader, 1986-1995*. Minnesota: University of Minnesota Press. 1993.

Haggard, H. Rider. *King Solomon's Mines.* 1885. Reprint, *World's Classics Series.* Oxford: Oxford University Press, 1989.

Hammond, Paul. *The Poems of John Dryden. Vol. I. 1649-1681.* London and New York, 1995. 1213-16.

Hegel, Georg Wilhelm Friedrich. *The Philosophy of History*, tr. J. Sibree 1858, New York: Palala Press. 2016.

Henry, Lord. *A Discouerie of the Sect of Banians Conteyning their Historie, Law, Liturgie, Casts, Customs, and Ceremonies.* London: De Capo Press, 1972.

Huddart, David. *Homi. K. Bhabha.* Routledge publishers: New York, 2006.

J.D. Fage. *A History of Africa.* Third Edition, 1955, 11. New Fetter Lane, London.

Jeal, Tim. *Livingstone.* Revised, Expanded Edition. Yale University Press, 2013.

Judith M. Brown & William Roger Louis. (eds). *The Twentieth Century: The Oxford History of the British Empire.* Oxford: Oxford University Press, 1998.

Kingston, William Henry Giles. 1871. *In the Wilds of Africa: A Tale for Boys.* T. Nelson & sons, 1914.

Kipling, Rudyard. 1901. *Kim.* London: Macmillan, 1981.

Loomba, Ania. *Colonialism/Postcolonialism.* Routledge, 1998.

Loomba, Ania & eds. *Postcolonial Studies and Beyond.* Duke University Press. 2005.

Macaulay, Thomas B. "The Hon'ble T. B. Macauley's Minute, 2nd February 1835." 14-30.

Mannoni, O. *Prospero and Caliban: The Psychology of Colonization.* New York: Praeger, 1964.

Massol, Clara de. "Postcolonial Climate Change: John Akomfrah and a Discourse of Difference". Muireann Crowley (ed). https://projectmyopia.com/postcolonial-climate-change-john-akomfrah-and-a-discourse-of-difference/

McLeod, John. *Beginning Postcolonialism.* Manchester: Manchester University Press. 2000.

Meath, Lord (1908) in Low, Gail Ching- Liang. *White Skin, Black Masks. Representations and Colonialism.* London, Routledge. 1996.

Meier, Allison. *How Cartography Helped Make Colonial Empires*, posted on Nov 22, 2013. https://hyperallergic.com/94793/how-cartography-helped-make-colonial-empires/ accessed on 30/09/2020

Michael A. Peters & Carl T. Mika (2017) "Aborigine, Indian, indigenous or first nations?", *Educational Philosophy and Theory*, 49:13, 1229-1234, DOI: 10.1080/00131857.2017.1279879

Mill, James. (1818). *The History of British India* (reprint), 3 vols. New Delhi: Associated Publishing House. 1972.

Milton, John. *1608-1674. Areopagitica: a Speech of Mr. John Milton for the Liberty of Unlicensed Printing, to the Parliament of England. Santa Barbara, Calif.: Bandanna Books, 1992.*

… 1608-1674. *Paradise Lost.* London; New York: Penguin Books, 2000.

Miner, Earl, ed. *Selected Poetry and Prose of John Dryden.* New York: The Modern Library, 1985.

Mukherjee, Pablo. 'Surfing the Second Wave: Amitav Ghosh's Tide Country'. *New Formations.* 59 (2006): 144-57.

Mukherjee, Meenakshi. "Interrogating Post-Colonialism". *Post-Colonialism: Theory, Text and Content.* Harish Trivedi & Meenakshi Mukherjee (eds). Simla: Indian Institute of Advanced Study, 1996.

Nandhi, Ashis. The Intimate Enemy: Loss and Recovery of Self under Colonialism. USA: Oxford University Press. 1983.

Northcott, Cecil. David Livingstone: His Triumph, Decline and fall. Philadelphia: The Westminster Press, 1973.

Nott, Josiah C. 1851. An essay on the natural history of mankind: viewed in connection with Negro slavery: delivered before the Southern Rights Association, 14th December, 1850. Dade, Thompson & Co Printers.

O' Brien, Karen. "Poetry against Empire: Milton to Shelly". Proceedings of the British Academy. 269-296. The British Academy, 2002.

Olson, James (ed). *Historical Dictionary of European Imperialism.* Westport: Greenwood Publishing Group. 1991.

Orwell, George. *Burmese Days.* Penguin Books, 1985.

........."Rudyard Kipling". *The Complete Works of George Orwell.* Accessed on 28/5/2020. http://www.george-orwell.org/Rudyard_Kipling/0.html

Poovey, Mary. "Ambiguity and Historicism: Interpreting Confessions of a Thug" *Narrative,* Volume 12, Number 1, January 2004, pp. 3-21. https://doi.org/10.1353/nar.2003.0025.

Porter, D. "Orientalism and its problems" *The Politics of Theory.* Colchester P. Hulme et al. University of Essex Press. 1983.

Quayson, Ato. *Postcolonialism: Theory, Practice of Process?* Cambridge: Polity Press, 2000.

Raj, Alok. "Colonial Fictions: Orwell's *Burmese Days*". *Economic and Political Weekly.* 18:5. 1983, 47-52.

Rajan, Balachandra. *Under Western Eyes: India from Milton to Macaulay.* Durham: Duke UP, 1999.

Roy, Rohan Deb. "The untold story of modern science is one of empire and colonial exploitation". Accessed on 3/6/2020. https://qz.com/india/1247577/the-untold-story-of-modern-science-is-one-of-empire-and-colonial-exploitation/

Rushdie, Salman. "Commonwealth Literature Does not Exist." *Imaginary Homelands: Essays and Criticism.* 1981-1991. London: Granta, 1991. 63-70.

Said, Edward W. *Culture and Imperialism.* New York: Alfred A. Knopf, 1994

.... *Orientalism: Western Conceptions of the Orient.* New York: Penguin Books, 2001

.... *Between Worlds, Reflections on Exile and Other Essays.* Harvard University Press; 2002. pp. 556–57.

.... *The World, the Text and the Critic.* Harvard University Press, 1983.

Selvon, Samuel. *Fore day Morning: Selected Prose 1946-1986.* Kenneth Ramchand, Susheila Nasta. (eds).Longman, 1989.

Spivak, G. (1985) "The Rani of Simur" *Europe and Its Others Vol. 1 Proceedings of the Essex Conference on the Sociology of Literature*, Francis Barker et al. Colchester: University of Essex.

.... (1985) "Three Women's Texts and a Critic of Imperialism". *Postcolonial Criticism.* Gilbert, Brat Moore et al. London. Routledge. 2013.

.... *A Critique of Postcolonial Reason: Toward a History of the Vanishing Present.* 1999.

Tamara.C.HO. "From Orwell to Rambo: International Affiliations and Transnational Antagonism in the Age of Human Rights". *Roaming Human Rights: Gender, Intimacy, and Power between Burma and the West.* University of Hawaii Press, 2015. 10-24. Jstor.

Taylor, Philip Meadows. (1839). *Confession of a Thug.* Oxford University Press, 1998.

Thiongo, Ngui wa. *Decolonizing the Mind: The Politics of Language in African Literature.* Portshmouth, NH: Heinemann, 1986.

Thomson, James. *The Seasons.* Eds. James Sambrook. Oxford, 1981, Spring II, 74-77.

Trilling, Lionel. *The Liberal Imagination: Essays on Literature and Society.* London: Mercury Books, 1961.

Viswanathan, Gauri. *Masks of Conquest: Literary Studies and British Rule in India.* Danbury: Faber and Faber, Incorporated, 1990.

W. Monk (ed). *Dr. Livingstone's Cambridge Lectures.* 1860.

Wallace, Edgar. 1911. *Sanders of the River.* Create Space Independent Publishing Platform, 2018.

Warren C., "Could First Fleet smallpox infect Aborigines? – A note", Aboriginal History 31, pp 152–164. Online: https://www.scribd.com/doc/49665744/Warren-AbHist31-2007

Westgarth, William. (1864). *The colony of Victoria: its history, commerce and gold mining; its social and political institutions down to the end of 1863; with remarks, incidental and comparative, upon the other Australian colonies.* U.S.A.: Kessinger Publishing, 2010.

Westermann, Derich. 1934. *The African Today.* Routledge. 2018.

Wilson, E. Argus 17th March 1856, in Harris, J. 2013, One Blood (electronic resource): Two hundred years of Aboriginal encounter with Christianity, Concilia LTD, Brentford Square, pg. 209.

Wood, Denis. *Rethinking the Power of Maps.* New York: The Guilford Press.2010.

Young. Robert. *White Mythologies: Writing History and the West.* London: Routledge, 1990.

Zbigniew Bialas, *Mapping Wild Gardens: The Symbolic Conquest of South Africa.* Verlag die Blaue Eule, 1997.

Index

O

P

R

S

T

V

W

Y